Pleasures of Provence

Pleasures of Provence

A Quest for the Secret to Joie de Vivre in La Belle France

GAYLE SMITH PADGETT

For Ralph H.

Also by
Gayle Smith Padgett

Passion for Provence: 22 Keys to La Belle Vie

The Birdwatcher's Wife:

A Quest across France for Birds and La Belle Vie

Author's Note

This book reflects true-life experiences, based on my written accounts and recollections. Any inaccuracies are entirely mine. For the sake of the narrative, some events have been reordered and the dialogue clarified. For privacy purposes, I've changed the names and identifying details of many of the characters. For the record, Ralph equals Ralph.

Contents

Introduction

Saint-Rémy-de-Provence, South of France

The journey to my *belle vie*—a Frenchified version of a good life—began on our honeymoon in the south of France over three decades ago. To celebrate our union, my husband, Ralph, an avid birdwatcher, had his hopes pinned on visiting the Camargue, the world-class nature preserve in Provence. As an Impressionist art lover who had only breezed through Paris and the Côte d'Azur and was eager to expand my repertoire of French adventures, I needed no convincing.

On that week-long trip so many years ago, our joie de vivre was sparked, and since then, we've held a torch for France. During our careers as US civil servants working in Germany over many years, we hightailed it across the border into La Belle France as often as we could. During each visit, we evaluated different destinations across the country as if someday we might make a life here. We developed a particular fondness for Obernai in Alsace and Beaune in Burgundy, but in retirement, we chose Provence.

Our decision wasn't based solely on *soleil* and rosé, although sunshine and blush-hued wine were part of the allure. In fact, we were drawn to the area for its unique combination of astounding natural wonders and vibrant urban centers, as well as its proximity to a wealth of diverse regions with distinctive dialects, traditions, and cuisine that kept our curiosity piqued.

After living in Aix-en-Provence for eighteen months, we settled in Saint-Rémy-de-Provence, where we've lived since 2012. Here in this little patch of Provence, we continue to shape our lives, one adventure at a time.

1

Stop in the Name of the Law

Saint-Rémy-de-Provence

Blazing blue lights exploded across Saint-Rémy's ring road, sparkling like festive fireworks against the inky February sky. But this was no late-night national holiday finale. The blinding illuminations screamed from atop multiple gendarmerie vehicles, blocking all traffic.

The startling encounter contrasted sharply with the mellow, multi-course dinner party we'd just left at the home of good friends, about a ten-minute drive from our home. Had there been an accident? Was a bandit on the loose? A drug bust under way? A protracted line of cars stretched before us with police officers engaging the drivers, but we couldn't see exactly what was happening. Minutes passed, but no vehicle budged.

I said, "Looks like our heads won't be hitting the pillows any time soon, at the rate we're going."

"Or not going," Ralph grumbled, turning off the engine.

Before Ralph could object, I hopped out of the car. "I'll see what I can find out—back in a jiff." Pulling on my gloves, I walked up the block until I had a direct line of sight to the first car. What I saw took my breath away. When the driver rolled down the window, the officer did not offer a polite bonsoir. In one hand, he cradled a small device connected to a tube, which he extended toward the driver. Without explanation, sans a *s'il vous plaît*, the officer issued the order to blow: *"Soufflez!"*

Oh my God, a breathalyzer test. I retreated quickly. Back in the car, I relayed the unsettling news.

"Are you kidding me?" Ralph said. "On a Tuesday in February?"

"I wish I were. You *are* fit to drive, right?"

"Yes, of course. I wouldn't drive drunk."

"I know you wouldn't. It's just that you don't need to be drunk to be drunk in France, if you know what I mean."

Ralph understood exactly what I meant. Our good friend Pierre had discovered this the hard way and had explained to us in painful detail how he had failed a breathalyzer test after three beers in two hours. The legal alcohol limit, Pierre told us, was significantly more stringent in France than in the US—more than 50 percent stricter, in fact. He's a conscientious guy, but he wasn't paying attention that night. Because of a prior conviction that he'd long forgotten about, he lost his driver's license for an entire year. To add insult to injury, he was slapped with a hefty fine of several hundred euros, and his insurance premium skyrocketed. He was relieved he didn't have to do jail time, which was a possibility if he'd met the next highest alcohol threshold.

"I'm sure I'll be fine. It's unlikely I wouldn't pass unless … I wish I hadn't had that last splash of *rouge*. Well, there's nothing we can do about it now."

Yes, there was something I could do. I could worry about the consequences of Ralph failing the test. I had no experience with breathalyzers and neither did Ralph—not here in France, where we had lived for over a decade, not in Heidelberg, Germany, our home for fourteen years, not in the Washington, DC, area, where we'd met and married three decades before, and not in California, where I'd grown up and passed my driver's license test on my sixteenth birthday.

This is not to say I was a stranger to traffic violations. Back in Virginia, I'd been pulled over for speeding, and had I been clocked a single mile more over the speed limit, I could have been charged with a reckless driving violation. Perhaps the officer had given me a break? In France, however, breaks were few. This I knew, especially after Pierre's debacle. He had paid a substantial price, but his French birthright protected him from the threat of eviction from his native country, an advantage unavailable to an American holding a temporary residency card like Ralph. Recalling that a pristine police report had been integral to our original visa application, my worrywart self wondered whether a worst-case scenario was now playing out. I could feel my heart rate accelerating as I considered how the situation might quickly go downhill.

The disconcerting implications of a failing grade loomed larger by the nanosecond. We hadn't tracked Ralph's wine consumption tonight, so we weren't sure whether he was pushing the legal boundaries. Regardless of his lack of intent to break the prevailing rules, ignorance didn't make for a strong defense in any language.

What moments ago would have seemed inconceivable now rested in the realm of possibility. If my fears were realized, it could mean that life wouldn't just become more complicated as it had for Pierre, who'd paid penalties and retired his car keys for a year. Instead, it could mean that France was finished with us and our Provençal dream.

As Americans, we lived here by the good graces of the capable, exacting bureaucrats of the French government. It wasn't as if they were evaluating applicants for annual membership in a theme park called Club France. They took their job seriously and expected the same of their constituents. One time, they rejected our annual renewal dossier, deeming it incomplete. The officials wanted more than the summary and signature pages of our lengthy rental contract, insisting on the entire document—all thirty pages. We dutifully complied with the directive, followed by another trip to the post office, another round of pricey stamp purchasing for our now even chunkier package, another acquisition of the return receipt notification, critical proof that the authorities had received the dossier, and another nerve-racking wait from the keepers of the keys to our French life.

We'd gone through this visa rigmarole every year for five years, each time asking whether perhaps we could get a ten-year visa. Each time, the answer was "Not yet." Only at the beginning of the sixth year were we eligible to apply for the ten-year version. Soon, we would need to request a renewal. But the requirements shifted every year, so no one could predict what they would be in the future. Chances were they would be tougher. That was the case with the language requirement for French citizenship, which had recently increased by an entire level.

If Ralph's test showed an alcohol content even a smidgeon above the legal limit, would that trigger the bureaucrats to rule that we'd outstayed our welcome? Would they then decline to renew our residency visas and show us to the proverbial *porte*?

We'd been so sure that living *la belle vie*, the good life, was our destiny. But was our French life simply a playdate, one with an expiration date?

Panic began to build as I recalled the wine-infused evening. Multiple bottles of *le bon vin* had made the rounds during the lengthy and lavish feast. With each delectable course, *vin rouge* had been offered, but crisp whites had ruled the repast for us. Plenty of Perrier had been poured as well, but how much had been drunk, I couldn't remember. What *did* stand out in my mind had zilch to do with wine consumption—it was the finale. The compote of kumquats decorated with glistening pomegranate seeds, all proudly produced on the property by our gardening buddies, was exceptional.

After the dessert, all the guests had adjourned to the living room, where we settled onto the overstuffed couch and chairs facing a mesmerizing fire. Many were eager for coffee, but for Ralph and me, a hot beverage held no appeal just then—even a decaf seemed jolting at that late hour. Instead, we opted for a glass of smooth, soothing red that our wine connoisseur host had highly recommended. We knew it would be luscious and surrendered to one last splash. It proved irresistible, just like the region, which went a long way to explain why we were here in the south of France in the first place—Provence offers temptations at every turn.

Following our thanks for the gourmet meal, we said our goodbyes and headed home. As usual, Ralph slid into the driver's seat and I hopped into the passenger's side without a single word about his driving fitness. That discussion hadn't occurred to me, as he appeared perfectly fine, and we lived but a short drive away. Typically, Ralph is Mr. Conscientious, and I rely on him to be reliable. And he always is. Well, unless my passionate birder husband is birding, which means all bets are off. Reality fades when he's following feathered friends, but there had been no birding tonight, just the distant hooting of a Tawny Owl.

Sometimes, to reduce our potential exposure to reckless drivers, halfway around the ring road we would veer off and zigzag through a residential neighborhood to reach our quiet *quartier*. Or if the traffic seemed calm, like tonight, we could continue around the boulevard, passing a string of lively restaurants and cafés, turning off in front of the town's church, the Collégiale Saint-Martin de Saint-Rémy, informally referred to as l'Église Saint-Rémy. The advantage of this route was the fun of seeing what was going on *en ville*. Tonight, caught in a routine traffic control, we were finding out. And it was far from funny.

It seemed to take an eternity to move forward even a single car length, and there were many more to go. I was dreading having to witness my heretofore law-abiding husband ordered to press his lips against the breathalyzer tube and exhale. The potential repercussions that could disrupt the precious lifestyle we had painstakingly shaped over a decade surged through my brain in a feverish spin.

Time seemed to freeze during the endless wait for our turn with the gendarme, and my mind flashed back to how our adventure in France had begun. For a year and a half after we landed in Aix-en-Provence, the marvelous university city of 150,000, we hustled this way and that to track down our Goldilocks house, a rentable version that was just right—or would be for a few years anyway. At that stage in our lives, we had no wish to complicate our situation with a foreign real estate acquisition. And besides, we wanted to take our time scouting out the region to ensure we selected the most suitable spot for us. We had fully intended to stay put in vibrant Aix, where we'd begun our Provençal journey in 2011, but no house met our requirements, the indispensable one being a pool. After two grueling summers there—sans *piscine* or even air conditioning—living in front of a fan had grown tiresome. So staying cool in summer was foremost in our minds. The other requirements were proximity to the town and a simple, unpretentious house that fit our budget, a place we could manage comfortably.

One afternoon, I received a call from a real estate agent. He'd found *the one*, an hour from Aix, in Saint-Rémy-de-Provence, a town we knew well. We'd discovered it on our first trip to Provence in the early 1990s and visited often. We'd eliminated it from our list of retirement contenders; with just ten thousand residents, we thought it might be too small for year-round living. But our perspective had changed in big-city Aix, and now we felt the tug to a smaller town.

The house the realtor had found was a brand-new two-level, three-bedroom build with a small pool, an enclosed garden, a garage, two bathrooms, and air conditioning. The partial view of the Alpilles Mountains from the second-story windows was not the expansive vista we'd had in mind. But we knew a compromise or two would confront us eventually, and this was it. And besides, the rent was acceptable and the location excellent—a tranquil, tucked-away enclave with just a leisurely stroll to the picturesque town center. Replete with restaurants, cafés, art galleries, boutiques, and a popular weekly market, Saint-Rémy was active throughout the year. It was nestled into the base of the Parc Regional des Alpilles, which was crisscrossed with hiking paths, putting nature at our doorstep. And perhaps most important of all, the village was situated just an hour from the Camargue wetlands, Ralph's happy place. We had wasted no time in moving in.

Now, more than a decade later, we cherished this small town in Provence. It filled us with joy day after day, year after year. The entire region and beyond seemed to possess a unique power to activate our delight receptors, enhancing France's allure. And we weren't finished living this *belle vie* yet—at least I didn't think we were.

My mind returned to the present. If Ralph's test results didn't result in the loss of our right to residency but the less traumatic outcome of a suspended driver's license, what would those implications be? The most obvious change would be that all the driving would be left to yours truly, though in truth we didn't drive around that much. Bikes and feet met the need for running many errands in and around town. But there were the big grocery shops and firewood-for-the-chimney runs, not to mention visits to the local wineries to restock our wine cellar. (Not that we possessed a proper *cave*, unless you counted a pair of tall metal racks in our back bathroom. It's the coolest room in the house.) Those were the times when an auto fit the bill.

Then an even crueler question arose in my mind. What would happen to our long-distance adventures? Maybe the train? We loved riding the rails, but trains were primarily helpful for visits to major cities, which typically didn't rank at the top of our travel wish list. Trekking into the wilderness and going off the beaten track were more our style, and such trips would be challenging to make with any frequency with only a single chauffeur, especially if that person were *moi*.

Our strong drive to discover meant literally *driving* to discover. In just a few hours from Saint-Rémy, we could be in Spain to the west and in Italy a few hours to the east. Going north, the Rhône Valley and the Alps awaited, and so on. Our to-go list kept growing as we learned more about enticing, distinctive new places not far from us. But if I were the sole driver, instead of swapping two-hour shifts at the wheel, all the road trip adventures would depend on me, slowing us down considerably.

And honestly, that set-up would be exhausting for Ralph. Blessed with a strong self-preservation instinct, he tolerated my driving "style" only by remaining alert when I was at the controls—no distracting himself with reading or relaxing. Rather, he assigned himself to driving-school duty and took his self-appointed position seriously. Staying constantly vigilant could be demanding, but he rose to the occasion with gusto. "Did you see the speed limit dropped to 110 km?" "Why aren't you passing this guy?" "Uh, the light turned green." "Red taillights up ahead—do you see them?" "Isn't the cruise control on?" "Oooh, you cut that close." Admittedly, most of the time he was right.

Soon, my stream of consciousness struck an even more sensitive nerve. Oh no, not the birds, I thought. Birds were off-limits. Untouchable. They were in a category of their own. Absolutely sacred. Nothing (well, almost) came between my ardent birdwatching husband and his avian friends. He could find many nearby birds but needed a vehicle to reach his beyond-nearby birds. If the policeman relieved Ralph of his driver's license, my beloved's birding would be severely curtailed. Unable to navigate independently meant gone would be his solo treks to the Camargue. For Ralph, knowing that during any season he could be in the marshlands spotting flamingos, stilts, avocets, and at least thirty other birds on a given day filled him with boundless joy. Public transportation didn't reach these remote corners of the Rhône delta with dependable regularity.

Of course, I could don the chauffeur's cap on the birding excursions, but Ralph's solo time would be compromised. And limiting that all-important personal space could lead to dangerous waters where our partnership was concerned. For peace and harmony to reign in our homestead, regular alone time was highly advised, if not downright essential. So it seemed that now, while Ralph was biding his time before blowing into the breathalyzer tube, not only was our day-to-day life in France hanging in the balance, but also our relationship.

That was when my fevered brain went into overdrive. *Perhaps*, I thought, *this whole ordeal is a sign that it's time to design a new dream.* Even if Ralph passed this test with top marks, was this the moment to reevaluate our Provençal lifestyle? Had it run its course? Had we arrived at the juncture scientists call punctuated equilibrium, where evolution happens in a spurt? Were we primed for a major change? Did we want to reinvent ourselves, make a fresh start in another foreign country, perhaps on a coast or in the woods? What kind of coast? Which woods? Did we have the motivation and stamina to begin again?

Dreams change, one friend had told me. After decades in France, this multilingual American friend with French citizenship had pulled up stakes and moved to Portugal, where she was sublimely happy. Would that work for us? Or was it time to head back to the motherland—the United States, the land of convenience? Several of our Eurocentric friends did return to the US after having lived most of their working lives outside their native country. They contended that one place wasn't better or worse. They were just different.

In the best of all possible worlds, people decide independently on a major lifestyle shift and aren't forced into it, particularly not by foreign authorities. Now the privilege of having the freedom to choose might well be vanishing for us, a bleak possibility I was loath to accept. Getting booted out of a country didn't top my bucket list.

Then, as suddenly as they'd appeared, my imaginings of a new adventure somewhere outside France withered. Instead, I was overcome with a profound sadness at losing our cherished French life. Now I could only think of what a bitter blow it would be. At this moment, it all depended on a different kind of blow—a transparent puff—one with the potential power to vaporize our *belle vie*. Poof, gone, as swift as a wave of a malevolent magician's wand.

Finally we moved into first place. Ralph rolled down the window and said, "Bonsoir." The policeman nodded and offered Ralph the tube. This was it. At that moment, I felt the full weight of what was at stake—the life we'd built in our beloved corner of Provence. Staring straight ahead into the darkness demanded every ounce of focus I could muster. I didn't dare glance at the policeman beside our car for fear of jinxing the critical test Ralph was undergoing.

Doubtless, the policeman had zero interest in our French fantasy. Not to mention the mysterious reason we experienced such joie de vivre here. The simple fact was that joie de vivre *did* happen for us here like nowhere else. Living this captivating French life for over a decade had enriched us in so many gratifying and sometimes surprising ways that we couldn't explain. But even if we couldn't deconstruct the winning formula for our rich yet simple life here, it was the slow-lane life we had chosen to make, and I knew we couldn't easily let it go. And now it was all up to this solitary gendarme to decide to let Ralph go so our Provençal dream-come-true could continue.

Closing my eyes, I silently made a heartfelt plea to the official shivering in the frigid night: "Please, Monsieur Police Officer, please free Ralph and send us on our way."

Trying to tamp down my dire what-if fears, I finally lifted my eyelids and turned to Ralph, bracing myself for the verdict. The gendarme was looking down at the merciless machine cradled in his hand. His chin rose and he stared directly at Ralph, his expression stern.

"Wait a moment. Don't move," he said, turning toward a police car parked nearby.

"Oh, geez, what's he doing now?" I said.

"No idea … probably consulting his boss."

"About what?"

"Maybe he's new and learning the ropes. Just breathe."

The gendarme motioned to his colleague sitting in the patrol car to roll down the window. They exchanged a few words, which we couldn't hear. Our officer pointed to us and continued the conversation before nodding and returning to our car. Without a word, he raised his arms and pointed both gloved hands ahead into the darkness. *"Allez!"* he shouted, signaling us to make tracks. He had dangerous criminals to catch. And Ralph wasn't one of them.

Cruising at ten kilometers under the speed limit, we wound our way the ten blocks home without speaking, shocked into silence by having landed in the crosshairs of the law, possibly jeopardizing our French future. After the garage door closed, we sat stunned, unable to budge, our seat belts still secure.

A couple of deep breaths later, we freed ourselves from the straps and turned to each other with matching what-the-heck-just-happened expressions frozen on our faces. Twisting to embrace in the tight space presented a challenge. But despite our bulky coats, once our hands touched, our arms quickly found their way to a full embrace, which we held until our breathing slowed and we felt restored to a sense of safety.

Ralph spoke first. "You okay?"

"I am now," I said, my tone solemn. "But for a while, it felt like we were on the verge of losing it all."

"Losing what, exactly?"

"You know … *it.*" I swept both my hands in front of me in a dramatic gesture.

"Our French life?"

I nodded.

"I felt fine to drive. I'd been cautious with the wine and drank lots of water, but frankly, I'd forgotten how strict they are here. I'm so sorry you were so worried."

"Yeah, I got wrapped up in a bit of catastrophizing."

"Well, actually, I was also uneasy about something else …"

"Really?" I was incredulous that there could be more to be concerned about. The car wasn't loaded with contraband, after all.

"My driver's license. It didn't occur to me until right before the test—I couldn't remember whether I'd put it back in that little credit card holder where I keep it."

"There's a fine, but you usually don't lose your license for that," I said, shuddering at the thought of the policeman finding him licenseless, even though that violation was near the bottom of the offense list.

Ralph extended his legs and pushed his back against the seat to allow some wiggle room as he dug it out of his pants pocket. "Yep, it's here. And our no-nonsense gendarme didn't even ask for it."

"Another crisis averted," I said, letting out a breath I hadn't realized I'd been holding. "But while we were in the lineup, our situation set off some pretty disruptive thoughts—unnerving, actually."

"I can see that," Ralph said. "You're shaking."

"A lot to unpack …" I said, taking my time. I needed some to process the realization of what we had unwittingly risked. We'd been careless, tempting fate. The police stop was a wake-up call, and I knew I couldn't ignore it, letting it go to voicemail. I had to pick it up and step up to take some sort of action. What, exactly, I wasn't sure. "Better to sleep on it."

"Definitely. It's nearly tomorrow."

Rubbing my hands together to generate warmth, I emitted a baritone *brrrr*. "Let's go inside now. I need to thaw out."

"Yes, but before we do, listen. We had a scare, but we know how to avoid the situation in the future. And we will. Nobody got hurt, and we're together. Let's celebrate that," Ralph said.

"You're absolutely right," I said. We'd been issued a warning, and it was up to us to heed it. "We can control this."

"That's not to say a meteor won't land on us tomorrow," Ralph said lightly.

"Hon-*eeeeee*, be serious." I objected to Ralph trivializing our close call and my reaction to it. But then I realized that in his inimitable way he had put the situation into perspective. We were fine and knew how to remedy the problem, and most importantly, our life together was intact. "But thanks for that—for the reality check. I needed that."

"Maybe this will help too," Ralph replied, twisting toward me. The first kiss was soft and reassuring, barely grazing my lips. But the second packed some heat—in genuine French fashion, of course, *bien sûr*.

2

Looping

Saint-Rémy-de-Provence

Before heading out the next morning, now known infamously as The Morning After, it felt de rigueur to convene a joint session of the key players of The Night Before to clarify our brush with the law. I needed to talk it out. What had it all meant and why did I feel the need to deconstruct it?

Over coffee, I said to Ralph, "About last night …"

Putting his mug down, he said, "Yeah, we should definitely discuss it."

"As you know, while you were in mid-puff, my mind was racing and bouncing between conflicting thoughts. I was playing out worst-case scenarios, mourning the loss of our life here as we know it. And on the other hand, I wondered whether it was a signal that it might be time to create a new life somewhere else, maybe returning to the US, even if you *did* pass the puff test." I further explained that the competing concepts swirled in my brain like a murmuration of a thousand wing-flapping starlings gone berserk. It was a royal mess.

"Wow," Ralph said, "I'm so sorry, honey. You took on some pretty heavy issues in a short period. I was mostly trying to remember if I'd grabbed my license."

"I'm so glad I didn't know you didn't know if you had it or not," I said. "That would have made things even worse. My anxieties were already accelerating at warp speed."

As we moved through our review of the unsettling encounter, we agreed on a few lessons. Number one, before hitting the road, we make absolutely sure we have our licenses and IDs. Number two, if alcoholic beverages are on the menu wherever we are going, so goes an abstaining driver, designated ahead of time. And number three, we take last night's lesson to heart for the well-being of all. I didn't fancy finding myself in the middle of another chaotic mosh pit of thoughts.

"Speaking of wild happenings," Ralph said, "do you really think it's time for us to move on—away from Saint-Rémy?"

"For the most part, no. But sometimes, yes. Especially when we're having a fun adventure somewhere else, there are moments when I wonder, What would life be like *here*?"

"Well, that's certainly something to think about. We've talked about finding a pied-à-terre somewhere for ages. We could get more serious about that."

"I think we should—we could test out a few places that aren't too far from here."

"But if returning to America appeals, could that be fear talking?"

"Hmm … yeah, and it had a lot to say. I felt so vulnerable while you were taking the test. Chills were shooting up my spine that had nothing to do with the weather."

"That's completely understandable. It was a potentially serious situation."

"That's an understatement," I said. From my perspective, it was a too-close encounter of the dream-depleting kind.

"On the other hand," Ralph continued, "that impulse to move to another foreign country—could that maybe be boredom?"

I paused to gather my thoughts so I could present them as precisely as possible, then said, "The truth is—"

Ralph interjected. "Wait a second, how about holding that thought—just let all those agitated ideas settle a bit? Let's see how they stack up after the Loop."

I loved the Loop. That's the name of the walking workout circuit that Ralph and I formulated during our first year in Saint-Rémy. We had several variations of the route, but they all included a balance of urban and rural features: the bustling historic center of Saint-Rémy, the Roman ruins of Glanum, Saint-Paul-de-Mausole, the hospital made famous by Van Gogh, the forests of the Alpilles filled with birdlife, hectares of vineyards, a winery, ancient canals, a snazzy five-star resort, a farm, and traditional residential neighborhoods. All the circuits were a pleasure and an integral part of our life here. Spending time in the fresh air beat living indoors no matter the season, though admittedly there was not much demand for snowplows here. It was more a question of bundling up or paring down a bit.

"Ah, so wise," I said, wondering why I hadn't thought of that, well versed as I was in the Loop's powers to calm and revitalize like an emotional reset. Although playing tennis and cycling were favorite outdoor hobbies, we often opted to walk because it wasn't so weather dependent and required no planning or prepping—no court to reserve or tires to pump. Just get out the door and go, maybe with an umbrella, always with binoculars in case something flighty merited a close-up. That explained why we'd probably done some version of this hour-plus town-and-country trek at least a couple of thousand times. And the calorie-burning route never failed to feel like a mini-adventure. With surprises tucked in everywhere, it reliably intrigued, inspired, and sparked smiles. And sometimes it led to double espressos at a sidewalk café, where we observed the perennially entertaining morning shift of the village stirring to life.

Today, after the nerve-racking Big Puff night, I was counting on the Loop to deliver its refreshing reboot. As we stepped out on the road, we agreed to ignore the previous evening's upset for now and start our Loop walk fresh—open to the sights and sounds around us. I needed my brain to relax into contemplation mode, so I planned to home in on what had made us fall in love with this place in the first place. Although it was a drab morning, my spirits were buoyed by our walk's sunny possibilities—or maybe simply by the fact that I wasn't at a police station posting Ralph's bail.

Since our morning trek through the neighborhood often happened in a sleepy trance, it was a relief that we rarely saw neighbors who expected a coherent chat. But we liked to check in at one house at the entrance to our *quartier*, a new addition to the neighborhood. It wasn't a new home for humans but a tiny hut-shaped habitat for books. The tiny library, built courtesy of the local chapter of a community group, was a sturdy, pitched-roof structure with a Plexiglas door supported by thick wood legs bolted to the asphalt. Above the transparent door, it read *CULTIVONS LE GOÛT DE LIRE*—"Let's cultivate the taste for reading." Based on the activity we had observed at other mini-libraries, they were a gigantic success.

Ralph plucked out a Donald Duck comic book *en français* and flipped through a few pages. The goofy tale set in Paris immediately proved to be a surprising vocabulary builder. After checking his phone translator, he learned that, in French, a *gratin* is not simply a type of casserole with a cheese topping, but also refers to the elite members of a population—the upper crust. So now we can read *"le gratin mange du gratin"* without confusion—understanding that it's an elevated socio-economic group that enjoys cheese-topped baked dishes. Ralph filled me in on the story's ending. A wealthy, *fromage*-filled Parisian couple walk off their indulgence by strolling through Luxembourg Gardens to a service at the world-renowned Cathedral of Notre Duck.

"You'll be chuckling your way to fluency, Duckie," I said.

"Whatever works," Ralph replied.

I agreed wholeheartedly. Improving my French was gratifying, and I suddenly realized I'd languished on a linguistic plateau for far too long. I was overdue for picking up the pace. I had some ideas about *my* best way to do that. It was up to me to choose one and get on with it.

Before continuing up the skinny lane just beyond the free bookshop, we carefully looked at the other three roads that intersected here because all sorts of vehicles come roaring through. We also needed to dodge bikes rented from the popular electric bike shop, often wiggling through a gaggle of adults and sometimes families with tiny tots in tow testing out bicycles or listening to the commentary delivered by Marcel, one of the managers. Last fall, as Ralph and I approached the shop, I'd spotted a helmeted man attired in Lycra standing next to a bicycle, clapping his hands and singing enthusiastically, "If you're happy and you know it clap your hands, if you're happy and you know it clap your hands ..."

"Ha, there's one tourist excited about buzzing into the hills," I'd said, drawing Ralph's attention to the upbeat scene. Upon closer inspection, I saw the man was clasping his baby's chubby fists as he sang while his wife adjusted the protective straps on the child. The father continued singing, "If you're happy and you know it, then your face will surely show it …" We proved no exception. Ralph and I couldn't get the ditty out of our heads, leaving us grinning like goofballs for the entire walk. Now, just thinking about it, the tune took hold once more. Of course, I had to clap, eliciting an amused smirk from Ralph.

Almost next door to the bicycle shop stood Le Petit Hôtel, formerly a distressed building, now a stylish lodging. While it was undergoing beautification, the owners had welcomed me onto the construction site to see the development. I was astounded to find a lush vast backyard with a stunning pool. It was so inviting and calming that once completed, it became a special spot to meet friends for an afternoon coffee. As we passed, the if-you're-happy-and-you-know-it refrain boomeranging around my brain instantly succumbed to my tranquil reflections. I imagined that more hidden treasures like this one were tucked in all over Saint-Rémy, just waiting to be discovered.

Up ahead, I saw that the new art gallery-in-the-making had donned a fresh coat of Tiffanyesque turquoise paint. When it made its début, it would join dozens of other galleries in town, enhancing Saint-Rémy's open-air museum quality. No ticket required, I noted with satisfaction.

My precious cinema, La Palace, displayed new film posters above the doors, so we grabbed a program even though I receive them electronically, a perk for cinema club members.

Being a film nut, I enjoy the challenge of reading all the movie synopses. I hope it's not just a delusion that I'll one day be able to breeze through all the offerings. It won't mean I've mastered French or can interpret the nuances of an entire French flick. But at least maybe I'll be able to follow the plot line sans crib sheets.

When we turned the corner at the fashionable Hôtel Gounod, I marveled at its history. In 1863, it was but a modest inn when French composer Charles Gounod wrote the famously popular opera *Mireille* within its walls, and now it's ready to pamper posh guests. Like Le Petit Hôtel, from the front you would never guess an expansive, Shangri-la garden replete with a pool is hiding behind the unpretentious façade.

The engraved plaque commemorating the operatic composer is easy to spot by the hotel's entrance six days a week, but Wednesday is a different story. That's the day of Saint-Rémy's market, one of the region's best, which explains why *marché* aficionados flock here, me included. On our trips here from Germany, it was always a top priority to experience the vibrant cacophony of the market, where the town comes alive. Stalls displaying clothes, shoes, straw carriers, hats, and table-cloths spring up right in front of the hotel and cover the entire Place de la République. The market booths encircle a glittery merry-go-round that is usually draped until the afternoon after the vendors pack up, and then it's a big draw. On weekends in warm weather, the carousel is abuzz with kids giggling while their grinning parents snap photos, the latter probably secretly yearning to take a ride themselves. Where would they take a seat—on the galloping stallion, rocket ship, or hot-air balloon?

A few years ago, I saw a little boy in a buggy pushed by his dad watching the rotating ride. As if for the first time experiencing the carousel's colorful figures swirling to a rousing tune, the boy twisted his chubby body around so he could take it all in, his eyes bulging with wonder and his little mouth agape. Meanwhile, his father was preoccupied trying to safely navigate the crowds, completely missing his child's wonderment. It wasn't lost on me, though. I knew the boy was enjoying one of life's standout moments. Had he been able to catch his breath and speak his mind, I would have heard something like "Papa, stop—please! What is this marvelous, magical thing? I want to try it!" He was clearly having his own joie de vivre moment, and I could relate completely.

Across the street at the Bar du Marché terrace, workers in paint-spattered overalls gathered to sip their morning espresso or pastis, exchange news, or read *La Provence*. I noticed the Albert Einstein look-alike, who we often saw pedaling his antiquated bike all over town, always without a helmet but sometimes with a beret, and occasionally smoking as he went. Now, he was hunched over a folded paper, pencil in hand, scribbling intermittently. I wondered what his backstory was as he concentrated on his crossword or Sudoku. Maybe he was a renowned artist, inventor, or land baron. In contrast, the guy sitting at the table next to this eccentric fellow was perfectly coifed, dressed in casual haute couture. All types, side by side, providing a fascinating scene for people watchers like us.

Pausing at the ring road, we considered which of the two main paths to take through the historic center. The "high" road led to striking Place Jules Pellissier, dominated by the Hôtel de Ville, the city hall, and the "low" road went past the more intimate Place Favier, surrounded by ancient chestnut trees that offered blessed shade in summer. The square was home to the Musée des Alpilles and several restaurants, including the stylish eatery Maison Favier and the family-run Crêperie Lou Planet. During the tourist season, on market day, the square was chockablock, mostly with artisans hawking all manner of handmade products such as jewelry, olive wood platters, lavender wands, and watercolors. Today, it would be tourist-free and aglow in the pale winter light, alluring in a tranquil way. I loved that Saint-Rémy had quiet corners just a few blocks from the hustle and bustle.

While we waited for the last in a string of battered delivery vans to pass, Ralph asked, "High or low today?"

"Today I'd like to see how my dolphins are doing," I said, referring to the elegant fountain called the Fontaine des Quatre Dauphins in front of the Hôtel de Ville on Place Jules Pellissier.

"Excellent choice," Ralph said as if I'd finally decided which ultra-expensive Bordeaux to pair with our three-star Michelin dinner. I appreciated him lightening the mood, helping to quiet the nagging questions about boredom tumbling through my brain. We'd agreed to hold off discussing the previous night, but I couldn't help a small reference slipping out.

"You know, honey," I said, "just for the record, I'm *really* glad you're not behind bars."

"That makes two of us. I'm happy just for a regular, routine day, like this walk. Is it working—you feeling better?"

"Yes, I'm off to a good start."

Ralph nodded, squeezed my hand, and we crossed the street.

As we walked by l'Église Saint-Martin, birds flew overhead, casting pale shadows that drifted across the walls, a soothing sight. Less than serene, however, were the church's concerts featuring its elaborate, humongous organ. Part of the town's musical heritage, the events attracted a devoted following. Although not organ music aficionados ourselves, we had attended a few times over the years and recognized the power of the pipes. That said, we were more likely to show up for the jazz, opera, or country-western events the city sponsors at various venues. All year round, no matter the month, there was usually a musical happening to tempt us into the swing of things.

Just beyond the ultra-chichi clothing store Souleiado, we passed a little lane called Rue Hoche. More of an alleyway, it was famous for one building, the birthplace of Saint-Rémy's most famous native son, Nostradamus. The privately owned house was plainer than plain, but a large plaque identified the renowned author of the treatise *The Prophecies*, who was born here in 1503. Busloads of tourists made long journeys to visit Nostradamus's home, but it was easy to take the history of the town for granted when you passed by the ancient walls almost daily. But today I saw them in a new light, and thought to listen to them, wondering whether they had any wisdom to convey. I'm not sure whether the walls were talking, but a question about longevity sprang to mind that impacted my thoughts concerning our life: What was fleeting and what endured?

Carrying along Rue Lafayette, we soon came to a former convent, long ago repurposed as the Hôtel de Ville. Dwarfed by gigantic plane trees, the *fontaine* looked as dazzling as ever. Regardless of the season, this graceful work of art was a show-stopper, deserving of a petite pause to pay tribute.

Popping out on the far side of the old town, we arrived at the Victor Hugo section of the ring road. Down the block to the left was the exceptional Maison de la Presse, which doubled as the town's heartbeat. Not only did it sell local, national, and international newspapers and magazines, but also stationery, greeting cards, toys, school and art supplies, and of course books. And since the recent change of ownership, with a vivacious young woman taking the reins, the store was even more vibrant and now included an English-language book section. It was such a treat to browse the treasure trove that you'd likely not leave without a few seeds of inspiration.

If we walked to the right, we'd find the beautiful Hôtel de l'Image, originally a movie theater opened by the French film director Jean-Luc Godard in the 1970s. Now, as a four-star hotel, its lobby showcased a massive vintage movie projector, a nod to its cinematic past. The real surprise was the "backyard." Right in the middle of town, the hotel grounds opened to an unobstructed view of the Alpilles. The panorama was wonderfully unexpected, like our life in Provence. Some days I still couldn't believe we lived here, and today was one of them.

Next we began the country portion of the walk. We followed a wiggly pedestrian lane to the big public car park and upward to the five-star Hôtel Vallon de Valrugues. Blackberries weighed down bushes along this stretch in summer, and we often gathered them as we passed by to use in smoothies or for jazzing up a flute of Prosecco. I had never thought of myself as a forager before, but in Provence, it felt completely natural. Now, I found myself anticipating the summer season's next crop.

At the canal, we paused and checked both sides to see whether anything was paddling by. Once we had seen a Little Egret fly out from under the bridge, its snow-white wings flapping gracefully, its bright yellow feet trailing behind. But most of the time we saw Mallards, and it was a kick to watch them too. Today, several were gorging on canal food as if they'd just finished a fast. As they voraciously sucked up the muck, I imagined that between the beak dips their enthusiastic quacks were dishing out compliments like "Yum, yum, how good is this pond scum?"

Often this was where, just downhill from the fancy hotel, we passed couples hand in hand, strolling to town, smiling dreamily as they looked around and took in the Provençal landscape. They had what Ralph and I called "the glow," as well they should. After all, they were on holiday in Provence. Today there were no tourists "aglow," but just as we reached the crossroads of Chemin Canto Cigalo, a fluffy-tailed red squirrel fired across the road and up a tree. We tried to follow the little fellow with binoculars, but he quickly disappeared into the foliage.

When the squirrel didn't reappear, we turned our attention to the farmyard next door. Here, we planned to pay homage to the lone *vache* who chewed her cud in the grassy patch by the road. I always felt an out-on-the-range freedom when visiting this farm, even though it was close to town. Several bovines used to graze here, and then there was just one. How happy cows looked, I wasn't certain, but *my* cow seemed especially forlorn after she'd lost her mates. I found her glumness particularly sad the last time we saw her, making me wonder whether she had sensed a depressing change afoot.

Whether she had or not, her hooves were made for walking, and that's what they had done. Today I found that my *vache* had vanished. The entire acreage, maybe two hectares, had been severely mowed and the whole place looked tidied up; even the boisterous dogs were tied up. With all the building going on around the city, I got a funny feeling that this extensive property had met with an auctioneer's hammer. I was suspicious that the transformation might herald impending construction.

At that moment, a woman arrived in a mud-spattered truck and parked beside us. As she unlocked the gate, she confirmed my theory. The property had sold, and my *vache* was not returning. I couldn't bear to ask where she was grazing these days, but hoped she occupied greener pastures. As melancholy as the bovine was, she had been a constant, an enriching part of the landscape's fabric, and the Loop was the poorer for losing her. I knew that adapting was key to maintaining a positive frame of mind, which is not to say my memories would evaporate. Au contraire. I conferred on the property the commemorative moniker Place Vache, and I knew that each time we passed by, we'd recall its better days.

Continuing south along Chemin Canto Cigalo, approaching the Alpilles, we crossed the Ancienne Voie Aurélia, often waiting for the cyclists whizzing down the road in this popular biking zone. We marveled at the new extension attached to an old stone house on the right. As much as we scrutinized it, we couldn't determine where the old part ended and the modern section began. Hats off to the artisans for their remarkable work at preserving tradition while embracing the new.

At this point, the road became a hard-packed dirt lane, and dwellings were few. As we marched past an olive grove toward the Alpilles, we arrived at a clearing scattered with tall pines and oaks. Like us, jays and woodpeckers liked to hang out here, where the views were marvelous. There was one particularly enchanting spot where a pair of limbs from small oaks had grown toward each other in two arcs. The heart shape framed a verdant vista of vines and olive groves with Saint-Rémy in the distance—the perfect place to steal a kiss. As our lips closed in on a smooch, a resident Eurasian Jay screeched, startling us. We turned in unison to see a brilliant streak of copper and dusty blue flash by.

"Just love that bird. Always such a pleasure to see one," I said.

"Me too, though that wasn't the best timing," Ralph noted.

"I'm not in a rush." I gave him a come-hither glance.

"Me neither." He leaned in to finish the job.

Our next pause took place above an olive orchard, next to a vineyard, offering another fab view of Saint-Rémy. There, we gave our favorite fruit a pep talk. "You go, vines!" I said. "Get a good rest and we'll see you next September for the *vendanges!*" Hopefully, it would be a brilliant harvest. Drinking wine from a local vineyard was especially satisfying, and with so many to choose from in Provence, we were spoiled for choice. Most of them were small family-run operations, dedicated to their craft, preserving tradition from generation to generation. Was that another aspect of life here I took for granted?

Down the road, we turned right at a lane that connects to the Chemin des Carrières, at the base of the Alpilles. It was a rocky, uneven path, so we had to watch our steps. An incline in one spot was so steep that only a tank could cruise across, so vehicles were rare. The lack of noise and exhaust fumes was a boon to the many bird species that filled up the forest around here, and when they chirped, our binoculars swung up. In summer it was a great place to spot electric-blue European Rollers. They tended to perch, inviting admiration. They were always a treat, and I always obliged.

Next up, we came to the home of another artist, one from long ago. Near the two well-preserved Roman structures called Les Antiques outside the ancient Roman city of Glanum, we turned down a dirt path running along a wall of

Saint-Paul-de-Mausole, the asylum where Vincent Van Gogh sought treatment. He was a resident for only a year (1889–1890), but in that time he produced over 150 works here, including one of his most famous paintings, *The Starry Night*. The Musée d'Orsay in Paris is its permanent home, but I hoped that one day at least one of the Dutchman's paintings would take up residence in the town that so inspired its creator. As we trudged along, I reflected on what the Romans would have thought of Van Gogh. Living millennia apart, they had something in common. They had both chosen to reside in the same dreamy neighborhood.

Provence itself was an invitation to dream. That was how our life here started. For years, we had dreamed about living in Provence, and now we were walking the Loop for the umpteenth time, each time experiencing something worth relishing. Usually lots of somethings, and each was extraordinary in its singular way. Did I appreciate them? Yes, in theory, when I thought about them. But did I appreciate them enough?

Halfway through the Loop, the walk's calming effect was taking effect. As my shoulders began to relax, my thoughts about our French life also began to take shape. Maybe by the time we were back home, *chez nous*, I'd have sorted out my answer to Ralph's question about whether boredom was a factor in our Saint-Rémy life. At this point, at least, one aspect was clear—Ralph's question really was about defining our future, and *that* was coming into focus. I wanted to reassure him that I was making headway so he wouldn't worry.

"This walk is working its magic," I said. "The fog is lifting from my thoughts. I feel like clarity is coming."

"I'm very glad to hear that. Actually, I'm not surprised. There's nothing like getting outside to clear your mind."

As we drifted downhill toward home on the rutted-out lane behind Van Gogh's monastery, we had to walk single file because it was so narrow. That didn't stop mountain bikers from blasting through. Sometimes if we'd timed our walk poorly and met a guided tour, we'd back ourselves into a break between the bushes to allow them safe passage. Striving to be good ambassadors for the town, we'd wish each of the dozen or so cyclists a *bonne balade*, a good ride. Sometimes we'd be stuck in there for a while. But all was clear today, so we picked up the pace. My ideas to share with Ralph were accelerating too.

We arrived at a busy crossroads, which we had named Russian Roulette Junction. There was no visibility around the corners and stop signs stood only on two sides, so cars blasted on through, relying on drivers going in the opposite direction to heed the signs. After witnessing a few near misses, we always mustered extra caution as we hustled across.

Usually, however, there was nothing particularly scary or dangerous about this walk, aside from a long, fat serpent I had once seen in the hills (I leaped over it before speeding off to safety). But the trail did have its hazards if one wasn't paying attention. Along this stretch, I often saw my friend Paula buzzing by on her bike en route to work in town. One day while Ralph was chasing birds in the Camargue, I was walking alone, daydreaming about an adventure, unaware of my proximity to a newly installed signpost. At that moment, Paula came from behind and shouted, "Bonjour, Gayle," racing by with a waving arm. Startled by the greeting, I swerved and conked my head on a metal YIELD traffic sign, or rather the smaller rectangle beneath it that read STOP 150 METERS. The sign clash set me back, though there was no gushing blood, thankfully. After hearing about my accident, though sympathetic at first, Ralph had been overcome with the comical irony of my collision with a Yield sign, remarking that that sort of tricky maneuver took talent. And impeccable timing, I'd added.

"But hon," Ralph had said, resting his forearms on my shoulders, "you really need to be careful not to lose sight of where you're going."

Tapping my tender forehead, I nodded my agreement. "Point taken—literally," I'd said ruefully. In order to carry out our down-the-road plans, it behooved me to concentrate on the road I was on. I needed to hold tight to that thought.

So today I focused, careful to avoid bonking my head on my nemesis sign, and Ralph and I safely turned right and walked by the kiddie park. This isn't your ordinary playground but more of a wood sculpture garden. All the "rides" are fashioned out of natural wood in the shapes of animals of the Alpilles, like the Eagle Owl slide with sprawling carved wings swooping gracefully to the ground. The park is an oasis for kids to slide, swing, and run around through art. It is popular with locals and visitors alike, and a variety of languages can often be heard. Today, Italian flowed from the direction of a big, beefy guy with a heavy beard who sat at one end of a seesaw, his knees practically touching his ears. At the other end, another large man held his hand lightly on the back of a preschooler dressed in a coat over a frilly pink dress with matching trainers and hat, clasping the handles and giggling as she drifted down and "flew" up again. The little girl's glee reminded me of my own frequent moments of joy and what a difference they made every day. When those unique moments filled with joie de vivre cropped up, life took on an extra layer of delight. I was certain that this distinctive feature of our life here was at the heart of what defined it and needed further investigation.

Cutting through the tourist office parking lot, we remembered the need for a key ingredient for the dish we had our hearts set on for dinner. The grocery store across the street was small, but it was well stocked and open daily, including Sundays, except for Christmas and New Year's Day. It was a godsend for last-minute menu creators like us. We could bike over to pick up whatever our pantry lacked. Since everybody forgets something sometimes, you'd often run into someone you knew. Or maybe a celebrity. Recently, a part-time resident, actor Omar Sy of *Lupin* fame, was taking selfies with the checkout clerk when my friend Julie stopped by. By the time she mustered the nerve to ask for one, the star had slipped out the door. Now, in the hopes of running into the acclaimed local, I stopped in the parking lot and dug around in my purse.

"Something wrong?" Ralph asked.

"No, just looking for my lip gloss."

"To go into the market?"

"You know …"

"Right. My best to Omar—and stay calm and carry on, please. I'll wait here."

With a tiny tub of crème fraîche tucked in my jacket pocket but minus a movie star sighting to report, we continued home. At the bus stop on the corner, boisterous screaming wafted over the wall from the elementary school playground. The kids were working up an appetite and we were envious, knowing they'd enjoy a delicious lunch—without a single *frite* or pizza slice in sight. The school's refined cafeteria cuisine had been featured on the British TV series *Simply Provence* with the acclaimed British chef Marcus Wareing. The program revealed how tender taste buds were trained from a young age, encouraging healthy food attitudes that would last a lifetime. How lucky they were.

Across the street, café terraces were filling up with coffee customers. I wanted to be one, but I wanted to be snug at home more. I'd brew a couple of mugfuls for Ralph and me before discussing the question of boredom, and how that meshed with our future.

As we moved along the quiet streets, past the post office and the community center where I took yoga, I sensed movement in my peripheral vision. An older monsieur sans helmet pedaled by at high speed on a thick-tired bike. He didn't exactly paint the clichéd French picture of a quaint villager—he wasn't wearing a striped shirt, espadrilles, or a beret—but a formidable baguette stuck nearly half a meter out of one of the tattered panniers straddling the rear wheel. Maybe he was late for an early lunch, but I hoped he'd take the corners slow so he didn't lose his loaf. After all, it was a mainstay of the daily *déjeuner*.

When we reached the safety of *chez nous*, not having been battered by an airborne baguette, Ralph said, "So what's your verdict on boredom?"

"You know, when you suggested earlier that I might be bored here, I was about to answer that the truth is, boredom is *not* a factor." My city girl side thought about Samuel Johnson's famous comment about London—that if you're tired of it, you're tired of life because the metropolis has all life can afford. As true as it may have been for the British writer, my country girl component had expanded over the years. "Granted, Saint-Rémy may not offer *everything* on my hometown wish list. I do miss not having the major cultural venues of a big urban hub nearby. But I love the variety of lifestyles and landscapes, the architecture and history—all the surprising contrasts—right here in our backyard."

"Or close by," Ralph added.

"You're absolutely right—how can I forget that?" I said, recalling a long list we'd compiled of intriguing places just an hour or two from home that we had yet to explore. I also thought about some of the adventures we'd had recently: a star-studded history lesson at the winery by Les Baux-de-Provence, a delectable Thanksgiving lunch at a counter in the Nîmes covered market, finding a wayward Siberian noble in an oyster village on a lagoon by the Mediterranean, a birthday bash in Bonnieux near Russell Crowe's château from the movie *A Good Year.*

I went on. "And when I stop to think about the *far-flung* French adventures we've had recently, well, we've actually covered a fair amount of territory."

Ralph recalled fun times we'd had in Paris, in a tiny town in the Alps, and on Corsica, adding, "And we didn't go just by car but also by train and boat."

"And boots and bikes. Let's not forget the Île d'Ouessant, the island at the end of the earth."

"I guess you could say we've *played around*," Ralph added with a wink.

I grinned in recognition of Ralph's double entendre. I knew he meant that we had traveled widely and not the spicy connotation of the phrase. Then I paused, remembering I *did* have competition for my birder husband's attention. My jealousy was manageable, though, as I was reasonably sure that the only mistress in our midst sported feathers and flew. "Yep, we *have* made tracks across France and racked up a mountain of joie de vivre moments."

These were the flashes of delight that continued to sparkle through the years. Before walking the Loop, my thoughts about what our *belle vie* really meant had wafted through my brain, but minus a Meaning-of-*La-Belle-Vie* tool kit, I was unsure of how to define it. Now, one thing was obvious—joie de vivre moments were key. The more we talked about it, the more we came to see that they were at the heart of our fascination with France, particularly Provence. Even if these memorable moments couldn't claim to be the bedrock of our *belle vie* or even weight-bearing pillars, they certainly represented essential building blocks.

"Ditto that," Ralph said.

"Every single one of these moments charges up our lives like a superpower," I said. Without them, life could morph from brilliant to bland. I told Ralph I felt in tune with the world here in Provence, a great base for endless exploring. It was as if the place were an adventurous soulmate.

Ralph said, "That explains why you were so afraid of losing it."

I agreed with him with a slow, deliberate nod.

"And now, you're wondering how or why these supercharged moments happen?"

"Yes. But, honestly, I think most of the how and why of these joie de vivre moments is like falling in love. You can describe it, but explaining it—well, that's for everyone to find out for themselves." It was probably best to leave that question undisturbed in the mystery department, at least for now. "So, however these exceptional moments arrive, when they do, it's marvelous and life-affirming."

I paused to consider what I'd just said. "Still, I feel like these experiences have been somehow incomplete—that I'm missing something crucial. It keeps nagging me. I've had this curious feeling—even before your puff test—that I've been overlooking some basic nature of these joie de vivre moments."

"How long has this been on your mind?"

"A good while, I think." The more I thought about the joie de vivre instances, the harder it was to fit them neatly into a box. They appeared in so many forms, running the gamut from an instantaneous combustion of glee, arriving like a thunderbolt, to a string of soulful seconds that slowly snuck up on me, to moments of wonder in between. Trying to summarize, I continued, "I've got the idea there must be some way to better connect to these special instances—to experience them on a deeper level. Whatever that something is, I can't help but think it isn't frivolous. I'm pretty sure it's *notable*, and also *knowable*."

"I have an inkling a challenge is coming up."

"I can't escape it," I admitted. I confirmed that his inkling about a challenge was spot on—the breathalyzer incident had been the catalyst. Maybe it was a fool's errand, but I needed to find this golden nugget of knowledge or *try* to find it. I couldn't just ignore my mind tugging at me that these joie de vivre moments held more than met the eye. They were the ingredients that made our good life, our *belle vie*, so fulfilling, yet it seemed these special moments had more to tell me. They seemed to be holding back, waiting for me to decipher some sort of message. Putting our French lifestyle in harm's way had underscored the importance of taking action. If I better understood the missing link between me and my joie de vivre moments, maybe I'd be able to do a better job of protecting our *belle vie*.

"You know," I said, "I didn't think I was taking our French life for granted, but now I know I was. Being unprepared for the traffic stop made that clear."

"Well, it's pretty easy to get caught up in the day-to-day stuff."

"I have a hunch there's a wiser way to manage things, and that hunch is hollering at me." Now, how to follow my hunch without an oracle to consult? "What exactly am I looking for, do you think?" I glanced out the window at sparrows flitting around an olive tree.

Ralph nodded, sensing that my question was more rhetorical and an answer was in the works, about to bubble up. I turned my attention back to him, and my words tumbled out. "I guess what I've got here is a *je ne sais quoi* quest."

"And if you figure out this I-don't-know-what, then you'll do *what*?"

"For starters, I'll bottle it—in a container with a sprayer."

"Of course—so you can spritz as needed."

"And I'll need a hefty supply since it's for making a better *belle vie*, which one hopes would last a lifetime."

"Well, I'm all for that. In fact, it occurs to me I know where to start the hunt." Ralph's eyes twinkled.

"Really?"

"Looking backwards for clues may point the way forward."

I looked at Ralph, puzzled.

He continued. "Joie de vivre has had its moments wherever we've been—during our big adventures and small encounters. You've documented plenty of them in your journals and books—they must hold a gold mine of memories and reflections. So replay your favorites from, say, the last couple of years. See what you find."

Turning over Ralph's idea in my head took only seconds. Doubtless, scouring our experiences for precious joie de vivre moments with my new mind-set had merit. Unveiling that notable *something* to try to connect these memorable moments could likely improve our lives immensely. And perhaps even more importantly, that *something* would work not just here in France, but wherever we might go. As if he had struck a gong, Ralph's suggestion rang true almost before the last syllable left his lips.

"So, to sum up," I said, waiting for the correct words to fall in line, "whatever I'm looking for … that notable something I know is knowable …"

"Your *je ne sais quoi*," Ralph said, filling in my blank with that quintessential French expression that describes the indescribable.

"Yes, my *je ne sais quoi* might surface if I look back at my best joie de vivre moments … which essentially translates to compiling my own personal highlight reels? Is that it?"

"Exactly," Ralph said.

"Okay then, let's go. *Allons-y!*"

3

Wine, Women, and Royalty

Les-Baux-de-Provence, South of France

Collecting my journals required some snooping. They were scattered about the house, tucked into bookcases in my atelier, in boxes in the attic, and in drawers in the hall closet. I stacked the jumble of hard-covered diaries and flimsy pocket-sized notebooks covering 2023 through 2024 and started to read. Occasionally, the most memorable highlights required dodging some lowlights—all mere hiccups except for one. But they all contributed to how our belle vie *came to be.*

Hey ho, we were off to Les-Baux, a cliffhanger of a village near Saint-Rémy. Like the Loop, it was full of surprises. Today, our hope was that the surprise would be the Wallcreeper, an elusive bird with bold crimson wing markings. In fact, the introverted bird was a regular here, according to the reports from France's foremost wildlife and diversity protection organization, the Ligue pour la Protection des Oiseaux (LPO). In this bijou village in the Alpilles, the bird frequently flew by to be counted. But never by us.

The striking bird had even escaped Ralph's view during his 2019 big birding year, during which we traveled all over France with the goal of seeing as many birds as possible. (That adventure resulted in my second book, *The Birdwatcher's Wife*.) Another year, we saw the Wallcreeper just once over in the Luberon Valley, nearly two hours from home. We'd been staying for a few days in the market town of Apt at a favorite holiday apartment called Cent Cinq and from there had hiked up to the picturesque hilltop village of Saignon. We weren't expecting to find exceptional birdlife, but we were treated to a gratifying surprise. For just a few moments, the secretive bird made several short flights from ledge to craggy ledge on the hilltop ruins, each time flashing its distinctive ruby wings.

We were always hoping to spot the Wallcreeper close to home, and this trip to Les Baux presented an excellent opportunity. It would mean a lot to see it in our very own stomping grounds, and we'd wear the accomplishment like a badge of honor, hard won over many years. Sometimes the fact that we had never seen it around here year after year generated feelings of failure, as if not seeing it was a character flaw indicative of a birder loser. Of course, nature wasn't keeping track of who saw what and where, so I knew I shouldn't take it personally. Still, as silly as it might seem, we were putting in the time and effort, so I couldn't help but ask, eyes lifted to the sky, "Are we not worthy, Wallcreeper?"

In the meantime, while waiting for the good old Wallcreeper to reward those of us who waited (and waited) with binoculars pressed to our faces, other flying feathered possibilities were the Blue Rock Thrush and Alpine Accentor. They were much more friendly, so our chances were good that we'd get lucky with at least one of them.

Prior to our trip, we'd learned that the château at Les Baux was currently open free to the public, presumably because the winter months drew few tourists and the few folks on duty in town probably welcomed the company. During our many visits to the ancient town over the years, we had always crisscrossed the vast Les Baux plateau with its spectacular vistas. We had never doled out the dough to visit the castle ruins, probably because we were certain they would not hold a candle to the awe-inspiring views that stretched to the Med, which were completely *gratuit*. This time we would close that gap in our Les Baux experiences.

Leaving the car in a free parking zone down the hill, we walked back up to the path that meandered beneath the pocked bauxite cliffs where our target birds were most likely to be found. But we saw nothing. Searching, scanning, scanning, searching—and nada. Not a Wallcreeper and no Blue Rock Thrush or Alpine Accentor either. Everybody was hiding, it seemed. Maybe it was simply too frigid for flying.

We moved on, continuing up to the entrance to the town, where I noticed a shiny plaque that referred to the Grimaldi family. I assumed it referred to the famous *famille* that presided over Monaco. But what did the exclusive principality have to do with Les Baux? I asked Ralph. No idea, he said, but maybe they'd donated that stone pedestal, pointing to the column near a viewpoint to the right. It was too cold to investigate, so we trudged ahead.

Tramping along the cobblestones, we passed *fermé* sign after *fermé* sign. The only commercial enterprise that appeared to be open was the Reine Jaune restaurant and a tearoom serving hot drinks and pastries, but not a single takeaway shop or one with picnic staples, which I'd counted on. Practically the whole town was on *congé annuel*, the yearly holiday, leaving us with a *déjeuner* dilemma. No worries, we'd get fed, I reassured myself. After our tour here, we could pop down the hill to Maussane-les-Alpilles, which did not close all its shutters in winter.

While looping around the plateau, pausing at the edges here and there to take in the massive view toward the Mediterranean, we scrutinized the rock faces for birds but still without luck. Inside the château ruins we looked for birds too, but only crows and jackdaws filled the sky, and nothing was coming or going from the crevices in the crumbling walls where there could have been Wallcreepers. The tumble-down structures were interesting, though, and I took loads of photos, which came at a cost. Each time I wanted to snap a photo, I had to remove my gloves, and my fingers froze, even out of the shadows in the full sunshine. Add to that the wind blowing me around, and I soon suggested to Ralph that we make our getaway.

As we moved through the town's narrow shadowy walk-ways, the temperature seemed to drop by the minute. Despite our discomfort, we felt compelled to be thorough about the birds, so we detoured past the church, where in 2019 an Alpine Accentor had revealed itself to Ralph. Once at the lucky bird-ing area site, we paid particular attention to a spot where there used to be lots of feeders. But there was nothing now, just a few pigeons flying around. Then Ralph saw something move. Could it be? Yes! The Alpine Accentor had not let us down. I saw it too because it flew in and remained pecking about just a few meters from us for five minutes.

Before it took off, I snapped a few close-up photos with my good camera, which I had lugged just in case, and in this case it paid off. Similar in size, shape, and coloring to a sparrow, the Alpine Accentor distinguishes itself with a black-and-white spotted bib and touches of chestnut on its sides. Not only had we achieved one of our bird goals, but as if this were a friendly reunion the bird pranced about for us, not sensing us as a threat, which was a special treat. Now, if it could just pass the word to the Wallcreeper.

By the time we got back to the car and buzzed down the hill to Maussane to find lunch, it was pushing two o'clock. All the boulangeries appeared to be closed, but we hoped that would not be the case at the popular Pizza Pont. As we approached the small shop, we saw that the shutters were open, a positive sign that they were in business today. Inside, we quickly checked out the menu, then asked a cheerful young man on the other side of a high counter for two *tartines*, a type of open-faced sandwich made with thick toasted country bread.

They were out of *tartines*, but a pizza royale was possible. While the pizza maker set to work, a small elderly man wandered in from the back of the kitchen area. He was wearing a knit cap, large glasses, a checked flannel shirt, and an unraveling mohair sweater that drooped off one shoulder. He began chatting with the staff, leaning in slightly, his hands clasped behind his back, observing how the pizzas were being assembled. The young chef's hands kept moving, scattering veggies and shredded cheese across the dough as he engaged the gentleman, asking gently, "How are you doing today?"

The man didn't brush off the question with a polite response but considered his answer, indicating that perhaps they had a close relationship. "Unfortunately, not too well. I have a bad back today."

"I'm so sorry to hear that," the chef said with sincere concern.

Signaling that he didn't want to dwell on his condition, the old man replied, *"Ça va, ça va"*—it's okay, it's okay, before shuffling to the rear of the shop.

Curious about this gentleman, I inquired about him when our pizza guy returned to the counter. Knowing that the family-run business had been around for years, I wondered whether the gentleman was part of the team, maybe even the original owner, deserving of utmost reverence. In fact, he said, the man was like the *douane*, the customs inspector—he inspected the finished product. Seeing my surprised look, he added, chuckling with the beginnings of a mischievous smile, "Actually, he's just a neighbor—he lives next door."

The pizza guys weren't just spirited kidders, having fun on the job as they patted their pizza dough and piled on the toppings. By being solicitous of an elderly neighbor, they also revealed a tender, human side. I sensed these compassionate cooks probably treated their dishes with special care too. My taste buds anticipated the best.

We parked in direct sun by the church in the middle of Maussane, where we unceremoniously scarfed down our pizza royale. With each bite of every cheesy, gooey slice, I also felt touched by the community spirit the young chef had exhibited. I couldn't help but think the product was the better for it. When it takes a village to prep a pizza pie in Provence, savoring is a must—even if they forget the 'shrooms.

Our impromptu in-the-car *pique-nique* hadn't included *le bon vin*, so we decided to follow up with a glass. On this day we didn't pop into one of our favorite wineries, Domaine Saint-Berthe, as we usually did when in the neighborhood. Instead we drove up the road to discover Mas de la Dame, a winery we knew had been around for ages but that oddly we had never visited.

Earlier in the week, I'd watched a movie called *Vigneronnes*, women winemakers, at the cinema in Saint-Rémy. After the Q&A with the filmmaker—a monsieur, by the way—I'd enjoyed a *dégustation*, a tasting, in the cinema's foyer with all the moviegoers, including some friends. The makeshift bar had been set up by the two female owners of the organic winery Mas de la Dame, the great-granddaughters of the founder. With our glasses filled, my friends and I retreated to the periphery, slowly threading our way through the dense crowd, careful not to spill. By the time we swallowed the last luscious drops, the wine table was engulfed, making it difficult to return to offer thanks.

This freezing day would be the one to correct that oversight. We knew precisely where the winery was, as we'd passed the entrance many times while driving between Saint-Rémy and Maussane. We turned onto the unobtrusive driveway next to a plain stone sign and parked outside the building. This wasn't a fancy winery like the Domaine de Valdition, near Eygalières, which has elegant iron gates and an impressive cypress-lined drive that winds around olive trees to a fabulous complex. No, this winery was modest and unassuming.

The tasting room was filled with prettily decorated tables stacked with wine, olive oil, and the makings for a gourmet *apéro*, a convivial drink with nibbles. The young woman on duty was helping the only other couple there. While we waited our turn, we wandered and examined all the goodies. Some stylish bottles of olive oil caught my eye, and I decided to take a few home. They were ideal to use as hospitality gifts.

When the young lady named Marie turned her attention to us, I asked whether the owners were around. Unfortunately, not today, she said. I'd hoped to meet them and ask some questions about the terrific film. Instead, I told Marie the story of watching *Vigneronnes* and how impressed I was that the dedicated vintners were carrying on for their great-grandfather and producing the inspired organic wine they had offered at the cinema. We were there to buy some. I explained that, sadly, I hadn't noted the exact name of the bottle of wine they had offered. Marie didn't know either, so in the interest of comprehensive wine research, we would give all the likely suspects a swirl-sniff-sip.

Marie poured, and we made our top picks. As we conducted the transaction, I gestured at a large picture on the wall of a woman standing in an olive grove and asked whether the woman was one of the owners. No, said Marie, but both proprietors were featured in a book about the winery. She pointed to an open tome on a small table. After flipping through the pages, I noticed a vintage black-and-white photograph on the wall before us. Was one of the family members in this photo? Again the answer was no, but Marie said the elegant lady wearing large sunglasses was Grace Kelly and next to her, Prince Rainier. The older gentleman in the photo was the mayor of Les Baux at the time and was giving the dignitaries a tour. It was taken in Les Baux, and the display of bottles outside a shop in the background was from none other than Mas de la Dame.

With that, she pulled out her phone and showed us a twenty-first-century color photo of the building that had once been the wine shop in the old photograph. The arch of the door was identical. I couldn't help but wonder how many cases the celebrity couple had taken back to Monaco. I didn't interrupt to ask about this detail, but I suspected the couple's limos had left Les Baux riding rather low.

Instead, I asked Marie, "So what were Princess Grace and Prince Rainier doing in Les Baux?" More than making a wine run, I felt sure. In that second, I flashed back to the Grimaldi plaque I'd spotted at the entrance to the village. *Of course,* I thought, *Rainier was a Grimaldi.* Marie explained that for a century or so, Monaco had owned Les Baux, and though France regained possession, the prince of Monaco still retained the title of Marquis des Baux and the keys to the town.

Marie's commentary on Mas de la Dame's famous associations was not over. She guided our attention to some artwork on the wall behind her. Unbelievably, it was a print of a painting of Mas de la Dame by none other than Van Gogh, in 1889, the same year the artist was staying in Saint-Rémy—at least according to local legend, which was convincing. The structures and entire scene looked remarkably the same as they did now—a road leading to a low-slung building surrounded by swaths of swirly vegetation below cobalt blue skies and the craggy Alpilles.

After heaping enthusiastic appreciation on our wine expert and her impromptu history lesson, we carried out several boxes of delicious organic wine and prettily packaged bottles of olive oil.

All of Marie's intriguing insights about Mas de la Dame piqued my interest, so I did some internet research at home. The history of the Monaco connection was one heck of a convoluted quid pro quo story. In the mid-seventeenth century

(1642 or so), French King Louis XIII granted the fiefdom of Les Baux to Prince Honoré II Grimaldi of Monaco for his support during the Thirty Years' War. Although France regained possession of the principality around the French Revolution, ties between the two vertiginous towns remained strong. This is evidenced by the Marquis des Baux title, which still belongs to the prince of Monaco, making the current reigning prince of Monaco, Albert II, aka Albert Alexandre Louis Pierre Grimaldi (born March 14, 1958), the Marquis des Baux as well. Who knew?

Another footnote Marie hadn't mentioned was that the French philosopher-writer Simone de Beauvoir referred to Mas de la Dame in her work, *La Force de l'Age* (1960): "The wind was blowing over Les Baux when I arrived there … A fire crackled in the Camino de la Reine Jeanne, where we were the only guests. We dined at a small table near the hearth, drinking a wine whose name I still remember, Mas de la Dame."

And even the Saint-Rémy-born seer Nostradamus mentioned Mas de la Dame in his best-known work, *The Prophecies* (1555), with a rather gloomy forecast about the end of the world: "The sea will cover the earth and stop at the stele of Mas de la Dame." As depressing as this vision might be on one hand, on the other, the predicted apocalypse indicated an upside—it spared the territory around Mas de la Dame. If this region's startling rugged beauty was the reason, who could disagree? *Pas moi.* The view of Les Baux, carved into limestone cliffs that tower over a patchwork of vineyards and shimmering olive orchards, is truly captivating. And that's just during the day. At dusk, when the imposing ruins of the citadel glow a golden halo, they take on a soulful, mysterious dimension.

There was no mystery, however, about the centuries-old magnetism of this exceptional patch of Provence. In addition to its striking natural beauty, this realm continued to offer a stream of surprises that enticed and informed, and the day's events were a reminder of that. This blustery winter day had begun with what we thought would be a simple, straightforward bird quest in a nearly deserted village just ten kilometers from home. Our modest objectives were to see a pair of common birds, while expecting the Wallcreeper to be its reclusive self.

What we hadn't anticipated, however, was a miniature time-travel odyssey à la *Bill and Ted's Excellent Adventure*. In the course of an afternoon, we'd engaged with some pretty heavy historic hitters who shared a past with Provence—from a sixteenth-century seer to a Post-Impressionist Dutch master to a twentieth-century French philosopher to a present-day royal family who had forged a geopolitical bond with Les Baux lasting nearly four centuries. There were a lot of layers of life to process, as if we'd unearthed a time capsule in our own backyard, filled with artifacts and symbols of illustrious lives spanning hundreds of years. I was at once embarrassed for not knowing most of this and enthralled about what else there was to discover. One thing I did know was that our adopted land possessed a complex allure that had been attracting luminaries for a very long time.

Provence put on a pretty face, but I was constantly reminded that it was not a district zoned exclusively for play. Its provocative backstory revealed deep, time-resistant powers of seduction that defied any "use by" date.

Joie de Vivre Highlights

A prancing Alpine Accentor
An endearing scene at a pizza place
A winery with an illustrious past
Les Baux's royal backstory
The legend of Van Gogh and Mas de la Dame

4

Train to Table

Nîmes, South of France

Celebrating US holidays abroad can be a tricky endeavor, especially when it comes to finding favorite traditional foods. Seeking satisfying substitutes may require creative solutions, like passing on firing up the oven and instead hitting the rails.

Cock-a-doodle-doo! Thanksgiving in the United States is typically synonymous with a turkey-with-all-the-trimmings feast. But *les dindes* in France are a Christmas specialty and are not readily available in November, except in chicken sizes. So one sunny autumn day, we decided to mark the occasion by not only dining out, but also by treating ourselves to a special day-long outing.

And I knew just the place—not just any old restaurant but an acclaimed restaurant in Nîmes. It was located inside the historic covered market and did not take reservations, so early arrival was highly recommended. And we would be traveling by train.

Departing Saint-Rémy after rush hour, we expected to arrive at the nearest train station in Tarascon in about twenty minutes. However, construction on the outskirts of downtown Tarascon had backed up traffic. This situation was not itself anxiety inducing because, contrary to our typical modus operandi for outings, on this occasion we'd allowed plenty of time to get to the station and park. But that changed when we discovered that the parking lot in front of the train station, half a hectare in size, was covered with slant-roofed wood huts—called chalets—in preparation for the opening of the Marché de Noël, marking the beginning of the festive winter season.

This meant we'd have to cruise the town searching for a spot, and how long would that take? We'd have to be quick about it and hustle back. Then, just as we turned toward the station, an empty slot on the road greeted us. Without hesitation we zipped in, with only one question: Were there signs restricting parking here? Yes, there were, but happily some temporary placards indicated that restricted parking would begin the next day, so we were good. If this lot had limited parking time, we would have been required to place our official blue cardboard clock on the dashboard, indicating our start time. But there were no signs to be seen—by our two pairs of eyes, anyway—so we skipped the clock and pushed on.

Winding through the parking lot-turned-Christmas market construction site, I began to worry. Had there been a sign we hadn't seen? Would we get a fine, or worse, get our car towed? That wasn't a far-fetched thought—we'd been down that sorry road before. Several decades ago in Nijmegen, Holland, we'd had our car towed and paid the equivalent of around US$250 to get it back—all my mad market money, plus our emergency stash. At the time, the sad irony was not lost on me that we'd come to the town for its Monday market and now, because we had unknowingly parked on the market square the night before the market, there would be no marketing.

After we'd paid the substantial fine with the scraped-together currencies we had with us, we regained possession of our car and returned to the crime scene to scour the area for No Parking signs. Nada, zip, *nyet*, which infuriated us—and we weren't quiet about it. A sympathetic Dutchman named Harry, a retired policeman who as a young boy had assisted the Americans during World War II, overheard us grumbling—as did many others—about our misfortune. In English, he explained that he very much wanted to help us sort it out.

When he couldn't locate any No Parking signs either, he took us to the police station to get some answers. Officers were dispatched, returning shortly with confirmation that the signs were missing. They had been taken down for some tarmac repairs and had not yet been replaced. Of course, all the locals knew not to park there. But that group didn't include non-clairvoyant winter visitors like us. And since the towing company was private, the police had no control over it.

Harry was undaunted. Next stop, city hall, where the mayor graciously offered sincere apologies. We thought that was the end of the sad saga, but Harry had another request that restored order to our world. Could I watch his bike while he accompanied Ralph to the towing service, which, according to the mayor, would refund our money? I did, and they did, in all the different denominations we'd paid with—Dutch guilders, plus our backup stash of German marks, and French francs.

Harry's thoughtfulness did not end there. His next kindness was to invite us to his house for cake and coffee, where we met his elegant wife, Marie. A long-term, long-distance friendship blossomed. We visited each other over many years while we lived in Heidelberg and corresponded by mail when we were in the US.

Meeting generous and helpful Harry had been a rare stroke of luck that was unlikely to happen again. Many years later when we were supposedly much wiser, it was up to us to avoid another parking fiasco. So when we reached the terminal foyer, I took action by engaging a smartly dressed woman who looked like a local on her way to work. She lived in Tarascon, which, in my hard-pressed circumstances, gave her instant credibility, as if anything she would tell me about the city would be tantamount to hearing it from the mayor. When asked about the parking restrictions, she answered that parking was free all day with no time limitation, and there was no need to place the cardboard clock on the dashboard. Offering thanks and wishing her a *bonne journée*, a good day, we felt we'd done a fair bit of due diligence.

But did this random bystander know the latest holiday parking rules? No idea. She had told us what we wanted to hear, so we went with it. Prudent? Not so much. If she were wrong, we'd face the music, maybe in court. I was dreaming to think I could defend a parking violation by stating, "Your honor, a lady at the train station said it would be okay." And that the judge would then slam her gavel, declaring, "So the lady at the train station said it would be okay—in that case, case dismissed!"

As we climbed the stairs in the station, Ralph turned to me and said, "It's not my dog," and we snorted in unison. He'd quoted a line from Peter Sellers as Inspector Clouseau in the classic movie *The Pink Panther Strikes Again*. After Clouseau checks into a hotel in Austria, he spots a puppy curled up in the foyer and wants to pet it. Before he does, he asks the elderly clerk, "Does your dog bite?" "No," the clerk answers. The inspector bends down to pat the scruffy mutt, prompting the pup to clamp his canines on Clouseau's gloved hand. He squeals, enraged, and yells at the clerk, "You said your dog didn't bite!" Without looking up, the doddering clerk responds mindlessly, "That's not my dog."

In the end, we threw caution to the wind and set off for our train. If our car was missing upon return, maybe we'd find a silver lining. But I knew that was just my rationalization talking.

Walking down the corridor to the train platform, we realized I'd forgotten to grab my beret from the backseat, and Ralph his allergy pills, stored in the glove compartment, so I trotted back to the car. When I returned, Ralph informed me that our 10:00 a.m. train would be five minutes late. But the 8:45 a.m. train was fifty minutes late and still on the track. We looked at each other and with a why-not shrug hopped aboard. This seat-of-the-pants decision seemed to be in perfect harmony with the jumbled way the morning had been going. So I topped it off with another lame due-diligence question. I interrupted a young girl wearing earbuds who was seated by the door to ask whether this train went to Nîmes. As soon as I said it, I realized I should have asked whether the train *stopped* in Nîmes, because some direct trains only stop at selected stations and surge through others. Maybe this one kept on truckin' to Perpignan near the Spanish border. She nodded with a smile and said *oui.*

Once seated, Ralph whispered in my ear, "It's not her dog either." An elbow delivered my response to Ralph's ribs—gently, of course.

A few minutes after the train was in motion, along came a young guy dressed in a dapper train uniform, replete with a jaunty pillbox hat straight out of a 1920s movie. As he approached, I said bonjour and started to open my purse to extract the tickets we'd printed this morning. Just then I realized that since we'd switched trains, I might have a problem, so I was pleased that after pausing slightly he waved me away with a smile. Maybe he wasn't on duty? Maybe he was an aspiring extra answering a casting call for a period film?

Finally, we were on board and moving, despite the Christmas market parking restrictions, engaging with a stranger about local legalities, returning to the car for Ralph's meds, and unsuccessfully searching for my beret. In the end, we departed three minutes early on a different train that was fifty minutes late.

The train held only a handful of passengers, so there was no wait for the WC, which offered its own surprises. The spic-and-span cabin was equipped with foamy soap, paper towels, and a designer toilet seat in imperial red, making this passenger feel like she'd scored an upgrade. We stopped briefly at Beaucaire on the Rhône River with its hilltop château and pleasure boat port, and also at Pont du Gard, though we couldn't see the fabulous ancient aqueduct. We'd kayaked beneath it once, which had been a thrill. I'd been scared at first and had rammed into little islands in the river, but once I got the hang of it, I loved it. Since then, we'd wanted to test out the waters by Isle-sur-la-Sorgue. Note to *moi*: Kayak the Sorgue.

Half an hour later, we hopped off at Nîmes and strolled down the wide pedestrian walkway toward *centre-ville*, passing the Musée de la Romanité with its antiquities, rooftop restaurant, and view of the exquisitely preserved twenty-one-meter-high Roman colosseum. The locals continued their workaday lives without giving the miraculous monument a thought.

Since we didn't see this marvel every day, we stopped to stare, not caring that we looked like tourists.

Early for lunch, we took advantage of the extra time to stop by the Brompton bike store. Ralph had one of these formidable foldable bicycles and adored it, but it was slightly too small for him. The manager brought out a model with a larger frame for Ralph to test drive. He rode it down and back the narrow street and said it felt great. If we acquired a second one, I'd inherit Ralph's old one, the benefits of which exceeded even its cruise worthiness. It would also ease my packing problem. They fold up so tightly that both bikes could easily fit in our car's trunk, whereas my current non-Brompton version was 50 percent bulkier. Since I couldn't manage *not* to overpack for any driving trip, having more room was a big plus. But these compact two-wheelers were pricey, so we had a discussion ahead of us, to be scheduled for another time. We thanked the helpful bike guy and assured him we'd be in touch. Now, off to lunch.

Inside Les Halles, Nîmes's vast indoor market comprising over a hundred permanent stalls selling all manner of culinary goodies, we found La Pie qui Couette, an eatery I'd read about in a favorite France-themed magazine by an acclaimed restaurant critic. I'd wanted to eat here ever since. This was it—our Thanksgiving treat. It was just barely noon, and only a few other lunchtime folks were seated at the horseshoe-shaped counter. A little boy with a hoodie sat at the far end, sipping soup as he stared at his propped-up iPad. Presumably, he was the son of one of the market vendors, "home" from school on his lunch break.

A young woman behind the counter greeted us warmly and motioned to various seats. We hopped up on the stools, ready for the culinary symphony to begin. She laid placemats, napkins, and cutlery in front of us, and soon a basket of sliced bread appeared. Then pepper and salt containers materialized, and last, she handed over the menus. We perused the options with interest, pleased to see that the grilled Galician peppers the restaurant critic had waxed poetic about were available. We ordered a portion of those to share as a starter, then *filet de merlu*, a whitefish, for me, and a chicken dish, *ballotine de volaille de l'Ardèche*, for Ralph. Plus a bottle of crisp local white. All set.

Promptly, the seats filled up, and owner-chef Emmanuel Leblay and his staff made tracks, welcoming diners, taking orders, and presenting the finished product. My fish arrived with crispy skin side up on large chunks of steamed potatoes surrounded by a thick swirl of golden aioli and topped with chopped spring onions and aromatic herbs. Simply beautiful and simply delicious. Ralph's chicken pieces were nestled in a veggie assortment bathed in a bright green pistou sauce. We traded bites that were bursting with flavor. We savored and sipped, sipped and savored.

For dessert we shared a scrumptious platter of *pélardon*, a local goat cheese, decorated with fresh chives and resting in a pool of herby olive oil, which we sopped up with rustic bread. Heaven. After we settled the bill, I explained to Chef Leblay how we had come to discover his restaurant and showed him a photo of himself from the magazine article on my phone. Beaming, he came down from behind the counter to chat. When I told him we lived in Saint-Rémy, he lit up, saying his sister Lucie had been working as a hairstylist in our town for years. I knew the salon well as we often passed it on our walks. It has always been popular, so it wouldn't be a surprise if we had friends who were her clients. I might have been one myself, but I adore my own hair guru. He's more of a well-being collaborator, so I'm very attached. Perhaps some of my buddies had the same relationship with Lucie. I made a note to find out.

This Thanksgiving feast wasn't the typical stuff-yourself-till-you-drop food orgy that was typical of our youth. We'd taken our time to choose our courses. We'd enacted our "slow to savor" motto. We relished every morsel and every swallow. It was a memorable meal in and of itself, but added to that was the friendly conversation with the chef, who seemed genuinely pleased to take a photo with me, which in turn brightened my non-turkey Turkey Day. We left filled with fabulous food and good cheer and looked forward to giving the talented chef repeat business.

We arrived early for our return ride, which was spot on time. Less than an hour later, we were back to Tarascon and back to the car, which, to our relief, was still in the same spot as we'd left it. But what was that small paper under the windshield wiper? Ralph and I looked at each other, frowning, wondering how bad the damage would be for whatever parking error we'd made. In addition to not wanting to shell out a bunch of euros for something we could have and should have avoided, I didn't want a costly parking ticket to mar what had been such a memorable day, all in a good way. A closer look showed that the small sheet was a colorful laminated ad for the Christmas market. "Thank you, thank you, parking powers that be," I whispered.

Now relaxed, Ralph couldn't resist recalling our past parking plights. "Not having our car towed might be a missed opportunity to make a special friend."

"I'm very grateful for the upsides to our missteps. But you are so right that we often get it so wrong. Maybe better to stop making a habit of taking parking risks?"

Over the next few days, I told some good friends in Saint-Rémy about our eventful train-to-table lunch, the gifted chef, and his sister Lucie. Unbelievably, two girlfriends who didn't know each other, as well as some of Ralph's buddies, had been regular clients for years. What were the chances? Were these just small-world-after-all situations, or did these connections carry a deeper meaning? Were they simple coincidences or significant ones? While pondering the value of both points of view, I sent friends the photo of the chef and me and asked them to please tell Lucie how gracious her brother had been and how much we enjoyed his restaurant. And that it was especially meaningful for Americans because it was a holiday called Thanksgiving, a day to celebrate what you're thankful for, and it usually involves quite a bit of feasting.

My friend Julie relayed my message the very next day during her hair appointment with Lucie and replied with happy news. Lucie's brother had just found out he'd been awarded a spot on a prestigious list of top international restaurants. We were thrilled for him and not surprised one bit.

Soon thereafter, I met Lucie, who turned out to be as charismatic as her brother, at her downtown salon. It was satisfying to personally tell her how thrilled I was for her brother's recent achievement and also for her own news. She was about to redesign *her* life. She was relocating to another paradise about as far from Provence as you can get—Tahiti.

Before Lucie departed, I popped into the salon while Julie was having her hair done by her favorite stylist for the last time. Not only did I want to wish her well in her new life in Tahiti, but I also wanted to show her something special. The glossy magazine accompanying the weekend edition of London's *Financial Times* contained an article about the world's best food markets.

"Guess what?" I said. "Your brother's restaurant is in it!"

Her eyes widened as I showed her the upscale magazine and the page listing the reference to the restaurant. It was written by the renowned food critic Alec Lobrano, who mentioned how popular the restaurant was. She asked me whether I thought Emmanuel knew. I offered a Gallic shrug as I handed her a copy I'd made of the article. "Maybe a special Christmas present for your talented brother?"

Even though this lovely woman I'd met by sheer chance was leaving the area and chances were slim that I'd see her again, my brief encounter with her had registered with me in more than a fleeting warm-and-fuzzy way. Simple or significant, it was impossible to say, but I was grateful for these coincidences in our small French world. They were like eager dots, anxious to be connected, and when we made the connections it deepened our sense of community, making us feel part of the fabric of this ever-enticing place we call home.

Joie de Vivre Highlights

Leaving the driving to the conductor
The Roman Colosseum
Lunch at La Pie qui Couette
A conversation with Chef Leblay
Connecting with a Tahiti-bound adventurer

5

The First Twitch

Bouzigues, South of France

Little did my non-birding self know that while roaming swamps, landfills, and scrub brush plains with my avid birder husband, I was nurturing a budding birder within. Years later, a magnificent kingfisher on a Camargue canal sealed the deal.

Hoopoes and harriers, rollers and ravens, puffins and pelicans, and loads of other fascinating feathered friends were relatively new to me just a few years ago. They and their relatives had always been flying all around me wherever I went, but I didn't know who was who until recently—2019, to be precise. That was when Ralph, my passionate birder husband of nearly three decades, persuaded me to hop on board his birding bandwagon to do a big birding year in France, where we'd lived for over a decade.

Toward the end of our year roaming around France in search of as many bird species as Ralph could find, schlepping the tripod and spotting scope from marsh to marsh, landfill to landfill, bird blind to bird blind, *it* happened. We were on yet another birding safari in the Camargue, the vast delta where the Rhône River empties into the Mediterranean Sea, so Ralph could reach his goal of at least two hundred species, when something miraculous occurred. Who would've bet that yours truly—someone who never dreamed that birds would command my attention—would have had a change of heart? I'd caught the birding bug, or it had caught me.

From one perspective, it seemed to come from nowhere. I was a non-birder one moment and a birder the next. But from a more considered viewpoint, you could say my breakthrough was like someone who's called an overnight success when in fact they've been working at their craft for decades, and then either all their hard work suddenly paid off or they just got lucky. The truth was, it took thirty years of marriage to an avid birder, meaning I'd had a zillion birding opportunities, before I saw birds in a new light.

On all our assignments while working for the US government, Ralph often birded in his free time and I would accompany him, seemingly only along for the ride. When we lived in the Washington, DC, area, the rich wildlife reserve of Huntley Meadows and the shores of Assateague were magnets for Ralph, and I would tag along sometimes. I'd see cute animals like beavers and ducks, but all that registered was the cute part. From our home in Heidelberg we crisscrossed the European continent, touching down in the Orkney Islands north of mainland Scotland, the Dutch island of Texel, the Spanish islands of Mallorca and Menorca in the Mediterranean, and the Greek Islands of Samos, Zakynthos, and Patmos. Also Tarifa, the most westerly point of Spain, the Algarve on the southern coast of Portugal, that country's main cities of Lisbon and Porto on the Atlantic coast, and on and on. Ralph always had binoculars around his neck, and he racked up a substantial life list of ID'd birds. Meanwhile, I was engaged elsewhere—wandering around villages, museums, or outdoor markets.

After our separate forays, we'd regale each other about what had impressed us. I might wax poetic about the oversized bowls of gleaming olives at the market, and Ralph would talk of the gleaming wings of a European Bee-eater. Had my brain been storing the avian info all along? Now, looking back, even though birding never clicked with me all those years, perhaps a foundation was being built, like an infant listening to human speech for two years before uttering a fully comprehensible word. I was the baby who required extensive prep. But then, I've always been a late bloomer.

The momentous moment arrived while Ralph was at the wheel, driving slowly alongside a Camargue pond, stopping now and then to press binoculars into use. During one pause, I was mindlessly looking around, thinking mundane thoughts like whether meatloaf leftovers would make a dinner, when suddenly I saw a flash of electric blue and squealed, "Kingfisher!"

So startled was Ralph that he lurched against the steering wheel as if he'd been given a hearty shove. Good thing a seat belt had him strapped in, or he would have slid off his seat. I had Ralph's hand-me-down binoculars in my lap and immediately pulled them to my eyes to study the spectacular bird dipping into the pond water and returning to the low-slung branch, over and over. When I lowered the binocs and turned to Ralph, he said, "Your eyes are sparkling."

"Really?" I said, puzzled.

"Yup. Do you realize you recognized the bird all by yourself?"

"I did, didn't I?"

Slowly I processed what Ralph had just said. Could it be that I, the CEO of non-birding partners of passionate birders, had just joined the flock? Had my recognition of the kingfisher launched me over the birding border? Maybe it meant nothing. Or did it mean something? After nearly a year of only half focusing on birds, I was sure it wasn't nothing. I'd never done that before. It felt different. Good different. Like pride, in fact. I felt proud, really proud. And feeling proud about a bird sighting was most definitely unexpected and a veritable something. I had come to name it my spark bird moment, the instant a bird and I connected joyfully, just the two of us. Although I didn't fully understand it then, it was during that split second that my birding journey took flight. Like a fledgling that flutters away from the nest under its own wing power, my birding had at last gotten off to a flying start.

Since then, my knowledge and appreciation of birds have skyrocketed. Which is not to say that I know much—just a mere drop in the bucket of birding facts—but a million times more than I'd previously known. Becoming interested in and appreciating what I see flying and trying to make sense of it has dramatically upped the fun factor of engaging in the natural world, which, frankly, I hadn't ever done a lot of. Even as a kid in Palm Springs, California, I didn't pay much attention to nature. In winter, I plucked grapefruit and lemons from our trees in the front yard and observed the hummingbirds at the feeder outside our kitchen window. Roadrunners scurrying helter-skelter across open sandy fields amused me, and I'd always pause to watch them. But for the most part I took them all for granted. They did their thing and I did mine. We might share one planet, but we both operated in different worlds.

BK—Before Kingfisher—when Ralph would point out a bird, I'd typically take a quick look and comment about its cuteness, but my enjoyment was fleeting and didn't coalesce into curiosity. Now I strap on my own binoculars for nearly every outing, anticipating what we might see. The surprises might arrive in the form of a gorgeous Eurasian Jay zipping between oaks up in the Alpilles, a sweet robin pecking on the trail behind Saint-Paul-de-Mausole, or in spring, the fabulous European Rollers in farm fields. Sometimes I might even spot a bird before Ralph does, which puffs up my feathers.

On one such occasion, along the Durance River north of Aix-en-Provence, I saw a large dark shape high in a tree at the water's edge. When we trained our binoculars on it, it turned out to be an Osprey, not a life bird for Ralph, but new for that year. It *was* a lifer for me because my bird list was short, with only a couple of hundred birds. Ralph, on the other hand, has seen, recognizes, and can describe in detail the distinctive features, calls, and behaviors of several times that number of birds.

So when our avian expert friend Gérard wrote me that the Grey-tailed Tattler, aka the Chevalier de Sibérie, had been reported for the first time *ever* in France, my bird radar system shifted to high alert. This was exciting stuff. I had the opportunity to see a bona fide rarity for France. How or why it had arrived here was a matter for speculation. Blown off course, most likely. Or perhaps this bird was a curious, gotta-be-me sort, forging its own path. Or maybe it had heard tales about the enticing Provençal lifestyle? Regardless, the unpretentious bird should have been with her flock in Australia. Yet here she was lollygagging solo on the Étang de Thau, a lagoon near the Mediterranean Sea that was only about ninety minutes from Saint-Rémy. It was an area we knew well because we often stayed at Mèze Maison, a stylish B&B in the nearby village of Mèze. Now I didn't have an overnight getaway in mind, but rather a birding adventure. I was enthralled with the Chevalier de Sibérie and itchin' to twitch.

But not Ralph. Nope, he doesn't count himself as a full-fledged twitcher, meaning a birder who drops everything at the first report of a rare bird and travels long distances hoping to catch a glimpse of that one bird. Not that we had much to drop—the day's agenda held no pressing imperatives. It was free of medical appointments, writing deadlines, social engagements, and visitor preparation.

It was to be a routine retirement play day—leisurely coffee, news update, both global and local, tennis or a bike ride or a walk—with binoculars, of course—followed by lunch and a free-form mix of activities like reading, playing the piano, studying French, cooking, house/garden maintenance, and trip planning, depending on the mood of the moment. Oh, and perhaps a short snooze squeezed into the demanding schedule before dinner, time permitting.

So it wasn't the agenda-disrupting aspect of twitching that bothered Ralph. His no-twitch policy, honed over many years, works for him for several reasons. First is the low return on investment of time, effort, and emotion. The payoff will be nonexistent if he travels a long distance searching for a single special bird that might well be on a flight of fancy and decide to disappear just after it had been reported and verified. Then, predictably, a hefty dose of disappointment is pretty much assured.

The second reason underscores his individualistic streak. While popular group twitches can reap tantalizing rewards, Ralph gets the biggest kick out of birding solo and identifying birds himself. The best birding scenario for Ralph is to consult the official bird sightings list over morning coffee, pick a zone that has a variety of good possibilities rather than just a single bird, arrive in the general area of the potential birds, and happen on them independently. This is when the gratification factor multiplies exponentially and his eyes dance. When I witness his bliss, it instantly creates a joie de vivre moment for me too.

As I pondered the Chevalier de Sibérie situation and Ralph's point of view, I considered going for it alone. I felt confident I could have found the spot on my own, but when I imagined witnessing the French début of this very rare bird without my bird-loving partner, my excitement dwindled. This wasn't any ordinary wild goose chase. This was the Chevalier de Sibérie that had been spotted for the first time in France, and I wanted to see it on my terms under the best of circumstances, if possible. I wanted to create optimal conditions for optimal joy for us both. It would have to be a team effort, win or lose. I would have to convince Ralph to trust me now and thank me later.

So how was I going to pull this one off? How could I persuade Ralph to twitch for me? To take on the quest for a single bird, and soon? A tall order, possibly requiring an actual strategy. Guilt? Bribery? Obligation? Squeaky wheel? All potentially effective tools under certain circumstances, and ordinarily I wouldn't hesitate to use them with a dash of humor, but would any be effective in this case? Maybe a novel concoction—two parts guilt, one part bribery, a pinch of squeaky wheel, shaken and stirred?

Then I recalled some small print in Ralph's personal birding bible, in the twitching chapter, that described some wiggle room. If the special bird was not alone but hanging out with some interesting friends, an exception to Ralph's No Twitch Rule might be made. In such a scenario—let's call it a semi-twitch—should the special bird fail to reveal itself, the odds would be decent for other good sightings. I considered the merit of my recollection. Were there any other interesting birds near the Chevalier de Sibérie? Unfortunately not. Reports on the newcomer showed nothing else remotely compelling flying in the nearby region. Gulls, gulls, and more gulls—nothing in the uncommon category.

By the end of the first day, I had to concede and agree with Ralph. Zipping off to a distant shore with only a slim chance of a peek at a lone bird with no special avian friends around didn't make a whole lot of sense. We would spend the entire day, incur the cost of gasoline and autoroute tolls, and probably face disappointment. Why not spare ourselves the headaches and expense and be content with vicarious enjoyment? The spotters were going nuts on the bird alert site published by the Ligue pour la Protection des Oiseaux (LPO), gushing gratitude and celestial appreciation for being in the company of the Chevalier de Sibérie. One by one I read the messages to Ralph: "Listen to this, honey. One guy called the researcher who initially discovered the bird a GOAT—the greatest of all time! Another wrote it was his best birding day *ever!*" Best this, best that, and on and on. These birders were raving with enthusiasm, and they were taking me along with them. But Ralph just nodded and remained calm.

As I read more reports overflowing with accolades, I could feel the reasonable objections to the twitch slip away.

My impetuous inner voice yelled, *To heck with the impracticalities of my idea. Let's go for it!* If only Ralph would naturally evolve to my heightened emotional state over seeing this bird … I took a deep breath and continued watching the daily bird sightings.

When the LPO sighting report listed the Chevalier de Sibérie the next day, my enthusiasm swelled again, but again not Ralph's. Any powers of persuasion I thought I had, I kept at bay. If he agreed under duress, the grumbling would cancel out the thrill of the adventure. Patience ruled. And the bird was still there the next day and the next. By Day 5, the Chevalier de Sibérie had hardly budged, an update so surprising that it jiggled something in my brain. Until now, I had forgotten the footnote to the patch of small print in Ralph's birding bible related to the exceptions to the No Twitch Rule: To embark on a search for an unusual bird with no special friends *is* worth it if the bird sticks around for more than a few days. We were now at that milestone—bingo.

That February morning could have been miserably cold, wet, windy, or all three, but the day brought sunshine and warmth. And all was calm—except me. I was bubbling over with excitement over the discovery of the liberating loophole. I presented it to Ralph by saying, "Honey, can you believe it? It's still there—in the same general area. After *all these days.* Remember the exception to your No Twitch Rule?"

Ralph's head jerked up from his iPad. "Really—it's still there?" he said. Clearly, the loophole light had flipped on. And the words I was waiting for from Ralph followed: "So what do you think? You want to go for it?"

"Yeah, baby!" I blurted.

"You realize it may not stay until we get there?"

"I do. It'll be an adventure!" To sweeten the deal, I suggested a seafood lunch in Bouzigues, the bijou village known for its oysters near the Chevalier de Sibérie site. We'd either celebrate or drown our sorrows, gazing at the shimmering view of the Étang de Thau by the Mediterranean Sea. Ralph loaded the spotting scope in the car, and we raced off, hoping that our rare bird would not race anywhere anytime soon.

By mid-morning, we'd parked in a semi-industrial zone beside the lagoon outside of sleepy Bouzigues, not far from the bustling seaport of Sète. As we tromped through the scrub brush to the water's edge, I revved up my positive thinking: *Please, with cherries on top, let the lost little blown-off-course shorebird be waiting for us.* Every few meters, we stopped and scanned the lagoon with our binoculars. Nothing. Walk, walk, walk. Stop. Scan the scene. Repeat. Twenty minutes passed and still, more nothing.

Then, in the distance about one hundred meters away, I saw a man moving away from the lagoon, carrying a tripod over one shoulder, binoculars resting on his chest. A woman followed close behind. Had they searched for the Chevalier de Sibérie, not found it, and were now going to try another patch? I had to know.

I yelled at Ralph, "See that man? Maybe he's seen it, or maybe he knows something. I'm running." And run I did, hopping over bushes, discarded buoys, and coils of fraying rope until I caught up with the birder. Panting, I nodded at the woman, then said to the man, "Bonjour, monsieur. Excuse me, but just a little question. Did you see the Chevalier de Sibérie?"

Grinning, he replied, "Yes, it's right over there" and pointed to the lagoon's edge about fifty meters away. I brought my binoculars up to my eyes, scanning for the bird we'd just driven an hour and a half to see, hoping it would stay put for a few moments longer. I couldn't spot it. Where was it? Had it seen me rush in, so it rushed off? Lowering his spotting scope off his shoulder, the man asked, "Would you like to see it with the *longue-vue?*"

"Yes, yes, yes, please. So kind, thank you!"

The man quickly set up his tripod, aligned the scope, peered through the viewfinder, made an adjustment, and stepped back. "Take a look."

And there it was, the Chevalier de Sibérie, the unassuming bird causing all the uproar—what an incredible joie de vivre moment! I could barely believe I was staring at this very rare bird for France, though it was hardly a stunner. Medium-sized like a Common Blackbird, but with longer, sturdy yellow legs, the Chevalier sported a lengthy beak, taupe upper body, and white underbelly. It leisurely pecked around the smooth rocks, took a few steps, then jabbed at the water some more. It appeared to be in no rush, fully enjoying its snacking, as if it had already adapted to the slower pace of the Provençal lifestyle and wanted to savor every morsel. I bonded with it immediately, making for a magical moment.

Thanking the gentleman profusely, I detached myself from his *longue-vue*, knowing that Ralph would be there soon with his spotting scope. Where was he? What was taking him so long? He simply *had* to see this. If he wanted to meet this first-time-in-France bird, he had to make tracks to twitch it before it continued on its merry migratory way. I scanned the bushes with my binoculars, finally spotting Ralph just rounding the bend. Excitement overwhelmed me, and all I could do was gesture furiously in the general direction of the pecking bird until finally I squeaked out, "There, there, there!" He had his scope up in a second and found the bird. "Pretty cool, isn't it, honey?" I said, letting out a breath.

"Yup, it sure is." He glanced over at me long enough for me to detect a smile. Even though my birder husband had just performed a twitch, something not listed in his private birding playbook, it was a moment to treasure. More than a moment, as it turned out. We followed the bird for an hour, along with about a dozen other birders and photographers outfitted with industrial-strength equipment. Beneath sapphire skies, the sun shining and a warm breeze blowing in an ordinary marsh, we were witnessing and silently recording an extraordinary avian event. Together.

"Thank you, honey," I said, wrapping my arms around Ralph. "I'll never forget this."

"Me too. I'm glad we came." Ralph squeezed me back. In mid-squeeze, I was tempted to add that I'd also never forget that, thanks to the Chevalier de Sibérie, he had officially twitched, but hey, why rub it in?

Before the kind gentleman with the scope and his wife moved on, I discovered that they lived close to Calais. Though madame wasn't a keen birder like her husband, the couple had taken a seven-hour train ride to Montpellier, booked a hotel, and rented a car—all in the hopes of catching a glimpse of this newcomer to France. That effort merited a gold badge from the twitching department, most likely not the first he deserved.

We celebrated our exceptional bird sighting at a popular brasserie on the waterfront in picturesque Bouzigues. Over fresh-from-the-sea grilled fish paired with a glass of *vin blanc* for me and a draft beer called a *pression* for Ralph, we reflected on our triumphant twitch. The drive had been hassle-free, we'd found the general area easily, the gentleman from Lille had been so helpful, and viewing the bird had been exhilarating. And we'd been impressed with the sight of all the bird paparazzi paying homage to the Chevalier de Sibérie, giving it the red-carpet treatment as if it were the hottest film star at the Cannes Film Festival, albeit ever so discreetly.

We knew that this sensation-causing bird's impromptu visit might have been a fluke and might not happen again. But I liked to think it had been drawn to the area by the allure of the Provençal lifestyle, was thrilled by what it had discovered, was able to find its way home, and might be reconsidering next year's winter travel plans. And who could blame it? A bird after my own heart.

Joie de Vivre Highlights

The arrival of nobility on wings
Ralph's twitch exception
Watching the Chevalier de Sibérie
The gentleman from Lille
A fresh fish lunch in Bouzigues

6

The Draw of a Dutchman

Paris, Part One

As a twenty-something backpacker, I waited in line in the rain to buy a ticket to the Jeu de Paume museum in Paris, home to Impressionist and Post-Impressionist paintings at the time. I adored those works then, and through the years, my love for them has only deepened, increasing my appreciation, especially when I'm dry.

Van Gogh made me go. To Paris, that is. Not that the City of Light needed any more allure than it already exudes to tempt me into a trip. From my first visit as a university student loaded with a bulging backpack to decades later when my husband and I stayed in a swanky hotel with an Eiffel Tower view, the mesmerizing metropolis has kept a distant but persistent hold on my heart. And by the TGV (Train à Grande Vitesse), France's high-speed train service, this magnificent city with its enigmatic pull is reachable in under three hours from Avignon, itself just twenty minutes north of Saint-Rémy.

So why now? For the first time, the much-acclaimed exhibition of paintings from Van Gogh's last months in the town of Auvers-sur-Oise (north of Paris) was in full swing at my beloved Musée d'Orsay. This former train station houses a treasure trove of magnificent masterpieces, but most importantly, my precious painters—the Impressionists and Post-Impressionists. Degas, Monet, Manet, Pissarro, Seurat, and Cézanne were my favorites, but I loved all the others too.

The collection had formerly been displayed in the intimate Jeu de Paume art center, where I'd first visited. I had returned many times over the years and could never get enough. Seeing them in person and up close was always mesmerizing and magical. The collection migrated to the Musée d'Orsay in 1986, and I'd been there a few times too. Their new home was terrific, and the paintings themselves, which I considered dear friends, had captivated me throughout the decades. The prospect of sharing time with them again put a spring in my step. The expo would end at the beginning of February, so this was the time for a visit to Paris if I wanted to witness this extraordinary collection by the Dutch master.

Even though the paintings were produced after Van Gogh's year in Saint-Rémy, the tortured artist is part of our town's celebrated history. I see the same gnarled olive groves that Van Gogh saw, I see the same blazing sunset over the Alpilles, the same cypress trees. As a Saint-Rémy resident, just as Van Gogh once was, I feel a certain responsibility to be well acquainted with the master's life. This would be a perfect opportunity to expand that knowledge and to pay homage.

I hopped on the Musée d'Orsay website to check out the booking possibilities. Availability was good for the potential time frame we were considering, both in the morning and afternoon, except for Monday, when the museum was closed. Although I was pleased to see timing flexibility, I wanted to go as soon as possible after arriving in the city. That very afternoon would be the best. Unlike saving the cherry for the last bite of an ice cream sundae, when it comes to excursions planned around special events, I find it's best to schedule the event early in the trip because you don't risk getting side-tracked with a tempting diversion or unexpected incident and miss the whole thing. But first, we needed a place to stay and train tickets.

Where to lay our heads in Paris was always a challenge. With so many enticing *arrondissements*, the choice of a neighborhood was daunting. We were no longer eligible to book a room at the elegant hotel where we'd stayed when we were US government employees working in Germany because the private establish-ment had been a work perk. I consulted many friends who visited regularly, and they all had their preferred *quartiers*. It was difficult to pick an area central to our designated activities because our interests were spread across the metropolis. In the end, I settled on the 8th *arrondissement*, not far from where we'd previously stayed. The residence I selected included a kitchen-ette, which is especially handy when you're on an extended stay. Sometimes after tromping around all day, you just want to put your feet up and have a quiet little dinner at "home."

After the accommodation and fast train tickets were booked, my anticipation for the long-awaited Paris getaway gained momentum. I started sorting out outfits, keeping in mind the winter climate, and compiling lists of different types of cafés and brasseries for the various areas we'd be canvass-ing that would match the moment's mood. Coffee here, *apéro* there, *pique-nique* yonder, dinner *chez nous*. Paris, here we come.

Several days passed before I focused on where to relax near the Musée d'Orsay after experiencing the superb expo. We'd have a lot to discuss. It was then that it hit me. I'd failed to book the exhibition tickets. The idiotic oversight clobbered me. The purpose of this Paris trip was the Van Gogh show, but I'd ignored *la forêt* for *les arbres*. What were the chances that I could just waltz into the ticket site and grab tickets for the last days of this world-class blockbuster show? I swallowed hard as I opened my laptop. Please, oh please, Musée d'Orsay, let there be tickets left. When the museum calendar appeared, my heart sank. The only slots available were at the end of our stay, a few hours before our departure—far from ideal. But I booked them instantly, printed the tickets, all the while thinking, *How on earth will we make this work?*

Ralph could have derived maximum mileage out of rubbing in my failure to execute the most obvious element of our travel plan. But since I was doing a darned good job of beating myself up all alone, he figured his help was superfluous, thankfully. Instead, he declared, "We can do it. We'll check out of the hotel, bring our luggage to the museum, stash it there—they must have lockers. Then we'll see the show and afterward, we'll take a taxi to the train station. It'll work." Calculating the time to get from the Musée d'Orsay to the Gare de Lyon, and planning backwards, we'd only have an hour—max—at the expo. Not optimal, but doable.

I shared my lamentable tale with my girlfriends at our weekly get-together at a café in Saint-Rémy. When I suggested the possibility of exchanging the tickets at the site for an earlier time slot, one friend urged me not to get my hopes up. "This is France, remember. They like to say *non*." And if no exchange was possible and we were stuck with our assigned time, that could be a problem too. She reminded me that just because our ticket indicated a specific time slot didn't mean we'd necessarily get in at the appointed hour. Reality check. At my friend's suggestion, we changed our departure to a later train for just a few additional euros. Even though we'd have to wait until the day of departure to see the show, at least we wouldn't have to check the time every second while attempting to commune with Van Gogh.

Without a hitch, the fast train delivered us from Avignon to Paris's Gare de Lyon in under three hours. Buying a multi-day metro ticket took longer. Well, it seemed to. The lines in front of the *billet* machines looped around the space where commuters charge across with purpose. *Stand back, we're coming through* was the urgent message their stern expressions broadcast like blinking ambulance lights.

But the metro got us to where we wanted to go quickly, and the hotel check-in was a snap. The spacious room was nicely appointed with a view of the Saint-Augustin Church from the small balcony. The bed was firm, and the compact kitchen was well equipped, plus the bathroom included a big bathtub. But we didn't dawdle because I had a plan. We were headed to the Musée d'Orsay.

The fact that our expo tickets weren't valid for several days didn't deter me on my mission. Just maybe, once on site and face-to-face with an actual person, we could exchange our tickets. Dismissing my friend's opinion about the dubious success of this approach, I mustered a positive mind-set.

And indeed, the ticket booth lady was particularly accommodating. First she explained in terrific English that she couldn't exchange the tickets because we had bought them online, and she operated a different system. Then she suggested we buy general admission tickets for today, proceed to the line in the expo area, and explain the situation to the person there. She said, "I think they will let you in … probably." I looked at Ralph, he nodded agreement, and two day passes later we crossed the threshold of the magnificent Musée d'Orsay.

How I adored this museum, and not just for its incredible collection. The building itself with its dramatic dome covering the central area is awe inspiring. We paused for a few seconds to soak up the artful ambience before marching on, following signs to the Van Gogh show. If I thought the line for the metro tickets was long, I thought again. Across a very crowded room, the mass of art lovers waiting to enter the special show wound back and forth four times in front of the exhibit's entrance, reminding me of an airport check-in after multiple flight cancellations. And behind that gathering was a feeder line for people with museum day passes, like us. We joined in.

For the next ten minutes, we heard repeated depressing announcements from a loudspeaker. Access to the special Van Gogh exhibit was running ninety minutes late. "Oh, man," I said, barely audibly. "Chances are they'll be running even later on Tuesday, since it's the last week of the expo." Even if we did return then, we would be out of luck since the entry time listed on our expo tickets wasn't guaranteed. But presumably our high-speed train departure time was.

Ralph and I stood amid that glorious temple of artistic wonder, making frustrated faces at each other and feeling helpless. Then I remembered the ticket booth lady's advice to explain our situation to the person in charge of the line. Considering the delays, that was imperative now. With all we wanted to do in the city, seeing the exhibition today was our only hope. Here we were just a tad early—a mere four days ahead of schedule. *Well, it's worth a shot,* I thought as I turned to Ralph.

"Honey," I said, "I'm going to see if the woman at the front of the line has a sense of humor. Save my place?" Realizing what I was up to, but likely aware this effort had emerged from the Hail-Mary department, Ralph wished me *bonne chance,* good luck.

Holding the expo tickets, I marched toward the young lady who was managing the line and occasionally dropping the thick cord to allow impatient patrons to pass to the next hopeful stage, as if granting them access to an ultra-exclusive secret nightclub. In my most respectful French, I said, "Bonjour, so sorry to bother you, but ..."

She listened to my sad saga, examined the tickets closely, paused, and asked, "Did my colleague tell you to ask me?"

"Yes, she did," I said, thinking she might confirm my answer with the helpful attendant at the front ticket booth who had sold us the day passes.

But she only asked politely, "Can you wait there for a moment, please?" She gestured to her side to make space for us while more people crossed over to the promised land.

"Of course," I said, taking this development as progress because she hadn't slammed me with a non-negotiable *non.* While she conscientiously attended to her rope control duties, I took a leap of faith that I was dealing with more of a pro-*oui* person, perhaps fresh out of PR training camp in preparation for the Paris Olympics. I motioned to Ralph to join me.

Miraculously, the line by the expo gallery had nearly disappeared, and fifteen minutes later, we were marveling at Van Gogh's vibrant portrait entitled *Docteur Paul Gachet* (1890), the first work that greeted us at the entrance to the hallowed hall of the exhibition. We had made it—along with a world of other Van Gogh devotees. Immersed in Van Gogh's visions of the world, we moved silently from masterwork to masterwork. Most of the collection featured scenes from ordinary life in Auvers-sur-Oise—the countryside, the wobbly houses, the plain villagers. As I studied the canvases, I listened as if I could hear the emotion behind the brushstrokes. Aware that the works were produced in the artist's last months of his life, I couldn't escape feeling what must have been his own feelings of anguish and despair. But then I reached *Wheatfield with Crows*. Over a brilliant swath of golden grain, birds fly through a sky rich with Van Gogh's signature blues. It struck me that the scene represented a glimmer of hope and promise. I wondered whether Van Gogh had experienced some joyful moments while painting it—if only just fleetingly? If only he'd had more of them.

During the following days, we crammed in as much as possible, excluding the main tourist sites because over the years, we'd been there, done that. Instead, we zigzagged throughout the city by foot, metro, and bus, taking in more art expos and visiting old haunts. Latvian-American abstract painter Mark Rothko's monumentally sized creations were impressive, but it was the structure that housed the works that took my breath away. Fashioned after a ship, the crazy cool Frank Gehry-designed museum Fondation Louis Vuitton sailed away with my heart.

On the other hand, the traditional manor house that was home to the Musée Marmottan Monet didn't upstage the stunning works by the French Impressionist painter Berthe Morisot on display there. Back in her day, Morisot had exhibited alongside the titans of Impressionism such as Cézanne, Degas, and Monet, but she never achieved their star status, likely due to her gender, sadly. But over a century later, if this expo was a sign, recognition for her gorgeous works was finally coming her way.

Although we hardly needed a topper for that gratifying experience, while we strolled through a nearby park, several neon-green Rose-ringed Parakeets cavorted in the trees, zipping past us as if trying to send a message: "Don't forget us— we're gorgeous too!" Smiling, I took out my phone, pointed it toward the beauties, and called up to them, "Ready for your close-up? Say *fromage*!"

Between the cultural activities, we meandered through the massive Luxembourg Gardens where adults relaxed in low-slung chairs, their chins pointing to the sun, oblivious to the kiddos sailing boats on the pond, squealing their hearts out. On the other side of the Seine, the atmosphere was sedate and contemplative at the Place des Vosges. With the agreeable weather, which was unexpected in the thick of winter, I could have stayed there for ages, admiring the stately arcades and people watching, imagining Victor Hugo emerging from his apartment at #6. But lingering wasn't listed on my demanding to-do list, which kept us on our toes.

Remarkably, we'd been clocking nearly twenty-five thousand steps a day—not necessarily a bad thing since we'd been overindulging—leaving the best for last. To cap off our Paris visit, we planned to have a bite at the lauded Le Train Bleu on our way out of town. But ahead of that gastronomic temple, we sampled yummy dishes at the opposite end of the foodie spectrum, like the falafel pitas we picked up at Maoz in the Latin Quarter. They were stuffed with fresh veggies selected from a serve-yourself bar and scrumptious. And munching them from a bench by the Seine—under sunny skies in February, no less—was an unexpected treat. Tourists stopped for selfies and legions of Parisians floated by, along with a string of cormorants patrolling the river for their lunch.

Another culinary winner was Brasserie Balzar, which I'd read about in *The New York Times*. Hemingway and his crew used to hang out there. We just happened to be passing by at the late end of lunchtime en route to the Luxembourg Gardens, but without a reservation at this historic haunt, which we assumed would be packed, we were prepared to either be turned away or offered a table near the loo. But lo and behold, a nattily dressed gentleman greeted us warmly, and after a quick check of the reservation book, he seated us without delay at a well-positioned table amid the happy hubbub.

The lively local crowd jabbering away *en français* somehow made my roast chicken, which I was savoring bite by succulent bite, even more flavorful. The scene looked like a cross-section of the weekend Parisian lunch bunch. Young moms and dads chased after escaped tots, infants squealed, thirty-somethings clinked flutes, and distinguished mature couples quietly conversed, while a young man sipped an espresso solo as he perused a newspaper by the window.

Nostalgia engulfed the room, so it should not have come as a surprise to spot a reminder of the good old days by the cash register—a bowl filled with matchbooks adorned with the Le Balzar logo. *Mais oui*, I nipped one. After all, a girl needs to be prepared, especially in the City of Light, where love especially loves a glow.

No fire starter was needed, however, to ignite romance while standing on the Pont d'Alma, staring at the Eiffel Tower, which puts on a spectacular twinkle show at night. When Ralph and I were there watching the flickering lights slide up and down Paris's most iconic structure, I felt a tingling sensation run up and down my spine. I leaned into Ralph for a tighter hug, keeping my eyes on the spectacular light show, enhanced by the reflections bouncing off the Seine and the *bateaux-mouches* passing silently by. It was about as dreamy as dreamy gets, though not exactly private. We were lucky to have snagged a spot.

Sharing Paris is to be expected, even in winter. After all, year after year, it's rated as the most visited city on the planet. But mamma mia, so many spaces in this popular city were packed with people jostling like robin nestlings vying for worms dangling from their parents' beaks. Tip: Avoid Galeries Lafayette on a Saturday during the last of the New Year's sales when it is a veritable madhouse. What were we, or rather, what was I thinking? Major oops. But even with the din of that commercial zoo, the soaring stained-glass dome was as glorious as ever. I thought so anyway. Ralph just wanted to escape the madness as speedily as possible.

A leisurely browse in the famous bookstore Shakespeare & Company would have been timely, but yet again a lengthy line stopped us outside. Another attractive idea was a pick-me-up coffee and a decadent indulgence at Angelina, the elegant Belle Époque tearoom/pastry shop. Sadly, thirty other potential patrons waited outside, hoping to be seated.

With the crowds, the distances we'd traversed, and my overprogramming of our schedule, it was no surprise that meltdowns happened between us. I'm not sure whether they started with Ralph or *moi*, but they engulfed us both. This was the time to invoke my brother's advice on my wedding day when I asked about his secret to a happy marriage: "Know when to keep your lips sealed." I'm pretty sure the steam shooting out from my ears divulged my frame of mind, but at least the record reflects silence, as icy as it was.

No blame game was under way. Responsibility for running us ragged in the City of Light landed squarely in my court, and I accepted it. Ralph grabbed some back, which I appreciated. But by then, exhaustion had taken over and humor had taken a hike, sending us both into a semi-sulky stupor.

Having managed to squash the dreamy Parisian spell, which by unwritten French law surely must be an offense worthy of a fine or at least a strenuous citation, we were subdued that evening. After all, a cranky climate isn't exactly conducive to *amour*, so a romance rain check was issued. My matches from Le Balzar took the night off.

Another day, living the libido loco would have its moment in the sun, or maybe under a moonlit sky.

Joie de Vivre Highlights

The Musée d'Orsay and Van Gogh's show
The Eiffel Tower's twinkling display
The Frank Gehry-designed Fondation Louis Vuitton
Rose-ringed Parakeets by the Musée Marmottan Monet
Roasted chicken at Le Balzar

7

Time to Reset

Paris, Part Two

My father had flair and a watch to match—a silver pocket watch. It spent its days in the breast pocket of his suit, kept safe by the chain that clasped to a little handle on the watch and a flat disk on the other end that fit through a buttonhole on his jacket's lapel. After I acquired it, I kept it safe too, for decades, taking it with me wherever I lived—Mexico, South America, and Europe. But it had never visited the City of Light ... until now.

Still in Paris, we banished every last vestige of grumpy pouting the moment we stepped into the Horlogerie du Passage, a Lilliputian watch repair shop I'd read about in *The New York Times*. Three young Parisians with a passion for watches who had studied watchmaking at the distinguished Lycée Diderot had joined forces to repair watches under the same roof. A sign posted above their workstations read IF YOU HAVE A WATCH, WE HAVE THE TIME. I was counting on this good-natured clan of artisans (one of whom is a woman) to find the time to squeeze me into their schedule because I did in fact have a watch.

It wasn't just any old watch but my dad's silver Longines pocket watch, which needed a jump-start. I have vivid memories of my father winding it by holding it in his left hand and gently rolling the crown back and forth with the thumb and index finger of his right hand, a hypnotic motion that practically put me under. He gave it to me when I was a teenager and he was in his late fifties, after he stopped working. While on the job, he cut an elegant figure at six feet tall, lithe with light brown, neatly coifed hair and always dressed in a well-cut suit—the slim Longines no doubt safely tucked away. Sometimes he swapped his tasteful tie for a bow version.

Once, I heard him say to my brother, "Clothes make the man," but I'm certain there was a wink-wink there, as he was a big kidder. He'd answer the phone by saying, "City Hall," or even "City Morgue," sending my mom into apoplectic fits. "Oh, Cash," she'd admonish, shaking her head. (I never heard her use his full name, Cassius, maybe because I never heard her utter an angry word at him.) And once, he told my older sister's date to "Get her home before the sun comes up." "He means midnight," my mom interjected. But I knew he was serious when he'd lean in over his plate at the dinner table, looking past two kids seated on either side, and say to my mom at the other end, "Have I told you today that I love you?"

And seriously sophisticated was how he looked dressed in an ivory double-breasted suit for their 1940 wedding, revealing a refined sartorial bent. But there was nothing remotely superficial about his intellect—it was solidly literary. Poetry tomes were the go-to gifts my dad and mom liked to exchange. When they weren't reading poems, my dad wrote them. If there was any doubt of his romantic feelings for my mother, the record was set straight with one of his works typed in duplicate that I found in my mother's papers after she passed away. It was titled "Midnight and a Time for Love," and it began, "Take my hand and come with me …"

In addition to his passionate nature, he understood the practical importance of impressions, and his dashing appearance suited his role as manager of the old Seattle cinemas that mimicked opera houses, with sweeping staircases on either side of the foyer leading to the balcony. Many had a storied history, like the 846-seat Music Box with its mammoth screen, constructed in 1928 by architect Harry Bittman and lamentably demolished in 1987. That was where I saw a refurbished version of *Gone with the Wind*. The last scene before intermission showed Scarlett O'Hara waving a dirt-encrusted carrot at the heavens, exclaiming, "As God is my witness, I'll never be hungry again." The iconic line reminded me it was time for a trip to the candy-stocked concession, so my older brother and I scurried off to find my dad, hoping to hit him up for some change.

Dad might have been a soft touch for his third-born, but he had little time to spoil me. Our journey as dad and daughter was brief. After we moved from cloudy, wet Washington state to sunny, dry Southern California, he worked away from our Los Angeles home for long stretches, following the good jobs to keep the family afloat. "You do what you have to do," he said. Soon thereafter, he was struck by a devastating disease and was barely fifty-nine when he passed away. Over the last few years of his illness, I watched my beloved, debonair dad's body contract like a folding lawn chair collapsing into itself in slow motion. But while he lost his form and ability to articulate clearly, he held tight to his humor, a stellar attribute demanding the utmost courage.

Now, decades after his demise, I would be dispatching the cherished memento from my father to a possible resurrected life in Paris, the city of Hemingway's *A Moveable Feast*. I was confident my literary dad would have approved, especially since he had a French connection, with his mother descending from a line of Huguenots named Michaux. Who knows—maybe my grandmother had bought the watch as a gift for my dad, lending my mysterious Michaux ancestry a role in drawing me to France in the first place? Surely the timepiece held secrets. Should I search for them? And what might I find?

For some time, I'd intended to don my Hercule Poirot chapeau and carry out a genealogy investigation, but for now, I wanted to see what these earnest young Parisian watchmakers had to say. They attempted to fix everything, advertising that no job was too small or too complicated. Clearly, they valued preservation of history over commercialism. This kind of sensitivity, coupled with a determined can-do attitude, dovetailed perfectly with my situation. The value of my timepiece was above all sentimental, and I'd transported it from Provence to Paris in the hopes of having skilled and understanding hands restore it. I had an inkling they would fully comprehend that without further explanation.

Before heading to Paris, I'd checked online to see whether the enterprise was still up and running, and it appeared it was. But I hesitated to make an appointment for a couple of reasons. Maybe they'd say *non*. Or that they were too busy, too short-staffed, or they needed a break. What a disappointment that would be. To be sure, it was a risk not to lock in a set time for evaluating my timepiece. But something about this particular undertaking found its place in the meant-to-be box. It almost seemed as if I'd be jinxing things if I tried too hard to make it work. Maybe if I physically appeared, even if they *were* too busy, too short-staffed, or needed a break, they'd instantly be charmed by my story and want to be part of it. Sometimes simply making the effort to show up brings home the trophy. Hopefully there would be time to try. A little French capital caper appeared on our to-do list.

Now, standing in front of the glass-fronted store, we saw loupes and other tools of the *horlogerie* trade spread across the worktables and instruments hanging on the walls like Julia Child's pans in her Provençal kitchen. Ralph and I looked at each other, grinning. Cloaked in old-world charm, the shop befitted a gray-bearded Geppetto. But au contraire—as soon as we stepped inside, young Matthieu popped up from his workstation and welcomed us with a gentle smile. I recognized him from the photo in the newspaper article. "Bonjour," I said, and explained how I'd found out about the shop. Then I extended my palm, which held the Longines watch. Knowing we'd interrupted him, I figured he'd appreciate receiving my "elevator pitch" without delay. "My dad gave it to me decades ago. It hasn't ticked in ages, and I can't set the time. Do you think you can restore it?"

I had my answer when Matthieu's eyes lit up as if he'd just been handed a Cartier crown. Anxious to investigate the new challenge, he deftly removed the back from the watch, examined it, and lifted his gaze. His eyes wide, he said reverently, "Madame, do you realize this watch is nearly one hundred years old?"

In that moment, my admiration for this dedicated lad swelled. From the article, I knew he had previously worked in the medical field but had swapped healing humans for a very different type of repair work. I sensed immediately that he was not only interested in renewing watches but also connections. In preserving treasured timepieces, he was preserving emotional history—my history. I wanted to hug him.

Instead, all I could utter was "That's amazing." I hadn't realized that what my dad had given me so long ago, knowing he wasn't long for this world, had traversed almost an entire century. And not only that, it had crisscrossed oceans and borders, clocking major kilometers in its day. From its origin in French-speaking Switzerland, not far from the French *frontière*, it had swapped the Alps for Mount Rainier, spent time near the sandy coast of SoCal and the shimmery sands of Palm Springs, accompanied me to the US capital, back to Europe, again to California, and finally settled in Provence. And then a few days ago, my shiny treasure had joined Ralph and me on a fast train to Eiffel Tower town. And perhaps one day soon, because of this little shop of second chances in the City of Light, the watch that had safeguarded memories of my dad for so long would have its heartbeat restored—and in analog fashion, no less.

As if Matthieu had read my mind, he smiled and added, "And not a *batterie* in sight."

Our watch expert explained that he would be able to fix it, to get it ticking again, *if*—and this was a big *if*—whatever was wrong was just a misaligned part. If a part was broken and had to be replaced, that could be a big problem because the parts from some exclusive brands were proprietary, costly, and took forever to receive. The value of the Longines resided in its emotional, not marketplace worth, but I didn't have to explain that to Matthieu. I instinctively knew he knew—no discussion was necessary. With that understood, we agreed on a maximum amount for the analysis and/or repair, but the critical question was how long the process would take.

If he could fix it, he'd want to keep it for several days, well after our departure. I'd anticipated that, but how would I get it back? Mailing it was out of the question because it would be too risky. Would I return to Paris for it? Yes, I would. I told Ralph I could make a round trip in a day if I had to. It would be time-consuming and expensive, but worth it, right? Absolutely, he said, no question. I nodded my thanks, grateful that Ralph fully supported my sentimental journey.

But wait—I had a sudden idea. "I have a friend whose daughter lives here in the neighborhood—she's doing a master's degree. Maybe she can pick up the watch. I'll call her mom and ask." I immediately got in touch with my friend Ellen, who assured me it would be no problem. Claire could pick it up and deliver it the next time she came home to Aix, but that wouldn't be until the end of February, over three weeks away. Did I mind waiting? Hardly controlling my laughter, I said, "Ellen, this watch has been in a drawer for decades. I think I can manage another few weeks." The Longines lingered in Paris.

Ralph and I, however, now had to make tracks—to the tracks. At the Gare de Lyon, home to the culinary temple that is Le Train Bleu, we would enjoy our departure meal. This historic restaurant is one of food critic Alexander Lobrano's top thirty restaurants in Paris, listed in his compelling book *My Place at the Table*, so I was keen to try it. There wasn't time for a relaxed meal in the opulent dining room—as this pricey option merits—so we headed to the extensive "bar" area, which offers much more casual and reasonable fare. The Caesar salad and club sandwich were sensational. And to top off our final Parisian experience, the greeter kindly snapped photos of us at the entrance, being very particular about positioning us to show off the newly restored room to its best advantage. Perhaps she was a photographer in her spare time, but her public relations skills were nonpareil. A highly recommended experience—both for the dining and photo opping. And feeling a bit like royalty, holding court in a Belle Époque ballroom.

A few days after we got home, Matthieu texted and said my watch was ticking and tocking. And, he reported, keeping time each day within ten minutes plus or minus. With the invoice sent and paid, it was now only a question of getting the watch safely back home. I couldn't wait to press it to my ear and listen to what it had to say.

I updated Ellen, whose daughter would act as the clock courier. The following afternoon, I alerted Matthieu so he'd have the watch ready, making the transaction as efficient and causing as little inconvenience as possible. To my surprise, conscientious Claire had already retrieved the timepiece that morning and would escort it safely home to Aix at the end of the month.

I wondered what the reunion would feel like. Would hearing my dad's timepiece tick, seeing the hands move and that it was keeping time—would this resurrect my father? Of course not. Yet I had hopes I'd feel some sort of renewed connection to my beloved dad, whose time on earth had been so heartbreakingly brief that I hadn't had the luxury of making many memories with him.

But even now, just the process of having his watch repaired was stirring up some of those warm memories of Dad. I recalled that when I was around six or seven, I discovered an open can of candy-cane pink paint in the garage that I, along with my assistant, the next-door neighbor girl, used to "beautify" a row of big rocks along our shared property line. My mom was horrified by my home improvement project, mostly because the paint was not just on the rocks but on the neighbor girl, the fence, and me. Irate, she insisted on punishment, but my dad with his flair for quips didn't even utter a "hell's bells," a polite expression of dissatisfaction at the time. My penalty, delivered by my pacifist father, amounted to a tête-à-tête about the virtues of tempering my artistic impulses when they involved an oil-based, indelible substance. The feather-light pat on my derriere indicated that, officially, I had hereby been spanked. My discipline-minded mom also grounded me. I'd always thought that the life-sized stuffed poodle presented to me by my dad the following day was primarily meant to keep me company during my solitary confinement. But in retrospect I see that Curly, the name I assigned my new friend, probably fulfilled several purposes. It assuaged my dad's remorse over the harsh sentence my mom had imposed and also cheered me up. But there was something else—my dad was a cheerleader for the flourishing of my free-spirited, creative side. Maybe it was a coincidence, but one clue was clear. Just like the paint, Curly was pink.

Another enduring connection to my father is not only burned into my memory, but also into a sheet of wood. He maintained a tradition of writing a poem for each of us four kids on our thirteenth birthdays. Mine goes like this:

HAIL TO GAYLE ON HER 13th BIRTHDAY!

Hooray! Hooray! Hooray!
This is the Day! This is the Day! This is the Day!
You're thirteen, thirteen, thirteen!
You're razor-sharp and plenty keen
For twelve long years, you've waited for this
Let Mom and Dad give you a kiss
You meet your problems face to face
You are a credit to the human race
For you, there's been no listless yearning
You've liked the way the earth's been turning
There's nothing but praise for your outlook on life
It's been great to see you eager for strife
You'll be a teener for seven short years
And when they're over, let there be no tears
You are entering this era with adventurous zing
We envy you the excitement the years will bring
No doubt stress and strain will be routine for you
But let your good judgment rule all that you do
You are growing up, your figure causes lots of noise
And that new hairstyle really numbs the boys
There's advice above if you look closely enough
We want your road interesting but not bumpity rough
Have a happy teenage career, above all, is our wish
Good luck, best wishes to you, our tender teenage dish
Hooray! Hooray! Hooray!
This is the Day! This is the Day! This is the Day!
Mom and Dad

Overall, my dad had correctly captured the spirit of his new teenager—with one exception: eager for strife. Did I really go looking for trouble? The pink paint beautification fiasco from my childhood aside, that didn't ring true. I usually stayed in my lane, well under the radar. Or did my poet dad simply need a worthy word to rhyme with life? No, he was always careful with words. In anticipation of being reunited with his keepsake watch, I reunited with his poem, reading it several times. After all these years, I stopped to consider the life-strife pairing and the advice it offered. I finally looked closely enough to realize what my dad had meant: Taking on challenges may be exciting, but they don't lead you down easy street. Speed bumps are part of the package, but rewards await. *That* interpretation made a lot more sense.

A week later, my friend wrote that her daughter was home and so was the watch. Since we were spending a few days in a holiday rental near Aix, it was easy to pop by. My excitement gathered momentum, as if I were being reunited with my father. On the short bike ride to Ellen's house, I reminded myself to take a deep breath, remember it was just a memento, and not to expect emotional fireworks. As soon as we walked through the door, without any fanfare my lovely friend handed me the pale gray velour case. Smiling, I opened the small box, and there it was, looking exactly the same.

I picked it up as if it were a priceless jewel, not surprised that the time wasn't correct. After all, it had been a while since it had left the watch shop. To be sure it wasn't ticking, I held it to my ear—nothing. Considering all the effort to restore the keepsake and my emotional investment, I hoped a winding session would do the trick. I set the time and rotated the bezel back and forth as carefully as my father had always done. Moment of truth.

Holding my breath, I pushed the watch against my ear. When I heard a hushed, rhythmic *shushing* sound, my exhalation brimmed with relief. But mostly I felt tranquility, the same feeling I'd had as a kid when watching my dad wind the watch. The calming effect lapped over me like a gentle ocean wave. I felt a sense of enhanced security, as if the soft ticking were transporting me to a safe zone, a protected place my dad would have wanted. A watch to watch over me, with its reassuring sound, steady as a heartbeat, not unlike his own.

Back at home, I found a novel use for my sentimental treasure that I think would have elicited a chuckle from my dad. My watch collection numbers five in total, but I rarely use any of them now that I carry a time-telling phone. But my mobile doesn't have a second hand. For precise timing, I always used my Swiss Army watch, but recently the battery stopped and I hadn't bothered making a trip to the jeweler to change it. Now the Longines lay on my desk, and I noticed as if for the first time that the clock face had a separate tiny second-hand dial between the center and the 6. I picked up the watch and listened to the rapid *shuh-shuh-shuh*, channeling my dad's can-do spirit and visualizing his impish grin as he witnessed my creative approach to problem solving.

I proceeded with the task at hand, lowering myself to the floor. I extended my arms, palms down, and one at a time stretched out my legs, balancing on my toes with my tummy tight, body board stiff. Normally, holding this awkward plank position for sixty seconds is my max, but surprisingly, this time I kept going, my eyes fixated on the tiny second hand sweeping away the seconds. I thought of my dad urging my primary school self to rise and shine, telling me, "Up and Adam!" I always wondered who this guy Adam was, but I never got around to asking my father. It wasn't until adulthood that I realized he had been saying, "Up and at 'em!" At this moment, in mid-core strengthening mode, I was more *down* and at 'em, but at 'em I was.

Thanks, Dad.

Joie de Vivre Highlights

A young Parisian watchmaker's admiration for analog
Ellen and Claire's supportive roles in the watch saga
Lunch at Le Train Bleu
The ticking of my dad's watch
How a treasured timepiece kept up with the times

The French Alps

Val-Cenis-Termignon, France, near the Italian border

For billiards and pool aficionados, there are undoubtedly important differences between the two. Whatever the name of the game, winning is sweet. And so is almost winning—perhaps especially when competing in a wild wonderland.

The white ball that I tapped ever so gently with my chalk-nubbed cue nudged my last one into the pocket. But before I could revel in my success, claiming victory over my experienced pool-playing husband, the *boule blanche* followed, disappearing down the hole.

"*Mais non!* That's bad, isn't it—I lost?" I lamented.

"Yup, sorry to say. It's called a scratch. Want to play another?" Ralph asked cheerfully.

"You betcha. I don't know much about pool, but enough to know I was nearly victorious. You've still got four balls on the table."

Engaging in a billiards challenge at thirteen hundred meters in an old-world holiday house in a small ski resort in the Savoie region was unexpected. We'd come here for a week to celebrate Ralph's June birthday. He'd chosen the destination as an extension of a family birthday tradition, which started with his mother's coconut cake. When he was a kid, he'd always been allowed to choose his birthday dinner, with dessert being the highlight. His choice invariably was coconut cake, a confection his mother prepared from scratch. Short of shimmying up a coconut palm with a machete, she created a classic coconut cake. She would buy a coconut, hammer an ice pick into its three indentations, drain the liquid, smash the shell, extract the coconut meat, roast the chunks, and then shred the meat. Unlike scratching at pocket pool, this from-scratch cake was a winner. But since *gâteau à la noix de coco* didn't figure in my repertoire and Ralph had conveniently lost interest in sugary desserts, I sweetened his birthday agenda by offering a getaway instead. Where would monsieur like to celebrate his special day?

The destination ideas in every direction from Saint-Rémy were tantalizing. I knew a metropolis wouldn't be Ralph's top pick, and there would be no black-tie events to pack for. My ball gown—if I had one—would stay behind. He'd choose a venue where cargo pants would comply nicely with the dress code, this I was sure of. In truth, going rural appealed to me too as a lovely change of pace. And one would be hard-pressed not to find an intriguing corner pretty much anywhere one went in France, not to mention a delicious local specialty. I was excited about the escapade, whatever it was to be.

Ralph considered some of our old haunts that we both loved, like Saint-Jean-de-Luz on the Atlantic in the Basque region, Île de Ré near Bordeaux, Hyères on the Med, Annecy on an Alpine lake, Barcelonnette, and Megève in the mountains—all accessible in an easy day's drive. He considered La Ciotat, but the one time we'd been there in mid-June, it was so crowded we couldn't find a patch of sand for our towels. Finally, Ralph decided on an Alpine getaway to the tiny town of Termignon. It's an authentic village in the Val-Cenis commune in the Savoie Department near the Italian border—a perfect setting for a nature adventure.

The area's main draws were that it was off the beaten path, boasted stunning scenery and cool temperatures, and promised new birdlife, especially some big birds that preferred soaring at higher altitudes. We'd head to the hills to hike and explore the natural, wild wonderland. Romantic mountaintop images rushed in. Clinking glasses of a mellow red on a terrace at sunset, the mountain peaks aflame. Dipping crusty baguette bites in a kirsch-infused fondue. A soothing hot tub under the stars, owls hooting softly in the distance. *On y va!* Let's go!

While I researched rentals, a property that fit the romance bill immediately caught my eye. Located just a few minutes' walk from the town center, the multilevel complex housed several holiday apartments, each with an enticing attribute. Of the units sized for two people, one boasted a little wood burner, a feature I adore, and the other a fab mountain view. The second option held additional allure—a corner Jacuzzi tub big enough for two. It was even outfitted with a pair of padded headrests. After a tough day hiking the hills and homing in on high-flyers, I imagined the bliss of sinking into a luxurious bubble bath.

Ralph would deliver a pair of flutes filled with fizz and settle in beside me. That was a formula I could get my arms around.

Highway A7, known as the Autoroute du Soleil, took us north toward Lyon for the first half of the journey, but well before the metropolis we cut east, passing Romans-sur-Isère, famous historically for its footwear production and in more recent times for its incredible shoe museum (worth a detour if you have the time!). After we skirted Grenoble, the majestic Alps rose in the distance and the road narrowed. For the last half of the journey, we sped along on a two-lane road that meandered through small villages, with little traffic and no scary heights to cause concern—so far.

Once in Termignon—population under three hundred— we looped through the compact commercial zone, noting a few restaurants and a ski lift before pulling up in front of our rustic home for the week. The owner had notified me she wouldn't be available to greet us but had passed along the entry code so we could check in by ourselves.

The building was partially built into the hillside, with our apartment on the third of four floors. The luggage lugging was daunting, but luckily the path that circled up and around from the parking area to a large patio was smooth. On the far side, we found our apartment. After we struggled with the door, it swung open to reveal a modern, spic-and-span kitchen, exactly matching the photos online. One step down, we found the wood-paneled living/dining/sleeping area. The room, though compact, was spacious enough to easily walk around a large bed covered with a quilted spread with a cheerful hearts-and-flowers motif, matching the thick curtains.

But it was what was behind the drapes that I was anxious to see. Drawing them back, I took in the magnificent mountain range topped by a lapis lazuli sky. The vista stretched over a lush garden patch, a flowering meadow, stone farmhouses, a church with a slate spire, and the still snow-dusted peaks. Never mind that we were in France, not Austria—the scene was so *Sound of Music* storybook perfect that I imagined Julie Andrews sauntering down the lane belting out "The hills are alive."

"Ooh, honey, look at this," I said, opening the windows and leaning out to breathe in the fragrant Alpine air.

Ralph followed me to the view and stood behind me, his arms around my waist, resting his chin on my head. "This will work," he said, noting a magpie flying across the garden.

"Yeah, not too shabby," I added. Remembering the Jacuzzi tub, which I'd planned to be a surprise, I took his hand. "Come with me, there's something else you have to see."

Inside the bathroom, I swept my arm across the scene, saying, "Voilà—the Jacuzzi. Think you could get yourself in there?"

"Pretty sure I could manage," Ralph said, smiling broadly and nodding his approval.

"Hold that thought, *mon amour*."

With our suitcases unloaded and all our stuff stashed away, we checked out the various outdoor areas, which were scattered with benches. We tested them all to identify the best mountain view vantage points for our morning coffee. Our exploration took us to the ground floor, where we found a huge garage featuring a wine-tasting area with a long wooden table and matching chairs, a room storing stacks of firewood with a space for bikes, a laundry cubicle, and to our surprise, a billiard room. What a treat! The low-key diversion would come in handy after a long day of hiking and exploring.

Although I was eager to wander around the village, my competitive spirit had kicked in. I'd nearly bested Ralph in the first game of pool, so I felt I was on a roll. It turned out that I'd been enjoying beginner's luck because Ralph destroyed me in the next two games. He had just needed a warm-up. So after the third loss I conceded defeat, and we headed to *centre-ville* for a close-up snoop to discover what we'd missed during our brief windshield tour earlier. On the way, we passed artfully designed informational signs incorporating vintage images of historic sites like L'Hôtel du Lion d'Or, built in 1810, and L'Hôpital, dating to 1494. A playfully decorated cheese shop with a small table and chairs beside the entrance was adorned with an anti-insect "door" of pom-pom strings. Inside, we found a full array of items made from local sheep's wool and hand-carved wood souvenirs from the area. For anyone in the market for an expertly made alpine craft, this was the place.

In front of the Hôtel de Ville, a formidable ibex greeted us—a life-sized wood sculpture with massive curled horns, a testament to the significance of wildlife in the community. The little chain grocery store was *fermé* and wouldn't open for a few days due to an annual vacation, so we were especially gratified that we'd come prepared with sufficient provisions. The tourist office was closed too, but just for the night. Peering through the tall glass doors, I could see it was spacious and well stocked, so I planned to return later to see what insider information I might find. I saw no dedicated bookstore or newspaper stand, which was a shame. I would have to forgo my ritual of buying a copy of the weekend edition of London's *Financial Times*, which was loaded with travel and cultural info.

But Ralph had chosen this location, so spoiled *moi* would deal with "roughing it" in the "wild." At least we weren't pitching a tent, something that had zero chance of happening to this outdoors-has-its-limits gal.

Having traversed the town, we'd worked up a thirst. We were pleased to see a bustling café terrace on a big open square and headed there. While we sipped our cool drinks, breathing in the refreshing Alpine air, I could feel all the tension of real-world worries, the drive, and hauling the luggage up to the apartment melt away. Our fun-cation had begun.

Suddenly the idyllic scene was punctuated by the clattering of hooves. Looking toward the cacophony, we saw a young woman run into the middle of the road and hold up her hand to stop traffic. A younger girl, maybe a preteen, did the same on the other side of the crossroads. From the mountainside came a mixed herd of sheep and goats parading down the main drag, dogs and a shepherd surrounding them, hustling to keep them together. A few curious animals hoofed it over and up onto the sidewalk to investigate a flowerbox, but the canine protectors did their job and expertly guided them back into the fold. I snapped some photos as they clamored their way through downtown, undoubtedly en route to their own evening aperitif.

Settling back into my seat after the rousing livestock show, I said, "Now we know where it's happening for Happy Hour in Termignon."

"I bet around here the action never stops."

Ralph's choice of words reminded me of a goofy game we had made up, like a competition for most implausible screenplay. We played it on vacation, usually when we were relaxed and feeling silly. I said, "Nor does the *action* stop in Scandal

Central—you remember, the fictitious town where life is always ridiculously complicated?"

"Sure I do. So you're up for that now?"

"You betcha!" I thought every prime-time soap opera script worth its innuendo should include a few wilderness episodes. "To refresh your memory," I said, "points for originality of the fabricated tale, suspension of disbelief obligatory, tone light, nothing excessively scary or dark."

"But smoldering is okay?"

"Of course. Like Mae West said, 'When I'm bad, I'm better.'"

"You start," Ralph said.

Glancing around the tables on the square, I saw an older couple in hiking clothes, walking sticks propped against their table; a young man and woman leaning toward each other over a table, their hands clasped, phones to the side; and a German couple in black leather motorcycle outfits. But my attention settled on the young lady with long blond hair and a bright smile who had brought our drinks. On my trip to the ladies' room, I'd seen her and the bartender hugging, with the handsome lad reassuring her it would all work out. Now I considered what *it* was that was going to work out.

"Well, our server is engaged to the bartender. The wedding is to take place in a couple of months *if* they overcome a slight hiccup."

"Which is?"

"He's already married and needs an annulment—from the state of Nevada."

"That constitutes a hiccup, all right."

"Our hero the bartender was in Las Vegas for a wedding. After a champagne-soaked reception, he shared an Uber with a bridesmaid to what he thought was a fast-food drive-in. In his inebriated state, he heard the attendant ask him whether he wanted fries with his taco, and he answered, 'I do.' Turns out he was in one of those ubiquitous Las Vegas drive-through wedding chapels and now has a lawfully wedded wife."

"Instead of a taco."

"Yes! Happens more often than you think. But you don't hear about it much. You know, what happens in Vegas, stays in Vegas."

"Okay, I think my suspension of disbelief is at capacity. Let's take a break."

"Wait, wait, you haven't heard about his evil twin yet—*he* was the one who was in Las Vegas, and *he* used his brother's name and ID info!"

"This is an episode that might be tough to top. I'll need to give it some thought over dinner."

"No sneaking AI help," I cautioned.

"Ha ha."

"Do you want to concede right now?"

"No, no, to be continued."

"Okay, but I think I got you on this one. Makes up for you blasting me at billiards."

The next morning, I swept back the curtains to reveal a sun-kissed scene under a cloudless sky, perfect for our foray to Lac du Mont-Cenis, one of the area's must-see destinations for Ralph. He hoped to spot a Golden Eagle and a Bearded Vulture. He'd seen the former but not the latter. I'd never spotted either one, making them both lifers in my bird book. I checked the battery strength for my camera and phone for all the photos I'd be taking, certain the landscape would be stellar even though reaching it meant paying the altitude price.

Whenever we embark on one of these Alpine treks, my internal apprehension gizmo registers somewhere between a mild twinge of trepidation and a hard pang of panic due to the Alps' propensity for fog and skinny hairpin roads with ultra-steep drop-offs and no guardrails. But today was sunny and Ralph assured me that the drive wouldn't be daunting, so I could relax. Also, I had done some mapping research myself and concluded that the ride didn't *appear* to be terror-inducing. It wasn't yet clear whether the other places on Ralph's itinerary could promise such a seemingly manageable drive, but today, despite some lingering doubts, I geared up for a fear-free day.

In reality, the switchbacks on the way to Lac du Mont-Cenis were only somewhat concerning but didn't scare me witless—a welcome surprise. Also surprising, not to mention impressive, were all the cyclists pedaling up the steep mountain road. Many were not Tour de France types but older folks, and several were on non-electric *vélos*. One might question the motivation to take on a challenge that requires such monumental physical and mental stamina. Most likely, the answer would involve a bucket list or, as the mountaineer George Mallory famously replied when asked why he wanted to climb Mount Everest, "Because it's there."

I had nothing but admiration for this hearty bunch, but for my part I was quite content *not* to be seated on a cycle saddle as we climbed higher and higher, the forests on either side safely tucking us in. Before we knew it, we were gazing over verdant pastureland to the starkly beautiful, impossibly turquoise Lac du Mont-Cenis. Treeless peaks creased with snow encircled the still, ice-blue water without a single high-rise structure. Our only companions were a herd of multitasking cattle roaming the grassy patch at the end of the road where we'd parked, munching while serenading us with a boisterous cowbell concert.

At the rate I was snapping photos of the surreal mountain scene, my phone would be out of juice in no time. I couldn't help it. The pristine lake was mesmerizing, an evaluation enthusiastically shared by Alex, the co-owner of the picturesque refuge Le Toët. While Ralph birded nearby, I paused for a coffee served by Alex's wife Nathalie at a picnic table near a swing set in the "front yard." As I was leaving, I chatted with her affable husband, who was taking a break from his lawn mowing. Sweeping my hand across the stunning lakeside landscape, I offered a serious understatement: "This is a very pretty spot."

Grinning with unapologetic pride, he said, "The best in the world."

In addition to the enchanting scenery, cheese was a source of pride for locals in this neighborhood, particularly Beaufort. It's similar to Comté, which I love for its firm consistency and rich, nutty flavor, so I was eager to try this particular Alpine version. I noticed a *fromagerie* snuggled into a cluster of buildings next to the visitors' center up the hill from Le Toët and hustled over. I didn't want to miss out on experiencing an integral part of their regional culture, especially one where I could sniff-taste-savor.

When I entered, the cheesemonger wore a dour expression, which didn't jive with the awe-inspiring lake view he could enjoy all day. I tried to lighten the mood with a question about the musical cows down the road. "Would it be possible to have some Beaufort from the bovines by Le Toët?"

Gesturing inside the case to a massive round of cheese that looked like a boudoir pillow, he said with a slight smile, "*Mais oui*, but their cousins helped. It's from a cooperative. Would you still like some?"

"Absolutely," I answered, pleased that his outlook seemed brighter.

"How much would you like?"

With my imprecise "Just a little bit," he positioned a wide blade on the big Beaufort wheel on a spot that would have produced a wedge weighing a kilo. Luckily, before pressing down on the cleaver, he asked, "Is this the right amount?"

"Oh, a bit smaller, please," I said.

He edged the knife a centimeter over to a place I agreed to. My "little bit" of Beaufort was more of a slab, sufficient to feed fondue to fourteen. Ralph and I savored its earthy deliciousness for the entire week.

When I reunited with my birder, he had great news. One of his target birds, a Golden Eagle, had paid him a courtesy call. I'd been too busy with the Beaufort transaction and missed the majestic bird, but I hoped it would make another fly by. Ralph hoped so too because it had been just a fleeting peek, but he was sure of his identification primarily because of the bird's deep brown color and sheer size—the biggest of eagles—and the higher elevation location. That's where they prefer to soar, a sure sign they have great taste in residential view property.

While the eagle hunted for lunch elsewhere, we returned to Le Toët for ours. As if the vast view of the lake and peaks beyond weren't gorgeous enough, a Rock Thrush hopped out of a thicket not far from the path. Dusky blue and orange, about the size of an American Robin, it thoughtfully stood still long enough for Ralph to note its longish tail and make a positive ID. I was daydreaming in the Alpine wonderland, looking in the other direction, when Ralph whispered, "Rock Thrush." I fumbled with my binoculars to focus on the hard-to-find bird, but it had vanished. All I saw was a blotch of blue sail away. It was a disappointing miss, but dwelling on it wasn't productive. Especially with birding, I knew I had to switch gears and embrace the promise of the next one.

I hoped I'd fare better with the much larger *aigle royal*—the Golden Eagle that Ralph had seen earlier. I wanted to watch for the large bird even while lunching since the restaurant had a sprawling terrace, but as the temperature was growing nippier, we opted to eat in the cozy wood-paneled interior. Giant cowbells hung from the rafters at one end and a pot-bellied stove stood at the other, separated by a bar and a room of sturdy wooden tables. No one else was there at first, but June is preseason, so that was to be expected. Nathalie cheerfully took our order—a cheese omelet for me, yes, with Beaufort, accompanied by a fresh garden salad. Ralph ordered a *salade* too, but with another form of *fromage*—goat cheese—melted on rounds of toasted baguette. The pretty salads on both platters displayed a designer touch—each was decorated with elaborate rosebuds shaped from carrot shavings.

While we were eating, a couple of young guys dressed for rugged outdoor work ordered beers at the bar. They were still there—likely on a second round—when we approached the cash register to settle the bill. While Nathalie was punching the credit card machine, I told her we were there to look for big birds, especially the Bearded Vulture. Thoughts of the bird may conjure up scenes of messy carnage, but it's a visually intriguing dark creature with a rusty undercarriage and longish black whiskers. Nathalie said to hang around there because our target bird, known as the *Gypaète barbu* in French, had flown through the property the other day. Surely it would be back.

"That's exciting," I said. Turning to Ralph, I suggested that perhaps we should stay where we were and let the bird come to us.

Unconvinced, Ralph answered, "And skip the thrill of the hunt?"

Then one of the young guys introduced himself as Tom and chimed in with some astounding information. He said there was a nest of baby Bearded Vultures outside of Bessans, near Bonneval-sur-Arc, on the mountain face near the parking lot for La Via Ferrata, meaning the Iron Path. This scary mountaineering endeavor relying on cables and ladders distracted me briefly, but my focus soon returned to the unexpected intel on the birds.

"Babies, truly?" I said, my jaw dropping.

"Yes," he said, "and you can see their little beaks pointing up out of the nest." To see a nest with baby birds—that exceeded any expectations we had, which were quite low, frankly. This was crazy good luck. After thanking Tom, we hustled to the car, excited about this insider tip.

As we backtracked toward Termignon, my thoughts returned to La Via Ferrata. Along with Alpine cycling, it was another sporty activity I'd happily leave to others. Maybe you get so used to the extreme exhilaration that relaxation sets in? I pondered this as we cruised through the hairpin turns and sheer drop-offs that had somewhat concerned me going up but now didn't faze me on the return trip. Funny how fear disappeared as I focused on not missing the turn to Bessans and potentially the bearded baby birds. We were on a mission, an avian treasure hunt.

I doubted I'd ever be a Via Ferrata fan, but in case that changed, I'd know where to find it. The sign Tom had told us about was unmissable, a low, thick, built-for-eternity wooden affair with the letters carved into it and painted bright white. More importantly for our purposes, next to it stood a large billboard that offered not just detailed Via Ferrata information, but also some critical facts about the Bearded Vulture.

The orientation map included a red rectangle indicating the Bearded Vulture protected area, the no-go zone, not that anything or anyone could access it without wing power. This was just the specific information we needed, and our hopes soared. We studied the map closely and then moved our gaze to that precise location on the pocked rock face. We searched methodically for any activity with both binoculars and a spotting scope. Hungry baby birds meant mom or dad would fly in and out with sustenance. The parents would be hard to miss with wingspans sometimes reaching almost three meters. But nothing was flying at all.

Refusing to give up, we continued to stare and scan, periodically returning to the info board in the hopes it would suddenly divulge a secret. But not only did studying the map not improve our chances, it drained us of hope because of the strange location of a You Are Here arrow. It pointed to the top of a peak. Since we were very much on the valley floor, this information didn't inspire confidence in the veracity of the signage. There was no way to reconcile that arrow with where our feet were, so the perspective was completely skewed. "We might be staring at the wrong rock face," I said to Ralph. "Or maybe some joker moved the arrow for fun, knowing folks would be twisting their heads around trying to match the map with reality."

"Well, then the joke's on us," Ralph said sadly.

"But I'm not laughing. Boo-hoo." Birds fly, that's what they do. They don't wait for you, unfortunately. We came up empty, but I awarded us an A for effort.

Disheartened that our "golden" insider tip for the special bird hadn't panned out, we tried to compensate by visiting the stone village of Bonneval-sur-Arc just up the road. A birder friend had told us not to miss this summer and winter resort, which boasts membership in the sought-after association of Les Plus Beaux Villages de France—the Prettiest Villages in France. With a population of under three hundred, the beautifully preserved village with its collection of gray stone chalets with slate roofs and wooden balconies is strollable in minutes. During our reconnaissance visit under what was now a cloudy, darkening sky, we felt an intriguing ghost town–like vibe. We were alone on the narrow streets except for a black-and-white *chat* with a spiky fur coat resembling a cartoon cat that had just pulled a paw out of an electrical outlet. Or maybe its edgy look was required for an audition for the role of sidekick to a dodgy, deceitful character from a whodunit? It would have landed the part, most certainly.

But as we turned a corner, the initial chilling ambience warmed up to cheery with a scene of log troughs filled with pink petunias in front of the tourist office. Thinking the staff might aid in our vulture quest, I hoped they were open for business. I jiggled the handle of the door but it didn't budge. Some women stood behind the desk in the back, and they waved in unison. Interpreting their greeting as encouragement to try again, I did. Nothing. Finally, one of the employees came to the door and opened it, but just a crack. She merely wanted to tell me bonjour and that they were closed, without further explanation. Perhaps she was leading a staff meeting and had to return *tout de suite*.

Still, I couldn't let this potential bearer of critical Bearded Vulture news disappear without making my request. As much as I wanted to stick my boot in the opening to prevent her from closing the door, I thought better of it. Such a menacing move would counter the friendliness I wanted to present in preparation for asking a favor. Without a nanosecond to lose, I blurted out my question with few pauses between words: "Bearded Vulture. I'm-so-sorry-to-bother-you-but-we-heard-about-a-nest-on-the-mountain-by-the-Via-Ferrata-sign. If you please, is-that-the-correct-location?"

As if on cue and without pausing, she recited a phrase that seemed rote, as if she'd rehearsed it ad nauseam: "I can't tell you where the Bearded Vulture is because I don't know." As if reversing the clauses would ignite understanding, she continued, "I don't know where the Bearded Vulture is, so I can't tell you. Really." It was delivered with a bright smile and an au revoir. Click.

What she left unsaid was "Even if I did know, I wouldn't tell you." I don't think she was clueless. Yet her knowledge was a secret for her to keep, not to share, especially with a stranger. She didn't know me—mum was the word. She couldn't risk abetting some sneaky surveillance that could endanger the birds. After all, maybe I had a drone up my sleeve.

Deflated for the second time in one day in our quest for the big bearded one, we left the idyllic setting of Bonneval-sur-Arc behind. But not without learning a fun fact. The authentic village is a twin town, a *ville jumelée*, with Les Baux-de-Provence, the cliffhanger village near Saint-Rémy where we looked for the Wallcreeper. I could understand the resemblance in one aspect at least—the two villages each had their own invisible birds. We hadn't seen the Bearded Vulture here, and we hadn't seen the Wallcreeper there.

En route to Termignon, we saw a billboard for a cross-country ski lodge and followed the signage, a last-ditch effort to gain some avian intelligence. At La Grange du Travérole, an older fellow walked out to the large parking area to greet us, followed by dozens of chickens, ranging freely. After the pleasantries, I asked about the Bearded Vulture nest. Using verbiage suspiciously like that of the tourist office lady, he said, "I can't tell you about the Bearded Vulture because I don't know where it is. I don't know where it is, so I can't tell you. Really." I believed him as much as the tourist office woman. He obviously was an experienced secret keeper too. I wish I could have convinced him that we could be trusted to scan from afar and that no remotely controlled aircraft was stuffed up my sleeve. Really.

The next day began with steady rain, putting a literal damper on our plan to venture into the woods. Like kids itching to escape outdoors but who are cooped up inside at a loss for entertainment, we turned to the large screen bolted to the wall. While I was refilling our coffee mugs, Ralph flipped through a dozen weather, news, and soap opera channels before settling on one.

Handing him his mug, I said, "So we've come high into the Alps, nearly to the Italian border, to sit on the edge of a bed and watch *The Simpsons*—in French?"

"It's only been three minutes and I'm practically fluent!" Ralph said.

Always keen to explore novel language acquisition methods, I said, "In that case …" and settled beside him. We were cracking up at far more of the jokes than I thought we would, but truth be told, that was probably because we know the English episodes so well. Twenty minutes passed before we realized the rain had stopped.

Although far from French-fluent by the time the sun arrived, we detached ourselves from the pixels to embrace what the day had left to offer. Since it was now late morning, we opted to snoop around close to home. Our target was Lanselberg, the nearest town with a commercial district, including some sports stores, which I was counting on. As far as Ralph's birthday present was concerned, I was guilty of proving right the adage of the six P's: Poor Prior Planning Prevents Proper Performance.

I hadn't packed a gift and hoped I'd luck out at the last minute and find a cool one in one of the sports stores. And if they happened to have some cargo-style hiking pants with lots of practical pockets for me and maybe an impractical, skimpy, lace-trimmed tank top to go with it, I wouldn't object. In one store, I found a broad selection from Le Slip Français, one of my favorite companies for guy garb for Ralph. I sent the birthday boy to browse at the opposite end of the store while I made my less-than-surreptitious purchase.

Before leaving, I paused to ask the cashier whether he could suggest a restaurant with a friendly ambience and authentic cuisine. "Right across the street," he said, pointing to a *crêperie*. "It's really good. We all go there often." Unlike the tourist office lady and the cross-country ski gentleman, I believed this guy. Had I thought about it then, I should have asked *him* about the Bearded Vulture.

After a laid-back, tasty mountain fare lunch, thanks to the salesman's recommendation, we moseyed along the River Arc, and that was where Ralph got lucky. Pecking along the rocks, a White-fronted Dipper appeared. The cute little thing had no snacking partners, but one was enough to make Ralph's day. And mine too. Watching its comical hop-and-dip, grab-a-bug antics was a hoot. In French theatrical circles, that bird rated a Molière, similar to a Tony Award—for Best Spunky Performance. It was the icing on the rainy-day cake.

On Ralph's special day, our destination was the Refuge l'Auberge de Bellecombe, just over twelve kilometers from Termignon. From the car park, we planned to hike to Plan du Lac, return to l'Auberge de Bellecombe for lunch, and then if time and energy allowed we'd check out the Lac de Bellecombe, which clocked in at an elevation of 2,755 meters, or over nine thousand feet.

The online directions revealed a squiggly rope of a road, which did nothing to calm my height phobia. I gave myself a little get-a-grip pep talk, trying to put my irrational thoughts aside. Ralph was a careful driver, and there was the stupendous scenery to distract me. This wasn't ziplining over the Grand Canyon, for Pete's sake. And for a final boost, I focused on the prize—the White-winged Snowfinch, a special bird that prefers thinner air. In addition, there might be a Spotted Nutcracker, Ringed Ouzel, Black Grouse, Rock Ptarmigan, Redbilled Chough, or even a Bearded Vulture. The bottom line was that sometimes adventure involved stretching the wings, I told myself. That was the idea of exploration, to go beyond the same old parameters. Today I would stretch a little. And hope not to tear a muscle.

The drive might have looked treacherous online, but thankfully that wasn't my experience. As we entered the torturous section, I distracted myself with a magazine article and managed to slip into some sort of Zen mode until Ralph turned off the engine in a vast parking lot that was filling up fast. Clearly, many others had made the same drive, and they were walking, talking, and laughing, seemingly excited to be there, and not at all traumatized. Apparently, for them, arriving at this altitude was simply a routine walk in the woods.

Only we were now above the tree line, so there wasn't a sapling in sight. We hiked up to the refuge overlooking the parking lot to verify it was open for lunch and continued toward Plan du Lac. A group wielding hiking poles and loaded with heavy backpacks walked single file along a path on the far side of the plain toward the towering peaks. Hearty souls they must be—certainly heartier than me. With only a small day pack, a camera, and binoculars around my neck, my goal was to walk to the lake and back, not a mighty trek at under six kilometers. I rationalized that the thinner air and undulating landscape meant the exertion required would be more demanding than it might seem on paper. That said, my future would doubtless hold no selfies from the summit of Mount Everest.

But this wimp had not freaked out on the drive up, so as far as I was concerned, I deserved a gold star. Still, I wanted to do my best to get to the lake alongside Ralph, who was in his element, stopping to scan the peaks whenever he detected a sign of movement. The path was wide, and we had it to ourselves for most of the hike. We frequently stopped to study the sheer majesty of the landscape, marveling at flora like the bunches of tiny electric-blue flowers that shimmered in the sunshine, brightening the drab scrub brush. Documenting the day with my camera and phone kept me busy, especially capturing the marmots that scampered about and lounged in the sun on boulders like they owned the place. And they did, in a way. This was their home, this incredible wilderness where we humans were but minute specks passing through, hopefully respectfully.

Pausing to take in the lake view, which looked like an otherworldly mirage, we could see the low-slung buildings of the Refuge de Plan du Lac in the distance. Once at the property, we claimed one of the picnic tables, where we sat and nibbled on granola bars while scanning the landscape. Just then a male guide, probably in his thirties, appeared with a group of about ten senior hikers carrying gargantuan backpacks, apparently prepared for a long haul. They stopped near us to take sips from their water bottles while listening to the guide's commentary on the area.

When he finished speaking and the members were chatting among themselves, I took the opportunity to pose a birding question to him, knowing *not* to pronounce the silent P in ptarmigan. "Excuse me, but did you mention the Rock Ptarmigan—do you hope to see one around here?"

"Oh sure," he said. "We'll hike for about four more hours and spend the night in a hut. At dawn the next morning we should see one."

"Well, that's great. All the best of luck!" I offered, stunned that those older folks were engaging in such a strenuous ordeal. The closest we'd get to that bird was right where we were.

Ralph hadn't heard the exchange, so I repeated the basics of what I'd learned, adding, "Bottom line, we toss the idea about the ptarmigan."

After I gave Ralph more details about the hut hike, I turned my head in time to notice a couple of birds flying over one of the buildings to the area behind it. We hustled over to investigate. Ralph stopped and stared at the pecking birds, pressing his binoculars to his eyes. "White-winged Snowfinches!"

"Seriously?"

"Both of them. See the large, elongated white wing patches and the black bib?"

I adjusted the focus on my binoculars. "Now I do. So this is the little guy that all the fuss is about. Nice to meet you, little finches."

Neither offered a response but continued pecking the dirt furiously, scurrying about close to the building where we stood as if our presence wasn't at all concerning. While they hunted, we hunkered down to watch. Seeing the target bird was a bit anticlimactic at first—it seemed like such a casual occurrence, like sparrows at the backyard birdbath. Just a routine happening. Which is not to disparage sparrows; they are a constant pleasure. Maybe that's part of the heart of travel, I mused—the extraordinary springs from the ordinary. The mundane made magic.

Back at the Refuge l'Auberge de Bellecombe, perched above the parking lot, we were the only diners, served by a teenager who was a summer intern learning the restaurant ropes as part of a larger educational program. From northern France, he was enthralled with the Vanoise valley and intent on a career as a guide. We could easily understand the allure based on just our limited introduction to the enchanting area.

For the last few years, the complex had offered hostel-like accommodation in addition to the restaurant that whips up local favorites like ham and cheese crêpes and local charcuterie.

It was open only during the summer, when it was a haven for the outdoorsy set. We learned it had been run by the same Jacquemmoz family for three generations, and they were proud of their heritage. While we waited for our meals under a fluttering umbrella at the picnic table, the intern brought us a family photo album to flip through. Some of the photographs showed the vivacious Celia, the property's current "guardian," in a parade as a broadly grinning teenager wearing a traditional costume, holding a sign that read TERMIGNON.

Decorating my crêpe was a toothpick with a little paper flag that read FROMAGE BEAUFORT, showing a hiker climbing a mountain with a backpack and a pole. The tall, strapping intern, I soon learned, carried a different sort of flag, a metaphorical one, indicating he took his duties of protecting this special place to heart. When I asked where the WC was, he pointed to the building with the washrooms, then asked me to follow him. We crossed the yard and went down some steps and into the accommodation building. In the entry, which opened to an inviting communal space with comfy sofas, he paused and pointed to a sign reading NO SHOES BEYOND THIS POINT.

"Madame, you need to take off your boots. You can put on those," he said, indicating some rubber slippers. I did as instructed while he observed my progress. He didn't want me to cut any corners and leave a trail of mountain mud on the pristine floors. "*Les toilettes* are at the end, on the right." He pointed down the hallway. "Okay?"

"*Oui, merci,*" I said, impressed with his serious but gracious manner and confident he'd learn his lessons well and would protect his adopted domain as proudly as any local.

Content to give the steep, narrow, rocky path to Lac de Bellecombe a pass, we returned to the car and headed south. After parking at the homestead, we were unloading our gear when the roar of motorcycles blasted us. Four fat-wheeled monsters pulled up, two stopping on each side of us. We were surrounded. Was France's version of the Hell's Angels moving in? Yikes. How would this impact our tranquil, romantic vacation space? Until now, we'd had the run of the property, choosing different spots around the extensive yard for our morning coffee and evening *apéros*. Now, begrudgingly, it looked as if we would have to share, and with some rough types to boot. But as they disembarked from their Harleys, we were surprised to hear friendly phrases—in English.

The jovial banter in my mother tongue reassured me that this group was a light-hearted one that invited interaction. "Hello, we're your neighbors, here for the rest of the week," I said. After introductions, we found out they were not a motorcycle *gang* but a motorcycle *club*, down from merry old England, having an easygoing holiday conquering the Savoie on "hogs," the nickname of the Harley-Davidson brand of motorcycles. I couldn't imagine attempting the narrow, twisty roads with no guardrails on one of those two-wheeled monsters, so I just had to ask.

"How do you ride on these crazy skinny roads and not get scared?"

"There's a trick to it," one of the men, a history professor, answered.

"This I have to know!" I said, stepping closer.

"You just steer where you want to go and not where you don't."

"Ah, so that's the ticket. That's advice I must commit to memory." After wishing our new neighbors a pleasant stay, we trudged up the path to our apartment, me repeating to myself the biker's straightforward road map for life advice: Steer where you want to go and not where you don't.

Our last night in Termignon was a winner in the cuisine department. At Le Trappeur, Ralph devoured an outstanding charcoal-grilled *daurade* with the most excellent fries ever. They must have been put through the fryer three times at least. Although I had ordered a dinner-sized salad, I was compelled to beg Ralph for a *frite* handout. And I kept returning for more—not just for the exquisite taste but to make a gastronomic determination. We had nicknamed a food truck in Saint-Rémy the Frites-Van because it churned out such delectable fries. Stopping there is an indulgence reserved for special occasions. No matter how many different plates of French fries we've tried all over France and beyond, our Frites-Van fries have always retained the gold medal. But now we might have a contender. I had to try just one more to be sure.

Later that night, the jury was still out on the Best Frites du Monde Award, but there was no doubt that the Jacuzzi tub bubble bath hit all the right buttons. Once the tub was filled, the foam mountains billowing, the jets massaging, and the champagne bubbles tickling, relaxation came to us both. Emitting soft *oohs* and *aahs*, we were settled in for an extended soak when a dazzling dimension of the bath *à deux* experience surprised us. Leaning back on a waterproof pillow, flute to my lips, I turned slightly to look in the direction of the tall bathroom window. We'd forgotten to draw the floor-to-ceiling drapes, and the glass panes were as transparent as if they had just been squeegeed. What loomed before us was the next-door neighbors' two-story house, which was thankfully dark. But what towered over the dwelling was not. In the moonlight, the snowcapped Alps twinkled as if sprinkled with glittery fairy dust.

"Oh, honey, look. We're together in a bubble bath and can see the Alps!"

"And the Alps can see you," he said, setting his flute on the tub's edge. "And so can I."

Packing up the next morning was much quicker than settling in a week prior because most of the provisions had been consumed, including the hefty hunk of local Beaufort. We bid adieu to the stunning, pristine Val-Cenis region, knowing that we'd just nicked the surface of understanding this layered mountain life and its variety of inhabitants closely entwined with the land.

To underscore the point, our departure was delayed. On our way out of town, just a few blocks from the apartment, we were stopped by a flock of sheep for the second time during our stay. A couple of shepherds blocked traffic while their woolly charges rumbled through, a raucous reminder that in this rugged Alpine retreat, the animal kingdom often takes the lead.

Joie de Vivre Highlights

Traffic-stopping sheep in Termignon
Beaufort cheese from musical cows
A Rock Thrush at Lac Val-Cenis
White-winged Snowfinches at the Refuge de Plan du Lac
An Alps view from the Jacuzzi with bubbles and bubbly

9

Worth the Detour

Southwestern and Western France

Our island destination in northwestern France was the big draw, but the breaks along the way held enticing surprises. Landlocked Montauban in the Tarn-et-Garonne department and the Loire-Atlantique coastal resort of Pornic each make a cracking case for creative routing.

*L*e bout du monde—literally, Land's End—isn't simply a single spot. Many places claim that title, scattered all over the planet from Argentina to Norway. The particular end of the earth where we were headed was the Île d'Ouessant, the dramatically beautiful island off the most westerly point of France. Ushant, its English name, boasts a population of under a thousand humans, probably nearly as many sheep, and few motorized vehicles. Most residents live near the capital, the island's solitary town of Lampaul.

The island is part of Finistère, the French department that is as far west as you can go and still be in continental France.

Visitors come to experience the magic of its spectacular scenery, with its dramatic coastline, luxurious solitude, and nearly four hundred species of birds that have been spotted over the years. It's a nature lover's nirvana, with hiking and biking trails crisscrossing the island. And the month of October offers a special allure—it's prime bird migration season.

Hundreds of birders from all over France and beyond pour into Ouessant for this exceptional event. They mainly aim to see vagrants and accidentals, birds that were headed elsewhere but got blown off course and ended up at the end of the earth by the sheer force of nature gone off the rails. Our French birder buddies visited regularly, and Ralph and I would join them this time. Not that we wore birding belts, but if we did, experiencing this event would put a notch in them.

Our plans for the long-haul trip—over twelve hundred kilometers by car from Saint-Rémy—had been in the works for months. From the few times we had been on such a far-flung journey, I knew we were in for a boatload of research. The first decision was to drive or fly. Flying directly to the island wasn't an option, but it would be easy to fly from Marseille to Brest, then take the ferry to Ouessant. Or we could stay farther west in Le Conquet, where the Brest ferry stopped to pick up passengers. I love ferries—a sea segment lends any trip a romantic aspect—so I was pleased that however we chose to go, a ferry would be part of the plan. Ultimately, we decided to take it slow by driving and stopping to explore along the way.

So where would the overnights be? I have a friend who doesn't mind driving fourteen hours in one go, but for me, after two hours of plowing down the autoroute, getting out of the car is a nice break. After four hours, nice becomes need, and by hour six, need morphs into misery if my feet don't touch terra firma. Judging by the total driving time estimate of between twelve and fourteen hours plus breaks between Saint-Rémy and Le Conquet, we'd need two overnights minimum.

Relying on a map application, I fiddled with various routes. I ended up with a first-night stopover in Montauban, a medium-sized city four hours from Saint-Rémy, and on day two, pushing the in-motion envelope to five and a half hours, we'd reach the seaside village of Pornic. That would leave three and a half hours on the last day, bringing us to Le Conquet, where we'd booked an apartment for a week. From there, it was just a ninety-minute ferry ride to Ouessant, where we'd spend one night at Land's End. The ferry arrived on Ouessant in the morning and departed in the early evening, so we'd have the better part of two days for an overview of the small island. We'd cycle all over and hopefully spot an inordinate number of feathered creatures that don't habitually frequent the south of France.

When I relayed our plans to Gérard, an ornithologist friend who had encouraged us to make the trek, he told me a couple of days on the island wouldn't do it justice. But bookings had been made. However, one of his travel tips was still possible to follow—the mode of transport on the island. We had first planned to take our foldable bikes on the ferry, but he said that the island's hills were demanding and that we would not regret full-sized bikes. Check. We could have strapped our own bikes on the back of the car, but it wasn't worth the hassle because the costs of transporting the bikes on the ferry and the bike rental on the island were the same. So I got on the phone and reserved the *vélos*, opting for nonelectric types. When asked whether I was absolutely sure about reserving regular bikes and not electric ones, I said yes—we enjoyed pedaling. But since I hadn't discussed the need for battery power with our experienced birder friend, I wondered if my snap decision was an invitation for regret.

On the day of departure, with the house prepared and car packed—cram packed, actually, including our foldable bikes—I took the first driving shift, nearly to Carcassonne. We stopped for a picnic lunch at a no-frills autoroute rest stop minus a gas station or restaurant but with a WC, plus a little lake. With the temperature at a pleasant 27° Celsius, we nibbled our tuna sandwiches while being entertained by some mallards paddling about under a sunny sky. We were off to a good start.

Ralph got us past Toulouse and over to Montauban, our first stop, a walkable city just off the autoroute. Before I'd started snooping around, trying to find a stopover around the four-hour mark, I knew nothing about this place. A magazine article I'd stumbled upon made it sound quite appealing, especially the main square surrounded by impressive brick buildings and double-arched arcades. Spending the afternoon exploring it would be a pleasure.

Our digs for the night, the former abbey-cum-hotel Abbaye des Capucins, provided easy parking in front of the main entrance, so we didn't worry about the car being stuffed to the rafters. (We'd bring in the Swarovski binoculars to be on the safe side.) The room was nicely furnished with a sofa, a table for two with comfy chairs, a huge bed topped with luxurious linens, and a spacious bathroom with a sparkling tub and separate shower. The only drawback was that beyond the driveway, our view featured a high-rise wrapped in scaffolding on which workers scuttled about. I trotted down to the front desk to try my luck at switching rooms. *"Je suis désolé"* was the answer from the polite professional manning the desk. He was sorry, but the hotel was full tonight. At least the room's two windows were double paned, so the noise wasn't obtrusive.

Next we were off to discover. The walk to the striking Place Nationale took just a few minutes. We spotted the restaurant I had wanted to try, Les 5 Bouchons, but at this time of year it wasn't open for dinner during the week. Regardless, we perused the posted menu to see what we were missing. If we could return one day, this would be where we'd go. But tonight, on to plan B. The first part of that plan was to enjoy an aperitif at one of the many cafés lining the bustling square that periodically becomes a liquid "mirror" when submerged geysers spring into action. After we'd settled into our seats overlooking the square, a young server welcomed us and took our orders. But when I ordered a glass of white wine, rather than asking whether I wanted a specific varietal like chardonnay or sauvignon blanc, she asked only whether I wanted *vin sec*, dry wine. In France, where most restaurants are particular about their regional wines, the question seemed odd. I surmised that the region specialized in sweet whites, so maybe it was the wine of choice for locals. Perhaps she'd pegged me as a foreigner and figured sweet might not be my "cup of tea" when it came to wine. I mentally registered this Montauban mystery, considering it a worthy case to crack.

I didn't have to wait until we got home to become enlightened. My phone immediately informed me that sweet Jurançon wines are indeed grown in southwest France, a few hours from Montauban, in the foothills of the Pyrenees. They boasted the Appellation d'Origine Protégée designation, which verifies that certain production methods are followed within a specific geo-graphic area. And Jurançon comes in a dry version too. In the world of wine, this informative tidbit might only be a drop in the proverbial barrel, but every drop counted.

While we sipped and people watched on the square, little geysers shot up in the center every half hour or so, sending steam swirling around tots who shrieked like they were on a roller coaster as they stomped the water, splashing each other. A pair of teenaged girls used it as a video backdrop. One ran alongside her friend, filming her as she charged through the water, swinging her arms and squealing like a carefree kid.

It was a happy-go-lucky scene, but we extracted ourselves for a serious reason—to find food. My second and third choices for restaurants didn't pan out—an attractive Lebanese place was also closed, and an Indian restaurant looked inviting but was a risky choice. Sometimes spicy cuisine doesn't suit stomachs that can turn temperamental when traveling. Sadly, a variety of countries worldwide lay claim to the dubious honor of having a City Where the Padgetts Tossed Their Cookies. Whenever someone tells a traumatized stomach story, we can usually match it and raise them one. 'Nuff said, as my mom used to say when further explanation would be too much for delicate sensibilities.

Deciding I needed some expert local advice, I asked Ralph to continue people watching while I poked around in a Red Cross shop that might hold a jewel, as well as the solution to our dinner quest. (A few years before, I'd found a vintage beret in perfect condition in a Croix Rouge boutique in the Basque town of Cambo-les-Bains.) Here, I spotted a pretty column candle, but the salesperson informed me it was for decoration and not for sale. *"Pas de problème,"* I said. Then while I still had her attention I put on my tourist hat. Did she have a favorite restaurant in the area? Maybe a nice Italian place, I suggested, thinking an Italian eatery would offer tasty yet mild options. The three ladies behind the counter turned to each other and jabbered away, considering my question seriously.

After an animated discussion, the youngest woman turned to me and said, "There is one and it's quite good, but we can't think of the name. But we know where it is—it's on Rue Fort." She whipped out her phone and all three huddled close, eyes on the map she brought up. "Here it is—Little Italy. It's a little expensive, though, and you must reserve." She handed me a note with the name, address, and phone number. I offered my thanks, and they all wished me a spirited bon appétit in unison.

Armed with the local recommendation, we set off to check out the restaurant on the opposite side of town, passing the Musée Ingres. I'd read that Jean-Auguste Ingres was a native son, and this museum dedicated to him housed several of his famous works, paintings that we wouldn't have time to see on this trip. We had to depart the next day before it opened. But it's always nice to leave something special for next time, and based on what we'd seen so far, I wanted there to be a next time.

As we approached Little Italy, we saw that the shutters were open, which was a good sign, but the front door on the main street was locked. We moseyed around to the side street, where we could see a covered roof terrace. The weather was so mild, eating al fresco would be possible—if there was space for us. Peering into the restaurant at the back entrance, we saw not a soul, but that was normal for 5:00 p.m. Maybe by the time we got back to the hotel, someone would be there to take a reservation call.

On our return to the abbey-auberge, while Ralph perfected his people-watching skills on a bench, I spent a few minutes in a designer *dépôt-vente*, a consignment store, with a stylish window display. I was greeted by an older woman with crimson lips, dressed in a tailored sheath and wearing bold black glasses. After sizing me up, literally, she pointed to the appropriate racks, organized by size, where I would find gems to fit me. Impressive. Obviously, she was a seasoned professional. During my brief overview, I determined it was fertile fashion grounds worth a closer look—when I wasn't on Ralph's clock. I was sure that by now he was ready to vacate his bench, and besides, we had evening plans.

Back at the hotel, I stuck my toe in the pool to test the temperature—deliciously warm. As much as a dip sounded great in theory, it would just energize me—not something I wanted right before my bubble bath and nap. The spa's sauna also looked inviting, but that too would wait for another visit.

We were lounging in the room by 5:40 p.m., when I dutifully picked up the phone and called the restaurant. Happily, it was open that evening, and we were set for 8:00 p.m. My bubble bath in the gleaming, new-looking tub was divine because I'd had the foresight to bring a bottle of Badedas. It's a terrific bubble bath from Germany, which I stockpile because the bubbles are so long-lasting, and it has such a fresh, herby, spa-like scent.

After my relaxing "spa" treatment and a revitalizing *sieste* for both of us, we dressed and headed to the restaurant on foot.

The young lady who greeted us asked, *"Avez-vous réservé?"*

"Oui," I said, giving our name and spelling it out. The greeter nodded and gestured for us to go upstairs, which

meant we'd be seated on the open-air terrace, precisely what we were hoping for. Customers already occupied a few tables, but there were plenty of seats left. Another hostess showed us a small table at the far end next to two big potted plants, which would come in handy later. It was the perfect vantage point for checking out the room as it filled, and judging from the steady stream of clients, no table would be left vacant.

We sipped on some agreeably tart Orvieto Classico while we perused the lengthy menu. I'd hoped for veal piccata, zingy yet simple, but it wasn't on offer. The spinach pasta with tomatoes got my attention, and the squid fettuccine grabbed Ralph's. We also couldn't resist sharing a dish of creamy mozzarella called *burrata* with tomato "soup." It arrived in a shallow casserole with grilled tomatoes on top. It was an exceptionally yummy dish, and we used the thick country bread to sop up the last drops.

When Ralph's bowl of fettuccine arrived, we were surprised to see that the ample mound of noodles was deep ebony. After a second we realized that was because of the squid juice, of course. But it was expected that my plate of spinach pasta would have a green hue. This heap of homemade linguine, however, was *strikingly* emerald, as if it were 99.9 percent veggie. The dish might very well deliver a week's worth of the suggested daily minimum requirement for vitamin K1. Topped with tomatoes and fresh spinach, my nutrient-packed dish was excellent, extra rich with all the parmesan I layered on top.

It was so excellent that once we dug in, sharing samples bite after bite, we didn't let up until we qualified for membership in the Clean Plate Club. We both sported satisfied smiles, utterly sated. Leaning back in our chairs, we gazed at our empty plates, realizing what we'd done. We'd eaten every morsel of both plates of luscious pasta. We stared at each other and simultaneously said, "Uh-oh."

While we tuned in to our stomachs, hoping they would remain calm, the personable owner worked the room, checking with each table to make sure everyone was satisfied. When he quizzed us about dessert, we declined, explaining we had no room left after the ample meal that had been so delicious. In that case, he said, he'd bring us some limoncello, *fait maison*. We could not refuse the sweet lemony liqueur—homemade—despite a potential gut revolt.

Within a few minutes, the hospitable restaurateur deposited two tall shot glasses on our table and said, "Enjoy" before turning his attention to his other customers. Throwing caution to the wind, Ralph took a healthy chug, while I took the smallest of sips, which was all I dared risk. The icy cold liqueur is great, but there's a time and place, and this wasn't it—for me, anyway. Ralph saw me glance at the potted palm to my side and knew instantly that I was contemplating the execution of a surreptitious watering.

"No," he whispered, slowly shaking his head. "Don't even think about it. Not cool. Besides, it might harm the plant."

"But I don't want to appear ungrateful …"

"Here," he said, holding his glass up for me to top it up.

"Are you sure?" I wasn't certain his limoncello capacity hadn't already been reached. But we weren't driving that evening, so I figured it was harmless and hoped his stomach agreed.

"Yup."

When the coast was clear—no one seemed interested in our table tucked in the back—I gave his glass a splash of the citrus liqueur.

"Still clear?" Ralph said.

As I nodded, he siphoned off a big dollop into his large water glass. This way, I realized, he showed his appreciation for the drink without having to consume it. A win-win.

"Nicely done, Sneaky Pete."

"You're welcome, Partner in Crime."

The stroll back to the hotel in the cool night air was the best digestif. We slept soundly, without disruptions from the activity on the exterior scaffolding across the driveway or our interior "scaffolding."

The next morning, after an extended wake-up shower *à deux*, we made coffee in the room, not rushing but not dawdling either. Our next stop, Pornic, was nearly six hours away, not counting stops, so we didn't want to linger over a long breakfast. Besides, we had to restore our appetite in preparation for our dinner reservations at an eatery with a Bib Gourmand designation, a special Michelin moniker that recognizes exceptional value for money. Under a bright sky and balmy temperature, we scooted north. Traffic was reasonable during both our shifts, and no scary bridges took my breath away.

The check-in at the modest Hôtel Beau Soleil in Pornic was a snap, though transferring our luggage and bikes took a bit more effort, requiring a two-pronged procedure. Since the parking lot was located up a hill near the town's austere tenth-century château, we first had to unload at the hotel and then relocate the car. But the parking lot was huge and *gratuit*, and the walk back down to town was easy.

What the room lacked in luxury appointments the view over the estuary made up for. We stood on the narrow balcony, letting a refreshing sea breeze caress our faces as gulls squawked, competing with the beep-beeping of scooters racing by on the street below. We took in the vista of anchored pleasure boats bobbing languidly, one with a cormorant swaying on the tip of its mast. Cyclists cruising the bike path running along the water swerved to miss clutches of visitors concentrating on their ice cream cones. Opposite the town, a forest of pines towered over waterside bars and surrounded sturdy stone and brick houses that marched up to the point. Except for the turreted château hugging the coast to our right, which didn't conjure up a quaint New England seaport, it seemed we'd landed in a French Nantucket. We were anxious to explore and so glad we were booked for two nights, giving us one full day to make some interesting discoveries.

After locating our dinner venue, L'Orangerie, and strolling around the commercial area, we stopped at the chic Marius restaurant on the water across from the boardwalk for an *apéro* and people watching. There weren't many customers, so tables were plentiful. And so were the waiters, all snazzily attired in matching black-and-white outfits. But they didn't take orders, as one patiently explained to us in more time than it would have taken to take our order. For that, we learned, one had to scan the QR code on the menu and order by phone. But another waiter finally did deliver a glass of white wine and a beer. Judging by the grand piano in the middle of the art deco–style dining area, this appeared to be a special event eatery that would be fun to frequent one day—not forgetting a phone, of course.

The welcome we received at L'Orangerie was huge, unlike the number of grilled scallops resting in a pool of pumpkin puree I'd ordered. But then, that's typically how it goes with scallops, and of course one can ask about a dish before ordering, but I usually forget to do that. Only a pair of scallops appeared, but they were plump, sweet, and entirely scrumptious. And so was Ralph's entire grilled whitefish, the humble *maquereau*, resting on a delicate cream sauce, topped with lithe roasted carrots. Together with the fresh-from-the-*jardin* first-course salad and before that an amuse-bouche consisting of two tiny pastry shells filled with vibrant beet cream and cubes of peppery focaccia, plus a small bowl of silky-smooth hummus, the memorable meal made its mark.

On our only full day in Pornic, one full of sunshine, we packed in a lot. First we walked along the coastal path on the far side of the estuary, pausing to snap photos of the bobbing boats with the picturesque town in the background and to watch a kids' sailing class, their boats outfitted with brilliant yellow sails. Once we rounded the point, we *oohed* and *aahed* at the stunning sea view, training our binoculars on the freewheeling terns, cormorants, and gannets that enlivened the scene. On our left, positioned above the path, stood house after impressive house, all with the Atlantic doubling as their front yard. One *maison* had our name on it: Champ des Oiseaux, Field of Birds. I could imagine living there. You'd feel like anything was possible every day—though maybe not in winter. Onward we walked to a huge spa complex called the Alliance Pornic Hôtel Thalasso & Spa to take in its vistas before circling back to town.

After lunching waterside on an exceptionally hearty salmon *pan bagnat* from a takeout sandwich place, we cycled on our foldable bikes along a canal. We passed a mural covering the entire side of a building of a jungle scene featuring a flying crimson parrot with blue wings, and took in a permanent out-door photography exhibition. One colorful photo by Didier Hamard, called *Canicule, Heatwave, Tharon Plage*, showed what looked like the entire Pornic population at the beach, some under striped umbrellas, others wading fully clothed in the shallow water. Overheating at the beach seemed a given, but another photograph was a total surprise. Christophe Rabreau's *Snow Day on the Old Port* showed the town enduring a blizzard on February 11, 2021. The beautiful photos captured a raw message: There was no ignoring nature. At a field filled with grazing goats, we turned around.

After pedaling up to the château, we struck out for Plage des Blancs Sablons. With bikes parked at the edge of the expansive beach, I removed my shoes before stepping into the soft sand and toward the water. In October, I didn't expect it to be baby-bath warm, but I couldn't leave Pornic without a dip, if only up to my ankles. *Oh là là*, that was one icy sensation I wouldn't soon forget. Two seconds satisfied my dipping requirement before beginning the trek back to Ralph. On the way, I passed a group of mature ladies in swimsuits heading for the water. Marching with determina-tion, they didn't seem to need a warning about the brisk conditions. I overheard one swimmer explain their motiva-tion: *"On doit profiter du soleil"*—one must take advantage of the sun. I couldn't have agreed with her more. It was just that sissy me with no Nordic blood would have preferred to *profiter* wearing a wetsuit.

It had been a long day, and we were taking off the next morning, so we headed back to the hotel to put our feet up before dinner. We weren't planning on making any more stops, but one sentimental scene demanded a brief pause. Below our path, a white-haired gentleman sat on a bench in the shade with a couple of elderly women seated at the other end. Strumming his guitar, he serenaded them, along with some grazing sheep, a few paddling mallards, and us. No concert ticket required.

Music may have been wafting through the air at Le Jardin de l'Olivier, the place the hotel receptionist had recommended for our last meal in Pornic, but we couldn't detect any tunes above the din. Whereas the ambience at L'Orangerie had been serene and dignified with everyone minding their manners, here it was let-your-hair-down casual. Young waiters dashed along their routes from table to kitchen while groups of mates clinked glasses, told stories, laughed, and cheered. It was a see-and-be-seen destination, and on this Friday night, it was packed. And so was my skewer—with no fewer than *six* seared-to-perfection scallops.

Quelle belle vue. The next morning, these were the three words on my mind, and I hoped they would spring spontaneously from my lips very soon. The striking images used to advertise the vista from the top floor of the multistory apartment we'd rented for the week dominated my thoughts as we approached the seaside village of Le Conquet. The photos had captured only the sweeping panoramic view of the estuary during the day, and I couldn't wait for the sunset version. Seeing it with my own eyes would be astonishing, I was certain.

The rental agency's young agent met us outside the apartment and directed us to the underground parking spot. Leaving everything in the car, we followed agent Odile as she bounced around a bend and down a hallway to an elevator. With all of us safely inside, she pushed the button and up we went, but only to the ground floor because she suddenly seemed to realize that we were not, in fact, inside the building that housed our apartment but in a separate sister structure that shared the single underground garage.

Next, she herded us outside to the courtyard and on to the entrance of our building. We loaded ourselves in the correct elevator, which whisked us to the top level, the fourth floor, home to two apartments. My excitement grew as the door swung open and she gestured for us to enter. My gaze immediately shifted to the scene at the end of the long hall. Through the floor-to-ceiling picture window and beyond the narrow balcony was nothing but blue—an expansive blue-sky view.

Ralph and I approached it without uttering a word, as if in a trance. "Oh, wow, look at that," I finally said, grinning.

Odile lifted the wooden rod from the track of the sliding doors and pushed one door open, and we stepped outside to survey the serene scene. Gulls swooped over the town's slanted slate rooftops, and small sailboats dotting the estuary barely bobbed. The verdant peninsula opposite was mostly undeveloped, with the spiky tip of the lighthouse at the end glistening in the sunshine.

"Pretty, isn't it?" Odile said.

"Pretty spectacular," I said, relieved and gratified that the reality of the view was even better than the online photos. The view was breathtaking and transporting, as if we had been ushered into another realm of possibility.

During the rest of the tour of the two-bedroom contemporary apartment, Odile stopped at the electrical box, carefully noting the readings, which reminded me that there would be an extra charge if we exceeded our allotment. Note to self: Make sure to turn off all lights when leaving. Oddly, the refrigerator didn't have a freezer compartment. However, Odile showed us the utility room outside the apartment, accessed by a separate key, which housed a giant one along with a washer and dryer. The only other apartment on the floor had its own designated washing machine, dryer, and freezer in the same room, so chances were good for meeting the neighbors. I'd be ready to properly greet them *en français*.

We piled back into the elevator and went down to the garage. Odile led us back to our car, perhaps thinking we'd gotten turned around with all the looping and wanted to ensure we knew how to get from A to B. Dutifully she asked, "Can I help you with the luggage?"

"No, no, thank you. We can do this," I said, slightly embarrassed that we had so much stuff, which looked like a disorganized jumble after only a few days on the road.

"Any questions?" she asked.

"Non, non, merci!" If we thought of anything, we were to call her, she said. Notebook tucked securely under her arm, she strode in the direction of the elevator we'd just left.

The apartment was well appointed and gleaming clean, and the wow view had made our hearts sing. But our stuffed car meant some work was ahead of us before the fun part would begin. "Okay, let's do this," Ralph said, popping open the trunk. As we began extracting our belongings, I grumbled that even though the building had an elevator, it would take several rides to transport all our "essentials."

"Probably four," Ralph said.

"One day we really must learn how to pack properly," I said. Ralph didn't comment, but I knew what he was thinking, so I said it for him. "Somebody might be guiltier than the other."

"And that's counting my spotting scope," Ralph said.

"As charged," I said, heaving a bag of boots out of the car. I immediately regretted how many I'd brought, so two pairs stayed behind.

A few minutes later, when we'd assembled enough stuff to fill one ride, the agent was back, crossing the garage at the far end. Looking up from my pile of assorted bags and suitcases, I must have looked surprised but just smiled and waved. She reciprocated but didn't engage us, briskly striding toward the elevator belonging to the other building. "Guess she forgot to do something," I said to Ralph.

"Guess so," Ralph mumbled, thinking nothing of it.

Once the elevator was crammed with our baggage and us, leaving little airspace, Ralph punched the button to close the doors. And again. And again. And again.

"Are we doing this right?" I said.

"There's not much choice. Close doors and push the floor button."

I tried it. He tried again. Again and again and again. The *porte* refused to respond. Desperate, we enacted a scene from the film *You've Got Mail* with Tom Hanks and Meg Ryan, jumping simultaneously on the count of three. More than once. It hadn't worked in the film, and it didn't work for us either. The next idea was to lighten the load, taking everything out except Ralph. Another failure. We tried it with only me inside, but with no luck. The doors were absolutely on strike. This elevator had left the building.

"This is crazy," I said. I felt like an idiot. It was an elevator, not a rocket. You enter, the door closes, you push a button, and bingo. But apparently, we *did* need a rocket scientist. At that moment, the realization hit me.

"Wait a minute!" I turned to Ralph. "Oh my gosh, this is why Odile returned through the garage. The elevator didn't work for her either!"

"And she said nothing," Ralph added, his words dripping with disappointment.

"She must have panicked, thinking we'd bail and she'd lose her commission."

"Or maybe she sized us up and figured we were so fit that four floors wouldn't faze us."

"So you take her choice to abandon us in the basement as a compliment?"

"Whatever, but in the meantime, take this," Ralph said, handing me a suitcase. "Okay, let's do it."

Since there was no phone signal in the garage and it would have taken ages for the agent to return or rustle up assistance, we faced the inevitable. Staircase, here we come. It was tougher than we imagined. The stairs to exit the garage didn't connect to the stairs in the building. We had to haul our luggage from the basement garage to the ground floor, follow a walkway around to the front of the building, go down a couple of steps to the entrance, punch in the code to unlock the door, move inside, glance longingly at the defunct elevator (which had worked for us just a half hour before), and only then embark on our trek to the fourth floor. The ground floor isn't numbered in France, which meant we were actually on the fifth floor. A vexatious misfortune times five, multiplied by four trips up and down to get all our belongings. When we finished we were utterly exhausted.

Next, I called the agent, describing the problem and our frustration. She agreed that the elevator hadn't worked for her either. Had I not been so depleted I would have unleashed a searing retort: "And it didn't occur to you that this tidbit of info might have been of some interest to us, your clients who have used a not insignificant amount of their resources to rent a top-floor dwelling with a functional elevator that now apparently was on strike, causing them to lug all their baggage and equipment via the stairs by hand and foot, one step at a time—seventy steps each way—and then repeat four times?" But before I could comment she added brightly, as if this was a satisfactory solution, officially concluding her workday so she could clock out and go home, "I've notified the owner, and I will keep you au courant."

"She'll keep us posted," I said to Ralph, disconnecting the call. Mean me, damp with sweat, wanted to post something to her forehead—a soft sticky note with a spiky message: Help your elders.

After that frustrating exchange, we took in a few deep breaths and the view. Our eyes were glued to its beauty and foreverness, and all the possibilities and freedom it suggested. Yet with a village waiting to be discovered, we gave our knees a pep talk and faced the stairs once again. The first order of business was to check out the ferry so we would be familiar with the set-up for our big voyage to Ouessant on Monday.

En route to the harbor, we strolled past a busy bakery, boutiques, municipal buildings, and sidewalk cafés—all picture-postcard cute. At the terminal we checked out the signage, confirming the ferry departure time, and then it was time for a well-earned *apéro*. We'd headed for the TDK (Taverne de Kermorvan), the pub Odile had recommended. As much as we appreciated the insider info, it only compensated a smidgeon for her lapse in judgment and consideration. Nonetheless, we owed her thanks because the tucked-away bar was friendly and fun and we might not have found it otherwise. We ordered inside the pub at street level, carried our drinks outside, mounted a flight of stairs—just one, fortunately—where we chose seats on an attractive terrace filled with rustic, mismatched furniture. Under a sunny sky, we sipped our drinks, let our bodies relax, and pondered our schedule for the following day.

Coffee the next morning on our balcony with the abundant *belle vue* was sheer bliss. We lingered longer than usual, enjoying the leisure boats floating about and watching the goats and chickens frolic in the backyard next door. Finally we tore ourselves away to hike to the lighthouse. Sunday morning joggers streaked across the central path in both directions, but we took our time, birding along the way and snapping photos, mesmerized by the rugged, austere beauty shimmering in the sunshine.

And during sunset, from the apartment balcony, the scene was simply astonishing. Before the blazing sun descended through the deep orange sky, a soft golden light bathed the peninsula, village, clouds, and sea. I'd read that the Ouessant sunsets were unparalleled, but I couldn't believe they could beat this. I would soon be able to judge for myself.

Joie de Vivre Highlights

The theater of life on Montauban's Place Nationale
Dinner at Little Italy
The seaside views in Pornic and Le Conquet, day and night
A guitar serenade on the beach
Grilled scallops at two restaurants

10

Oh Là Là, Ouessant

The Island of Ushant, Northwestern France

What prepares one for an otherworldly experience? After tip-toeing out of my comfort zone, I still did not know for sure. But one thing I did know was that returning to this magical place for a longer stay was a no-brainer. It was simply a question of how soon.

Timing. It was advantageous that we had ours down on the morning of our cruise. We arrived at the ferry terminal half an hour before our 9:45 a.m. departure, joining the queue of about twenty-five people. Minutes later, a packed bus arrived, unloading dozens more travelers, most equipped with binoculars or cameras. Fifteen minutes before loading, a linebacker-like ferry worker arrived, scanning tickets with his handheld machine, which made a delicate beep with each swipe. A jolly chap, he engaged with regulars, bantering and beeping through the long line.

Boarding, on the other hand, was overseen by a bronzed, thirty-something mariner, a buff model type who would heat up the cover of a bodice ripper—not that I owned any, mind you. But my prim, literary mom had a few and wasn't shy about them. Once, I'd urged her to read me a paragraph aloud, and she obliged, throwing all her stage experience from a teenaged thespian summer into it. It ended with a crescendo: "Keep your distance, you arrogant scoundrel!"

And so I was thinking about my spunky mom while I watched, bemused, as the "scoundrel" attended to the task at hand. Fist over fist, he hauled the heavy rope over the railing of our ferry that would transport us—and memories of my mother—to the *bout du monde*, Land's End.

Finding seats required a mad dash. Hordes of people from Brest had already filled up most of the interior cabin, which didn't bode well for seats on the bow, where we figured the best views would be. We scampered to the front quickly, but spotting a double-wide space was not to be, so we wriggled into separate spaces on bench seats a couple of rows apart.

At the little island of Molène, the only stop before Ouessant, the couple seated in front of me started to rise as if to disembark. Immediately I took my cue to hustle, sliding into their places. They had barely straightened up before I was warming their former seats. Good thing they had not just been stretching their legs.

I waved to Ralph and he moved in swiftly. Seated, we couldn't see anything except the pale blue sky, and only if we tilted our heads back and looked straight up. Ahead of us where there was standing room only, a petite blond woman conversed with a tall guy who, by his slightly accented English,

I guessed was Dutch or maybe Swedish. Unsurprisingly, the topic was birding on Ouessant. The man told her about the Yellow Warbler that had blown in from the US and how special it would be to see it. Ralph used to see them routinely outside his office in Virginia, so it wouldn't be a great bird find for him. But an ordinary bird in one place may be an extraordinary bird in another. As the lady earnestly logged the information in her notebook, she asked the man to spell *warbler*. He named some letters, but they didn't add up to *warbler*. After a few minutes, they finished talking, and the birder turned his attention elsewhere. I tapped the notetaker on the arm and showed her my little booklet where I'd written *warbler*.

Smiling, she sat down next to me, where a space had been vacated. She said she was on assignment for a major newspaper based in Paris, writing about the birding culture on the island. The article would be published in about a month. That explained all her notes. All the way to Ouessant, Annette continued to scribble copious amounts of them, recording my answers to her litany of questions about how we had ended up living in France, my husband's passion for birds, the Camargue, his big birding year in 2019, and getting to know two of the ornithologists who authored a fantastic French bird guide, which inspired our Ouessant visit. When her tousled-haired photographer Alain joined us, his huge camera around his neck, I was in the middle of an explanation. I was trying to describe how I had managed to be married to an avid birder for thirty years before becoming a birder myself. Alain piped up, saying, "No one's perfect!" which cracked *me* up. He was a kidder, which I appreciated. I'd heard that phrase a few times in France and it always underscored the friendliness of the encounter, putting everyone at ease.

He wasn't kidding, though, when he posed a question. Could he take photos of Ralph and me once we arrived at Ouessant? Honored to be asked, I answered without hesitation, *"Avec plaisir!"* As the words left my lips, my thoughts went into overdrive. This lovely journalist would write lovely things about the lovely American couple birding on lovely Ouessant. How cool would that be? A happy coincidence. Reading my mind, Ralph gave me a look as if I had been hallucinating. I snapped back to reality, which was that this journalist would be interviewing loads of people over the next three days on the island. Based on the speed of her note-taking, she appeared to be a master, so she would have tomes of material. In all likelihood, our small story would settle on the cutting-room floor.

But in the meantime, I reveled in the improbable, gratifying encounter. Until I remembered the picture-taking part. We were on a ferry headed to the End of the Earth for a rather rugged nature adventure with only one small backpack each. Of all the activities I'd anticipated having on the island, doing a photo shoot for a French journalist from a popular, polished publication hadn't sprung to mind. I instantly regretted leaving behind my hairspray.

Before we reached our destination, I returned to the topic of the bird guide. I'd told her one of the authors was on the island, and that we were going to meet him that evening. I didn't know whether he was available to give an interview, but I was happy to ask him if she wanted me to. Yes, she said, but she'd understand if he wasn't available. We exchanged contact info.

The entire time we'd been chatting with the journalist, the boat sailed along without so much as a single jarring bounce—utterly smooth, softened even further by a gentle breeze. So, it was jolting to suddenly see the massive cliffs that plunged into the sea at Port du Stiff, a scene made even more dramatic by the sun highlighting the deep, craggy gashes cut into the rock face.

Like the embarkation, the disembarkation proceeded smoothly, as if all the travelers were seasoned. Everyone had kept track of their belongings and was moving politely and calmly toward the exit. Nobody except us appeared frazzled with excitement to have finally arrived at Land's End. Having waited for the ferry to dock before preparing to jump ship, we scrambled to inventory our gear. For the third time, we rechecked our seats for an escaped phone, sunglasses, or the indispensable long-billed caps. Satisfied we had it together, we feigned composure and crossed the plank.

Backpacks in place, bike helmets in hand, and wearing our binoculars in cross-body fashion, we hiked up the hill to find our bike rental place, Cycl'Evasion. With all the birders and naturalists descending on the island and making their rounds by bicycle, it must have felt more like a biking *invasion* for the islanders. But like the birds we hoped to see on this far-flung speck, our stopover would be brief, and we wished not to be invasive but welcomed.

At a little information hut up the hill from the ferry, I told the woman behind the counter that we'd reserved a couple of bikes under Padgett. She checked her list and handed over a ticket that read "Reservation," then pointed to an area a bit farther up the hill where all the lime-green bikes belonging to the company were stored. I showed my ticket to the man in charge, who swiftly ushered us to our two-wheelers, mine with a basket but Ralph's without. A pannier rack was attached to the back of his bike that could have carried a backpack strapped on with bungee cords, but being bungee cord-less, we made do. No hairspray, no bike basket, no biggies.

The first hill rising from the bike rental area wasn't alarmingly steep, which was a huge relief. I surged ahead of Ralph, pedaling furiously, giving it my all, thinking we'd be okay if that were as bad as it could get. But very soon, bad as it could get got a whole lot badder. The succeeding hills were much more daunting and required some stand-on-the-pedals posture. Even though our hotel was under five kilometers from the port, the terrain proved to be demanding—for me, anyway. As we passed some grazing sheep, one glanced over at me and seemed to shake its head in an I-told-you-so sort of way. In retrospect, I'll bet it was reading my thoughts: *What a rookie. You seriously believed you could crisscross this island of hills and see everything you wanted to see in two days—sans a bike battery—without ending up in an exhausted heap?*

Even without a hairspray can, my loaded backpack weighed heavily and became weightier with each pedal push. At last we found our hotel, La Duchesse Anne, situated on a point along the rocky coastline. Bikes were parked everywhere and none were locked up, but we'd brought our bike lock, so we dutifully put it to use. The receptionist processed us quickly and showed us to our room beyond the breakfast area on the ground floor. It was furnished minimally but with one maximal characteristic. Beyond the weathered deck and a swath of emerald grass was a breathtaking view of the cobalt-blue sea. It melted into the sky, creating an endless vista, like a life of boundless possibilities. They say the sky's the limit, and *this* was that infinite sky.

Before we headed out to explore, I tried to text our expert birder friend, Noah, to let him know we had arrived and to explain about the journalist. But the local cell service was inter-mittent, which I hadn't anticipated. I kept trying. When I finally got through, he said he'd be happy to talk to her, which was a relief. Birding and nature need all the good publicity they can get, and I was pleased that my chance encounter might turn into something positive and not just the thrill of a photo shoot. We agreed to meet at 6:00 p.m. at our hotel, and I would schedule the journalist for half an hour later.

Back on our two-wheeled steeds, we rode past sheep—you can't *not* ride past sheep on Ouessant since they are ubiq-uitous—to our destination, the lighthouse Phare du Créac'h. Without backpacks, cycling was a dream—at first. A few kilo-meters later it became a workout—but so worth it. At the impressive black-and-white striped lighthouse tower, Ralph found a Winter Wren posing on a post. This bird is fairly common in Provence, but it rarely finds Ralph. In fact, he didn't spot one during his entire year of focused birding, so it was an exceptionally satisfying "get." Just down from the lighthouse, he saw another target bird, the big black Red-billed Chough. Two of them were hungrily pecking around in the grass with abandon, giving us plenty of time to wit-ness the show. It was gratifying to spot them and observe how oblivious they were to us. We all had plenty of room to explore, sharing the same windswept space, so dramati-cally different from the Alps or any other place we'd been in France, for that matter. It felt like a place where everyone and everything could run wild, including my imagination. How would it feel to spend a season here, away from the things of humans?

We rode back to the hotel by 5:00 p.m. to transform our-selves. Noah arrived an hour later wearing dark green wellies, the footgear of choice for experienced birders. After all our exchanged emails and reading his bird guides, one of which included literary references, I felt as if I knew him. It was like meeting up with an old friend. Ralph went inside to order some drinks—beers for Noah and himself, and a glass of white wine for me. While we chatted, he kindly signed both his books for me. They had been heavy to haul, but I admired this expert's work so much that it seemed a fitting way to pay homage. I was nervous watching the clock, wondering whether Annette and her photographer Alain would arrive on time. After 6:30 p.m., I had just begun fretting that they were going to skip us altogether when I got a text. They were running late due to the discovery of a rarity—the Baltimore Oriole. Ralph got a kick out of this because, like the Yellow Warbler, he used to see this bird routinely while living in the DC area. But here on Ouessant, the stunning ebony-and-deep-orange bird was making headlines.

Noah had seen the bird earlier that day and was relaxed about waiting for the newspaper folks. But how long would the wait be? I wrote Annette that we'd stay put, but to please hurry, if possible. I didn't want the rendezvous to dissolve, possibly disappointing Noah and making all the coordination in vain (not to mention the struggle to tame my hair without any lacquer).

We finished our drinks and Ralph ordered another round. I was becoming increasingly worried as time passed. Then, two sips from draining our glasses, the journalist and photographer appeared. Thank goodness!

After apologies for their tardiness, they took turns gushing about the magnificent island. Noah and the reporter spoke in English until Annette commented on how funny it was that two French people were talking to each other in English. Realizing this was out of consideration for us, we assured them English was unnecessary. We'd listen with French ears. *Pas de problème.* Even though we wouldn't get every detail, we'd get the gist, which would suffice as long as they didn't submit us to a quiz at the end.

Annette took notes at warp speed as Noah passionately described how perilous the situation was with so many bird species in danger of becoming extinct. An environmental engineer by training, he advised architects about ways to adapt structures that support biodiversity, such as restoring ancient buildings to allow for swifts to nest when their original homes have been removed. He explained that birds were arriving on the island at unusual times due to abnormal weather conditions, which was concerning.

At that moment, Alain was concerned about the fading light. He escorted Noah toward the sea with his lighting equipment, including a block battery—the guy was prepared. During that photo session, Ralph and I chatted with Annette about the hundred or so birders going nuts over the Baltimore Oriole. She showed us photos on her phone—it was a mob scene. She'd witnessed the exuberance of the birders, jostling into position to see the very rare bird. Seeing a rarity was heaven for birders, but there was a sad flip side to nature's wild side, which Noah had explained earlier. For the blown-off-course birds to survive and thrive, the odds were long. To beat them, these birds had to find their flock, find their way on their own, or find ways to adapt. That last option was something I knew something about. And it wasn't always smooth sailing.

When Alain finished with Noah, it was time for our close-ups. We had been advised not to miss the glorious sunset at the Duchesse Anne, and not only did we not miss it, but it was the backdrop for our professional photo shoot. After taking lots of snaps of us, Alain was kind enough to photograph the group, and then Ralph took one of me with Alain. I knew I wouldn't believe this had happened when I got home if I didn't have concrete proof.

Finally, we bid farewell to the dedicated duo, wishing them luck with their story research and telling them we'd watch for the article. Before we said good evening to Noah, he gave us some tips for our potential birding discoveries the following day. We'd discuss our findings over coffee in town late the next afternoon before our ship sailed.

Our adventures weren't over for the day, however. Next up were some discoveries of the culinary kind. I'd been tipped off not to miss a meal at Ty Korn, a popular pub in town, but alas, it wasn't open on Monday or even for Tuesday lunch. No matter what birds flew our way the next day, the dramatic scenery and checking the Ty Korn box were reasons enough to extend our stay, but our ferry reservations couldn't be changed. We'd have to settle for a plan to return another day.

Our second dinner option was a good runner-up. Keeping it simple, we dined right there at the Duchesse Anne. The menu was printed on a single sheet clamped securely to a clipboard. Ralph chose *Pesked ha Farz (le kig ha fars de la mer)*. For those lacking Breton language skills, like us, an explanatory note in French was helpful. Translated into English, it read "For those not familiar with this dish, it's a *pot au feu* with a base of fish, mussels, langoustines, shrimp, smoked sausage, lard, and accompanied by *lipig*, a sauce with a lot of butter and onions, and *farz*, a base of rye flour and *froment*." At the time, we didn't know that *froment* was one of several different grades of French wheat flour, each having a different degree of gluten. But Ralph figured with all that seafood, the dish had to be a winner. My dish was much more straightforward, a whitefish called *lieu*, which arrived piled with a gigantic heap of veggies over a pool of delicate béchamel sauce. Both were excellent.

By the next morning, the sun had bid Ouessant au revoir, leaving behind a murky blizzard of mist but thankfully no rain. The ambience was eerie yet hauntingly alluring. Despite the less-than-stellar conditions, our exploration continued, undaunted—we had to make the most of the limited birding time we had. Carving our way through the thick gray haze, we headed north to the peninsula across from the Île de Keller.

We were on the local bird alert roster, so our phones steadily pinged as we cycled. Pausing to read every notice would have prevented us from reaching our destination. But each time I got a chance to check, the news was heartwarming because the birders shared their experiences with either unbridled jubilation when the subject was a bird sighting or, in the case of lost or found binoculars, bikes, or backpacks, a caring sense of community.

The landscape itself further complicated our cycling. It was a challenge not to stop to snap photos every time an intriguing scene appeared: sheep jogging along a coastal path, a slate-topped stone house with bright blue doors and window shutters, birders shrouded in mist peering through spotting scopes and cameras with massive lenses, or improvised parking lots of bicycle rentals, each in a different color. Finally, however, we made it to the northern coast. Ralph didn't have his spotting scope, which would have come in handy to see the seabirds, but he searched as best he could with his binoculars. After he'd scanned the rocks and the thick scrub brush dotted with wildflowers, it was time for nourishment. With our backs against the Blockhouse, a massive former fortification, we nibbled our sandwiches, staring out past the jagged cliffs to the endless sea. Weirdly, it wasn't intimidating, even though I felt so small. Without all the distractions of urban bustle, I relaxed into the natural space as if blending with it. I didn't want to withdraw from the comforting, warm embrace feeling, but our time on the mesmerizing island was winding down.

Back in the enclave of Lampaul, Ralph and I split up, each to meander on our own for a while. As much as I was drawn to the coast, I also wanted to get a feel for the "city" scene, and Ralph felt pulled to the marina. I popped into a couple of shops and the austere church, and I paused to admire a long-abandoned boat surrounded by big blooming hydrangeas. On the outskirts of town, I admired a fanciful mural featuring a lighthouse, cliffs, and ships covering a house's entire façade.

As planned, we met Noah for a late-afternoon coffee at a café in town. We chatted about the birds we'd seen on this wild isle and those we hadn't, including the Baltimore Oriole. That off-course bird most certainly would have made the highlight reel for the loads of lucky birders who witnessed it, as well as for the journalist. We hoped she would consider her Ouessant experience as extraordinary as we considered ours. We'd have a few weeks to wait until publication to find out.

Saying goodbye to our dedicated biodiversity friend was hard because we didn't know when we'd see him again, but the *Fromveur II* would not wait to sail. Our ferry workhorse had a schedule to keep and kilometers to cruise. We'd be at the dock for the all-aboard signal.

One more time with feeling, we heaved on our heavy backpacks and sped through town, over the hills toward the bike turn-in point. The last climb before the port had somehow morphed into a mountain since we'd sailed down it the day before. Ascending it was daunting, requiring me to stand tall on my pedals. I pushed myself hard, willing myself to reach the crest. Then, panting as if I'd just finished a Tour de France time trial, I put my shrieking back and calves on mute as I screamed down to a screeching halt at the bike place. At first no one was on site, so we looked around for the best place to stash the bikes. A few minutes later, I was relieved when a guy appeared to verify our turn-in. I didn't want to worry about getting charged for two disappeared bikes. From there it was a short downhill stroll to our ferry ride. Giving my aching back a break, I carried my backpack in my arms.

We joined the line behind just two others, so the odds were excellent that we'd have our choice of seats since Port du Stiff was the departure point. Once on board, we chose to go to the bow, port side, where no lifeboat blocked our view as it had coming over—not that we could have seen anything with the crowds. But with fewer passengers today, chances were good we'd be able to bird a bit.

As soon as we got settled, I told Ralph to save my seat while I searched inside for a socket to recharge my phone. It was running low after all the photos I'd taken that day out on the range and in town, and I hoped there'd be more photo ops on the return trip. By the time the ferry horn bellowed, it was charged up, and I returned to my place next to Ralph. After we heaved ho, we celebrated the conclusion of our Île d'Ouessant adventure with a private *apéro*. It consisted of only warmish white wine from plastic water bottles, but we savored the sips just the same. Just as we clinked our "glasses," several gannets flew close to the ship, showing off their impressive two-meter wingspan as if to salute the finale of our journey to the end of the earth. I wasn't able to get my recharged phone out fast enough to capture their majesty digitally, but the spectacle fit snugly into my memory bank.

The ocean minded its manners all the way back to Le Conquet. En route, we reflected on the trip's many highlights. It had been a kick running into the journalist and doing the photo shoot, and particularly gratifying to meet Noah in person, especially on the wild isle where he was in his milieu.

And what an astounding milieu it was. Now we understood the magical allure. The dramatic cliffs, windswept plains of scrub, free-range sheep, and terrific birdlife all cast an other-worldly spell that I did not want to shake. I hadn't wanted to leave, and not because we had yet to eat at Ty Korn. As we had been warned, one overnight wasn't nearly enough. We'd only covered a small portion of Ouessant, and now all the other areas beckoned like a siren call: "Come, discover us." We were keen to do just that and further explore this mysterious and rugged—and woolly—isle.

The end-of-the-earth island's ambience was on the far side of the spectrum from Provence's gentle *soleil* and rosé lifestyle. But maybe that stark contrast was what made it so fiercely captivating.

Joie de Vivre Highlights

Coastal views from every angle
Bonding with our ornithologist friends
A photoshoot at sunset
Sheep trotting along the coastal path
Red-billed Choughs

11

Le Conquet Caper

Brittany, Northwestern France

We anticipated cycling to sandy beaches and seafood restaurants. Hiking to a Michelin star wasn't on the agenda, much less jumping to conclusions about mysterious happenings. This far-flung seaside enclave wasn't so sleepy after all.

※ ※ ※

We drew up to Le Conquet's dock at 6:30 p.m., and with our packs back on our backs we pushed ourselves the few blocks home. Since the elevator had not miraculously sprung into action in our absence, we took to the stairs, all four flights of them. After riding our bikes around all day and having my face in the sea air during the ferry ride, I felt particularly sticky and grimy. A shower would feel so good, not to mention the Côtes du Rhône that would follow while gazing out at our splendid view from a terrace chair. The trek to Ouessant would become a magical memory, well worth our exhaustion.

Unsurprisingly, the stairs hadn't gotten any easier with practice, but I trained my thoughts away from the drudgery of the trudge and centered on the creature comforts that awaited. Each time we entered the apartment, I was drawn to the view and walked, trancelike, down the long, narrow hallway through the living room to the expansive terrace. This time was no different. But seconds after we walked down the hall, those relaxing thoughts vanished like feeding sparrows spooked by an intruding cat. Instead of feeling dreamy, I felt frantic thoughts take hold. Something had gone amiss on the patio.

The neatly arranged terrace table and chairs we'd left two mornings ago were crammed together in a corner as if they had been shoved there. But the jumble of outdoor furniture wasn't our primary concern. Orange straps hugged the balcony railing, attached to an industrial-strength ladder that extended to the ground.

"Oh my God," I said, "have we been burgled?"

We were dumbstruck that we might have become robbery victims. Our bodies remained immobile even as our minds raced. Ralph noted that there was nothing of significant monetary or sentimental value in the apartment. We'd taken our cash, laptop, and Swarovski binoculars with us. What else was worth potential jail time?

After dropping our load, we forced our limbs into action, performing a slow sweep of the apartment. The first order of business was to check the sliding door to see whether the wooden stick we'd placed in the track was still there. It was. But was there another way in? Not unless the culprit had come through the front door. After a thorough evaluation, we deemed the front door fine. And the same for the living and dining room area, as well as the bedrooms and bathroom. All seemed to be in order.

What the heck was going on? Out on the terrace, we found the answer—a gun.

And it was smoking all right. It told us everything we needed to know. Although it might have been reckless, since I knew I'd leave fingerprints, I fearlessly picked it up and waved it at Ralph.

He put his hands up in front of his face, palms facing me. "Honey, don't point that thing at me. It could be loaded," he said with mock horror.

This instrument might have been made of metal, but it didn't shoot bullets. What it shot wouldn't be fatal—unless you choked on the rubbery gunk it contained. It was a caulking gun, found beside a pile of metal strips, along with an assortment of empty water bottles and a squashed paper sack, probably filled with lunch remains. In a flash, realization struck—repairs were in the works. Our private abode with its mesmerizing water view would by day evidently become a buzzing building site.

On the positive side, sans burglars, there would be no kerfuffle with criminals, no knock-out punches, no frantic emergency call, no police intervention, no handcuffs, no trial testimony, no demolishing a crime ring, no placement in a witness protection program—yes, I can have a tendency to catastrophize—so there was relief in that. But on the negative side, strolling out on our private terrace in the morning to contemplate the exquisite view of construction workers would require a hard hat.

More than mildly miffed, I said, "Oh, yippee, tomorrow morning at breakfast we'll have the pleasure of the company of workmen." So much for wearing my lacy, racy robe and matching thong to *petit déjeuner*. Or maybe I should. Why not give *them* a surprise?

Worn out from the trip, the stairs, and working through what might have transpired had we confronted intruders, I pulled myself together and texted the news to Odile at the management company, not concerned about the hour. The agent wrote back a chipper note saying that the work being done was news to her. She offered thanks for the update but no solution, as if she didn't see any problem. The supervisor was away, but she was keen on keeping us posted, she assured me. To this unhelpful response, I was tempted to reply, "So happy to be of assistance."

It might have been a revelation to her that, as selfish as she might think it was of us to text at that hour, our purpose for renting the apartment was not to deliver the staff a refresher on Holiday Rental Management 101. Obviously, the company needed a policy that ensured updates on repairs for units they were renting. But at this point, our concern was not company policy. We needed a single action—a delay of the repairs until after our departure. Certain that any complicated suggestions about company responsibility would be ineffective, I took a deep breath and dialed Odile's number, hoping to find words not soaked with sarcasm, simple terms that would prompt the clueless agent to make the required calls to postpone the renovation work.

"Odile," I said, "do you have something to write with?"

"Just one second. Yes, here's a pen."

"Great. Please write this down," I said.

Breakfast with bulging biceps and a pronounced six-pack attached to a stranger didn't fit with my intimate *petit déjeuner*

à deux agenda. Nonetheless, around 9:00 a.m. a young man wearing cutoffs emerged from over the terrace wall, exposing a large tattoo of an albatross on one calf. Immediately I went out to greet him in my lacy, racy robe with a matching thong. Just kidding. The thong didn't *match* exactly. In fashion parlance, one would say the pieces *coordinated*. Truth be told, I thought better of startling the poor man, possibly causing him to trip on his rebar, while I explained our presence and questioned his. With safety and hospitality in mind, I stepped onto the terrace, extending my offer of a cup of coffee, wearing sweatpants and a zipped-up hoodie—an actual matching set, in fact.

That was how we met Serge, a metalworks expert. He told us he had been laboring at the complex's railings for several weeks, starting from the ground floor and working his way up. Since this wasn't an emergency service but a lengthy maintenance project, there was even more reason for the management company to have been aware of it.

Leaving Serge to his repair work, we retreated inside to pour ourselves some coffee and to review the situation. Failures to communicate were mounting, and so were our grumbles. First, the agent hadn't told us about the elevator going belly up, leaving us to fend for ourselves at considerable inconvenience. Now, the agency didn't know about the ongoing repair project, leaving us to fend for ourselves again. Fending for ourselves at home is life, but when you're on holiday from life, it's the host's job to do the fending for you. That's part of the beauty of being *en vacances*. How long would this project take anyway?

As if reading our minds, Serge tapped on the glass slider to get our attention and delivered some good news. He assured us he'd be finished and out of our hair by noon. Judging from the repairs yet to be completed, I doubted this. But we thanked him and bid him a good day, wishing he would spend it any-where but on our balcony.

Even from inside the apartment, the *belle vue* over the cluster of pitched slate rooftops against the blue sky and shimmering sea was enchanting. But Serge moving back and forth through our picturesque scene dissuaded us from wanting another coffee refill. Also, the promise of adventure motivated us. With the town at our backs and the tide out, we walked along the estuary beyond the pedestrian bridge, where we spotted curlews with their long curved beaks and scarlet-legged stilts making the most of the mud. Over the hill at Plage des Blancs Sablons, on this weekday morning we were practically alone on the pristine, seemingly endless beach. Although not many other species flocked to see us, it was a pleasure to see many striking black-and-white oystercatchers with their prominent orange bills frolicking along the water's edge.

Leaving the beach behind, we retraced our steps over the estuary bridge and then cut through some residential neighborhoods, following our noses. We didn't have an exact plan for the day, but Pointe Saint-Mathieu came to mind. We knew it was not to be missed, especially at sunset. Still feeling a tad tuckered out after our on-the-go Ouessant trip but aware that only three full days remained in Le Conquet, we thought we'd better get ourselves over there *tout de suite.* We checked a map app on our phones and saw that it was nearly an hour's walk, but we were pretty sure it would take us longer considering our penchant for wandering off-piste. It was a mild, sunny day, perfect for a carefree chug along the glorious coastline, birding as we went.

The path by the sea offered incredible views of rocky cliffs and sandy beaches. On one—fittingly shaped like a horse-shoe—a lanky young woman wearing jodhpurs and tall riding boots, her long auburn hair unfurling behind her, was leading a white horse by its reins along the water's edge. Was Ralph Lauren shooting a commercial on location? Nope, no film crew was in sight. I knew I couldn't preserve the preciousness of that scene with my phone, but I made a mini-movie myself just the same.

As we approached Pointe Saint-Mathieu in the enclave of Plougonvelin, it was lunchtime, so I immediately scanned the scene for food outlets. The lighthouse loomed large next to the former Benedictine Abbey of Saint-Mathieu de Fine Terre—in ruins for over a century—but there didn't seem to be much else. The town's name may have been long, but it seemed short on eatery options.

Surely there would be cafés in this beautiful spot, *n'est-ce pas?* I spotted one with a terrace filled with tables, but not a soul was to be seen. It was Wednesday, a popular day of rest when primary school children typically don't attend class, often to pursue non-academic pursuits like tennis or sailing. I feared the establishment was closed. But as we rounded the front of the building with floor-to-ceiling windows facing the sea, I saw people inside. Hooray! Now, would there be room for us wanderers?

Ralph studied the menu of Bistrot 1954, posted by the front door, and I bounded ahead, not worrying about what cuisine was on offer or the cost, for that matter. We would have been grateful for any kind of sustenance. But a dress code could be problematic—we were in hiking gear. If we *were* out of place in our puffy jackets and hefty boots, I'd cope just fine with feeling like an idiot. I was vastly overqualified in that department, as reflected in my impressive faux pas-filled résumé, honed to perfection over our many years in France.

I peeked through the glass door and saw an inviting dining area with attractive minimalist décor, not posh at all. This didn't appear to be an extravagant eatery, and several tables were empty, though none by the big windows looking out to sea. No matter—I could see the water from where I stood at the entry. Ralph was still perusing the menu, but I hurried inside—it was late for lunch, and I hoped we could order before the kitchen switched off the oven. I smiled, said bonjour to the gentleman wrapped in a starched half-apron who was standing behind the counter, and asked whether a table for two was available. Dreading the have-you-reserved question, I braced myself, and it came as expected. When I replied regretfully no, he checked his reservation book, scanned the room, looked at my hopeful face, took a slow breath, and said *oui*, indeed there was space. I hoped my grin revealed my gratitude.

When Ralph entered I relayed the good news, and we followed the gracious greeter to a natural wood table sans tablecloth in the middle of the room. A visibly nervous young man who may have been in training tentatively handed us menus. Would we want something to drink? he asked politely. After our hour-long walk along the sea, the answer came quickly—*mais oui*.

I ordered a glass of white wine and Ralph his usual beer. To quench our thirst, we also asked for a carafe of water. I certainly wasn't going to hydrate with my chardonnay. A young girl appeared next with a ceramic bowl filled with thick, lattice-designed potato chips. After just one, I wanted a whole bag. Scrumptious.

Judging by the inventive amuse-bouche, we'd lucked out. Today, our culinary expectations had not been high by any stretch. We'd moseyed out farther than we had expected to without a thought of where we'd end up at lunchtime, but since we were in a populated area, we'd expected to find some local, albeit ordinary fare. And lo and behold, by sheer serendipity we'd stumbled upon what promised to be a memorable meal. *Quelle belle surprise.*

Ralph ordered the plat du jour—usually the best bet because it's sure to be fresh. It consisted of a pair of thick pork medallions topped with crumbled black sausage called *boudin noir*, all placed between slices of gently spiced poached apples with peppery arugula scattered over the top, plus a separate cup of small roasted potatoes drenched in velvety olive oil. And this astoundingly delicious dish set us back the equivalent of a nondescript pizza from the frozen food section of a chain supermarket.

My *merlu* was slightly more expensive, but the portion was generous and beautifully presented. The plate arrived with two thick chunks of fish covered with a thin pasta sheet and topped with crushed roasted hazelnuts and sage, all floating on *beurre blanc*. Scattered sprigs of arugula added bursts of color, making me pause a second to process its sheer loveliness. I also received my own bowl of roasted potatoes—thankfully, because otherwise Ralph would have been pressed to share. They were delectable—every single one. Magnificent-looking desserts arrived at other tables, but our main dishes with the sides had satisfied us, so we enjoyed the sweet fare vicariously.

After we finished our outstanding meal, we gushed our enthusiasm to the waiter and the gentleman at the register. It was Michelin-star quality in our epicurean black books. As a dear friend used to say about happy stuff happening unexpectedly, "It just shows to go ya." Sometimes when you orchestrate the heck out of a project with research and making a reservation months ahead, and you dress up and have hopes up, the experience fails to measure up. And then when you wing it, you find a wonder, just like that.

Following the marvelous meal and back outside on the pavement, facing the roaring sea, I longed for a quick lift home for a dreamy nap.

"Dream on," Ralph said, jolting me out of my reverie.

The next bus wasn't due for hours. I hadn't hitchhiked since I was a teenager, but as I watched the occasional car whiz by, the idea of sticking out my thumb didn't seem far-fetched. On second thought, I realized the linguistic risk factor was too much. Speaking French to a stranger for twenty minutes straight would have required full-on brain power, and my mind was in pre-nap mode. I imagined we could have Uber-ed ourselves home, chat-free, but neither of us had thought of downloading the app on our phones, which was just as well. With this extraordinary scenery, a return mosey wasn't an obstacle but an opportunity to revel in the seaside beauty. And everybody knows the return trip is quicker. At least, that was the tactic I used to persuade myself to get moving.

As we turned toward Le Conquet, I recalled that this return-trip situation was no comparison to the pickle we'd gotten ourselves into a few years before on La Rhune mountain near Saint-Jean-de-Luz in the Basque Country. We'd ridden the cog train to the top with the plan of hiking back down to our car, but we followed the wrong path, which quickly became an extremely steep slope. When we realized our error, we had to hustle ourselves back *up* the extremely steep slope to catch the last train back down in the fading light.

Today, there was no steep incline in sight, and we only had to follow the coast back in the opposite direction we'd come from. On the way out, the water was on our right, and now it would be on our left. Even under the influence of some seductive chardonnay, the chances of retaining that straightforward thought seemed fairly strong. With a *sieste* awaiting, we were like motivated cows heading to the barn, but with a few birding detours.

At a small cove, we walked to the water's edge and paused for a few minutes to check out some waders, mostly oyster-catchers. Ralph was ahead of me as we trudged back up to the trail. At the top, he started moving south, back toward Pointe Saint-Mathieu.

"Honey, wait, water on the *left*—L-E-F-T," I yelled.

"Ha, gotcha!" he said with a grin, pivoting around. "Yes, I'm paying attention!"

And then in unison we recited a Russian proverb, "Trust but verify." Ronald Reagan had used it frequently when dealing with the Soviet Union in the '80s. Apparently, in return Gorbachev would show off his knowledge of American literature by quoting Ralph Waldo Emerson: "The reward of a thing done well is to have done it." I'm not sure how particularly well we'd done the round-trip walk to Pointe Saint-Mathieu, but within an hour, we found ourselves back in Le Conquet. We'd completed our mission to check out the point, and that knowledge was indeed satisfying. But with all due respect to Emerson, in my humble opinion our reward for having done something required a little topper-upper. And it sounded like this: ZZZZzzzzz.

It was a particularly rejuvenating *sieste* because we were alone in the apartment. Our balcony buddy Serge had cleared out as promised. But the ladder was still in place, orange straps securing it, which begged the question: Would he be back in the morning? We'd keep that thought in mind before we emerged from the bedroom in birthday suits.

Our day's "work" at Pointe Saint-Mathieu was not over yet. It had been lovely to experience the rugged area under sunny skies, and now we'd drive back to add a dusky version to our memory banks. Our birder friend Gérard had insisted that the après-sunset coast was a premier sight to behold, which is no small compliment coming from an extreme world traveler. If the weather held, following the *coucher du soleil* many of the lighthouses along the coast would be visible. This was our best chance because there was no telling what the weather tomorrow would bring, and Friday night we had to pack up and prepare to say au revoir to this striking landscape.

We drove back to Saint-Mathieu just before sunset so I could pop into the terrific restaurant to pick up a souvenir calling card. I'd forgotten to do that after lunch when I was so caught up in chatting about the incredible meal with the staff. The same gracious gentleman from the afternoon shift greeted me when I entered, and he plucked the small memento from a card holder on the counter and passed it to me. I thanked him, and as an afterthought asked him to jot down the chef's name in the little notebook I carry with me. The first name was a Breton name I didn't recognize, increasing my curiosity about this far-flung eatery. It crossed my mind that perhaps whoever was working the magic in the kitchen was a woman, but I didn't take the time to confirm that. A sunset awaited. Turning to join Ralph, I thanked the accommodating man again and said I hoped we would return one day, wishing that day could be tomorrow.

Ralph and I positioned ourselves as far out on the point as possible and stared down the coast. Clouds had rolled in, and a beam from a single lighthouse appeared clearly through the grayish-blue mist. We waited a while, hoping some other *phares* would light up, but the sky grew a denser gray by the minute, making for mostly blurred photos. The lack of clarity of this world-class, worth-a-detour view made for unfinished business, which meant one thing. We *would* be back. At least I hoped that was what it meant.

Before we turned off the lights on another day in this surprising Finistère outpost, I took a moment to research the restaurant. I was pleased to learn that not only was the chef a woman and a young one, she was one of the few female chefs in France who had been bestowed a significant honor—a star from Michelin. I wondered whether *étoile* number two was in the works. It wouldn't be a surprise.

Unbeknownst to us at the time, we'd wandered into a gastronomic eatery attached to a hotel complex, the Hostellerie de la Pointe Saint-Mathieu, which houses the restaurant and is directed by Nolwenn Corre. She's a granddaughter of the original owners who opened the property as a restaurant and grocery store in 1954. Ms. Corre took over the complex from her parents in 2018 and one year later received the coveted star. The more casual bistro, where we'd eaten the excellent lunch, enjoys a Bib Gourmand label from Michelin, a gratifying coincidence since I usually organize our stays around Bibs wherever we go. They're less pretentious and don't break the bank. This time I'd done zilch and still found one—maybe my nose was trained for Bibs? Indeed, we had followed our noses today, but the Bib discovery credit goes to serendipity. It was simply one lucky off-course wander. And a delicious one, at that.

On our next-to-last day in Brittany, we explored the rugged coast to the north. En route, we paused at the tiny outdoor market at Lampaul-Plouarzel, which primarily sold produce and fresh fish. In need of a little mid-morning pick-me-up, I investigated the crêpe truck. A smiley lady selling sweet and savory crêpes wore a crisp apron with ENVIE DE CRÊPES—desire for crêpes—stitched in cheerful primary colors across the top. I ordered a cheese buckwheat version and eyed the jars of *caramel au beurre salé*. Salted caramel would be perfect for gifts back home in Saint-Rémy. To encourage the sale, the spirited entrepreneur assured me that they were *fait maison*—homemade. I stocked up.

We tromped around the coastal paths at Porspoder, marveling at the vast, wild natural area, which is fiercely protected, as evidenced by ubiquitous signs listing acceptable and prohibited activities. Picnics were fine, overnight stays not. Near Lampaul-Ploudalmézeau, at the magnificent stretch of deserted beach called the Beach of Three Sheep, Plage des Trois Moutons, we encountered no woolly creatures. But we did witness a mass of Sanderlings putting on an impressive aerial show, taking off in starling murmuration fashion, making massive swirling movements through a grayish sky. Luckily, no rain threatened.

After dinner, we thought long and hard about our plan to meet Gérard in Brest the following night for dinner. We were disappointed that our schedules hadn't clicked so we could have crossed paths on Ouessant. As a consolation prize, we would meet him for a meal after he flew into Brest. It was a logistically challenging plan: His flight didn't land until 7:30 p.m., so the soonest he could make the restaurant would be 8:00 p.m., meaning we'd be driving an hour back to Le Conquet late at night. Then the next morning, after checking out of the apartment, we'd drive the same route back to Brest and head home. Although all that driving wasn't ideal, we were looking forward to talking birds with our birder buddy, fresh off our Ouessant experience. We wouldn't have experienced the terrific adventure on Ouessant if it hadn't been for Gérard.

But the more we considered our plan, the harder it was to hear the constant reports of air traffic controller strikes. They were happening everywhere in France and getting worse as the weekend approached. For our get-together to succeed, every-thing would have to work without a hiccup, not even a micro one. When a national strike was called for Friday, October 13, the day of our rendezvous, it was not a hiccup but a severe whooping cough. What would be the chance of Gérard's flight out of Montpellier not being affected? If he didn't arrive at precisely 7:30 p.m., he couldn't make our dinner reservation a half an hour later. Ralph and I looked at each other, shaking our heads. A command decision was made. I wrote an email to our friend. And then another. By lights-out time, I'd received no word back. Sleep didn't come easily.

The next morning, there was still no response from Gérard, so I sent a few texts via different platforms. He had to know we wouldn't make our dinner in Brest. The thought of him sitting in the restaurant alone, thinking he'd been stood up, wasn't acceptable. A delayed response from him was highly unusual. I tried not to worry, but that was useless. To distract myself, I started packing, checking my phone every ten min-utes. Finally, late in the morning, I got the vital message—he was fine, understood the situation, and told us not to worry. It didn't seem as if he was concerned about the flight being can-celed, which made me feel worse that we weren't even going to try to make our rendezvous.

But the judgment had been made, so we focused on the task at hand—preparing for departure. Since the elevator was still throwing a tantrum and the underground garage was secure, we decided to pack the car the night before. With this approach, we could take our time scaling the stairs and avoid rushing in the morning.

With that job completed, we rode our bikes to lunch at a beach shack we'd spotted earlier in the week, not in town but inland along the estuary. At Le Hangar du Pêcheur, the menu was inviting with lots of fish choices, and the price of the two-course daily special menu was less than a single main dish anywhere in our usual stomping grounds in Provence. We were welcomed warmly and seated right away. It was a good thing we'd arrived early because the roomy dining area filled up quickly and later arrivals were turned away. Clearly, it was a popular destination, and it was easy to see why. We thoroughly enjoyed the hearty fish fare accompanied by loads of veggies, served by attentive staff in an authentic setting. As we cycled home, we talked about the restaurant's down-to-earth formula and how hard it was to find eateries with similar concepts in our local patch down south. Or was it? Could they be hiding in plain sight? Was it that we didn't expect them, so we didn't see them?

Even though the Brest trip was a no-go, it made sense to stay home on our last night for two reasons—to rest up for the trek the next day and to clear out the fridge, meaning less to haul home. To that end, we'd planned a simple menu of salmon, spinach, and some remaining *haricots verts* (green beans), which were stored in the big freezer the agent had instructed us to use. We had bought the salmon and the bag of chopped *épinards* the previous day, freezing the spinach with the green beans and placing the fresh fish in the fridge.

While Ralph prepared the salmon, I took the key to the utility room where the freezer was located to retrieve the veggies. Upon swinging the door open, I saw that the freezer door was open. Oops. Had I not closed the door properly the day before and now the veggies would be a stinky, melted mess? Peeking inside, I saw nothing, and then I noticed the freezer had been disconnected. The other freezer, which had not been running when the agent showed us which one to use, was now humming, so I looked inside. To my amazement, it was empty as well. Our veggies had gone AWOL. First, the elevator had gone belly up, then Serge showed up, and now the freezer had freed up our food. This latest episode was a puzzler. Who on earth would do this? There was only one other apartment on our floor, but we hadn't heard or seen anyone the entire week. We assumed it was either vacant or the owner was elsewhere. Who would have a key? Apparently, a vegetable thief was at large.

Had we used the wrong freezer, and the sly owner had then applied the possession-is-90-percent-of-the-law reasoning? But then I wondered why that person would not have placed the frozen food in the appropriate freezer since they had gone to the trouble of plugging it in. I walked back to our apartment empty-handed and related the sad tale to Ralph.

"What?" he said. "There's a veggie poacher in the building?"

"It appears that's the case. Maybe we'd better reconsider using the washing machine for a last-minute load. Whoever's behind the looting might lift our laundry too."

This latest turn of events landed so squarely in the incredulous category that we had to laugh about it. I imagined contacting Odile with an absurd request. "Sorry to be a bother, but somebody stole our side dishes for dinner tonight, so would you mind sending over a couple, preferably spinach and green beans?" No, I'd leave Odile to enjoy a work-free Friday night; besides, she wasn't programmed for commanding actual results. She'd never reported back on attempts to delay the terrace project, and her idea of making the elevator repair a reality was informing us that OUT OF SERVICE stickers had been stuck to the elevators. In fact, she'd emphasized, she'd placed them *on every floor*, as if that commonsense action deserved commendation. No comment. I put off the disheartening texting task till the morning. We'd be leaving, so there would be no more of our possessions to pilfer, but I knew the agency would need to know or should *want* to know.

The salmon was lonely on the plate, but our attention was drawn to what was happening outside, and it wasn't a dazzling sunset. A magnificent wind that was in full rage mode—up to eighty kilometers per hour, I learned later—felt like it intended to smash things. Forget the broken elevator, workman, and pilfered food. I hoped that the building would withstand the thunderous forces.

Some of the terrace chairs didn't look like they would, though. They weren't properly tucked under the table, so while Ralph was washing the dishes, I rectified that situation. It would not end happily if the furniture took flight from the top story. The gulls soaring about would not have been pleased with the intrusion, nor the chickens and goats in the backyard next door. While I was wrestling with one of the chairs with my back to the terrace half-wall, which rose about waist height, a mighty gust hit me—thankfully not blowing me over the new railing so carefully installed by Serge but onto the terrace. Yikes! I was screaming on the inside as Ralph grabbed me. We staggered around practically on our knees, folding each chair and laying it flat on the deck. Clinging to each other, we lunged to the safety of the apartment.

Hugging me but issuing reprimands at the same time, Ralph said, "Honey, you shouldn't have gone out there by yourself. Thank goodness I turned around and saw what you were doing. That was frightening."

"That's an understatement," I said, trying to restore my breathing.

"Don't do that again, okay?"

"No worries. Thanks for saving me."

"I'd say with pleasure, but that was no picnic."

"No kidding. Provence's mistral doesn't have anything on this wind. With gusts this fierce, it must have a name. It definitely deserves one." I discovered later that the storm that night was probably due to the *galerne*, or *gwalarn*, a sudden and violent northwest wind in Brittany.

"And we deserve a good night's sleep."

"Right. Big day tomorrow."

Lying in bed, we discussed how relieved we were that we had given up going to Brest and weren't driving through the brutal storm, probably dodging tree limbs flying over the road. Just then I received a message from our birder friend. Fifteen minutes outside the Montpellier airport, Gérard had received confirmation that his flight was canceled. His new plan was to try to get to Paris and then take a train to Brest, hopefully snagging a spot on the ferry to Ouessant the next evening.

In the end, we had made a good call about the Brest trip, but we hoped Gérard would make it to Ouessant. I knew that for him, every day not birding on Ouessant during fall migration would be hugely disappointing. Now, having experienced the enchanting aura of the island firsthand, we took on some of that disappointment too. I'd check on his progress the next day, and hopefully he'd have good news.

On departure day, our not-so-trusty agent was a no-show, which was an excellent development. Because in her place was an office manager, Mr. Simonet, who appeared right before 9:30 a.m. After friendly exchanges and raves about the apartment and views, I proceeded to *not* sugarcoat the variety of ways the agent had let us down, including how she had abandoned us in the garage and avoided helping us haul the luggage to the top floor.

"That was very unkind and unprofessional of her, "he said, in excellent English. "After months of training, she should have known how to handle the situation. She should have contacted me for advice, but she probably thought she had it under control." At any rate, he explained, her contract would not be renewed.

I suddenly felt bad about Odile losing the job. Surprising myself, I sprang to her defense. Perhaps it was my guilt talking, but I told Mr. Simonet that she had been generous with information about the town. Not wanting to be the cause of the termination of her rental management career, I said, "Maybe she *does* have potential, but she just needs more experience?"

"Actually, she's on a limited contract that's due to end anyway. And besides, her heart is with dogs—her dream is to be a trainer."

"Well, good for her," I said, genuinely pleased for the young woman and somewhat relieved. Not only did this information erase any potential responsibility I might be feeling, but also her experience with us humans probably reinforced the rightness of her career move from property to pets. Hopefully, she'd spoil her new clients so they wouldn't ever feel compelled to file a formal complaint but rather deliver nothing but woofs of approval.

As for the freezer debacle and the veggies on walkabout, he was sure the culprit was the elderly owner of the adjacent apartment, who rarely visited it. Over the years, communication had proved a challenge, so there was no easy explanation. Putting on his detective's hat, the manager posited that the old gentleman had likely checked the freezer before turning it off and took the food, not remembering it wasn't his. He then turned on the other freezer as a neighborly gesture. As unlikely as his positive spin was, I nodded in agreement, not wanting to rain on his community spirit parade. And besides, all in all the mishaps amounted to minor inconveniences in comparison to the extraordinary wonders we'd encountered around Le Conquet and on Ouessant. I hated all the stair climbing, for sure, but with every step I kept telling myself it was good for my glutes.

After returning our security deposit, Mr. Simonet apologized again for all the headaches, including the terrace repairs, adding that he was confident he could convince the owner to offer us a partial refund. "What a marvelous thing that would be," I said. He then offered another idea—to help us with the luggage. "That would be great," Ralph said, handing him two suitcases.

With Le Conquet and its related mishaps in our rearview mirror, we recalled the special experiences we'd had in the seaside village. The annoyances faded fast when we focused on the extraordinary walks, food, and views, especially watching the orange sherbet sun melt into the horizon beyond the light-house. For many kilometers, as we flew down the autoroute, our happy-o-meters were pinging nonstop, each note heralding a different dimension of delight.

Joie de Vivre Highlights*

A lone pony on a horseshoe beach
Lunch at Bistrot 1954
The making of a Michelin star
Wandering on the Plage des Blancs Sablons
A Sanderling show at the Plage des Trois Moutons

Despite some pesky lowlights

12

Tiny to Mighty

Velluire, Western France, and Carcassonne, Southwestern France

The speck of a village called Velluire is far from the tourist trail. Nestled into the department of the Vendée, named for the river that meanders through it, the enclave provides an idyllic setting for a country auberge with a gourmet restaurant. Our second destination was Carcassonne, a UNESCO World Heritage Site that welcomes nearly four million visitors annually. There, in the shadows of the grand medieval citadel, we united with globe-trotting friends.

From Le Conquet, Velluire wasn't an exceptionally long drive at five hours, but it was far more exciting than we'd anticipated—an unexpected heart-pounding episode awaited me. After we filled the car with petrol and our stomachs with tuna sandwiches, which we consumed in picnic fashion in a grassy area behind the gas station, I took the wheel. In a section near Nantes that should have been totally flat—I'd consulted the map beforehand—what looked like a huge bridge rose to the sky ahead of us. Those tall curvy ones get me every time—inciting big-bridge phobia when I'm the driver. Without a place to pull over, I shakily continued on as Ralph reminded me not to stray from the middle lane and to follow the leader.

"You've done this before; you can do it again," he encouraged. "And this isn't as bad as the Millau bridge, and you did that."

It would have been much better if he hadn't mentioned the cable-stayed Millau Viaduct, the tallest of its kind in the world when it was built in 2004. It's a thousand meters high—or seemed like it anyway (343 meters, actually). The one time I drove across it a few years ago, I nearly hyperventilated with fear of flying off into the yonder beyond. Regarding automobiles—Formula 1 and their ilk aside—*exciting* and *driving* are two words that should never meet in the same sentence. And here I was executing an exciting drive. Sitting up ramrod straight and gripping the wheel tight, I tailgated the van in front of me until we were back to the reassuringly flat freeway. I knew the driver was a guy because I'd noticed when he'd passed me earlier, so I sent my silent thanks to Van Man—he'd saved the day.

Before checking into our hotel in Velluire, out of sheer curiosity we cruised the city of Fontenay-le-Comte, just east of the autoroute exit. Going the extra mile, or in this case, driving the extra nine kilometers, to check out an area while we were nearby made a lot of sense. It just might hold a treasure.

I had such complete confidence in my good friend's recommendation of a particular countryside auberge that I'd booked not just a room but dinner too—so there would be no last-minute switcheroo and we would follow through with our reservation, no matter how outstanding Fontenay's charm factor. I had been more than prepared to be impressed with this newfound town, but our windshield tour left us cold.

"That's a relief," I said. "We aren't missing out."

"You're relieved not to be charmed? Isn't that a little junior high?"

"Good point," I said, though still feeling like a thirteen-year-old who had just found out a party for the "in" crowd I wasn't invited to had been a bust.

Ralph gave me an if-the-shoe-fits look, so I added, "I may look like a grown-up, but apparently I'm still in the developmental stage."

"You're making steady progress, though," he said.

"I am now preparing to adore the auberge."

No preparation was required. The Auberge de la Rivière, tucked away in the lushly verdant Venise Verte, charmed us at first sight. Smothered in ivy with white shutters peeking out, the hotel sits above the grassy banks of the tree-lined river Vendée, close to a picturesque old bridge with graceful arches. Across the parking lot from the main building, our room was in an equally inviting building with a wide glass-paned door leading to a deck decorated with cherry-red planters, cushioned chairs, and a direct view of the river. On the opposite shore, three little boys managed fishing poles, an endearing down-home scene reminiscent of a Norman Rockwell painting.

After all the time in the car, we wanted to stretch our legs before dinner, so we strolled along the canal-width river. A teenaged girl and a younger version of her—probably her sister—emerged from a backyard gate onto the path about fifty meters ahead of us. The older girl held a pair of orange paddles and the little one hugged a basketball. They scrambled down the bank and climbed into a small rowboat. Across the river in the distance, we could make out a sports complex, presumably their destination. No need for mom or dad to drive them to b-ball practice. The self-sufficient kids would paddle their way over under their own steam. We waited while they put on life jackets to see which way they'd go, but they didn't go anywhere. We figured they were progressing through a lengthy safety protocol, so we continued on our way. By the time we circled back, they were gone. Probably already shootin' some hoops.

No other boats were on the narrow waterway, much less an Uber rowboat. One would have come in handy to hitch a ride to a nature park nearby. On our stroll, we'd seen the preserve on a posted map and wanted to check it out, hoping we'd spot some birdlife. So we had to drive, but it took only a few minutes to locate the "observation" area. But we found no observation deck. It amounted to a plaque and a parking area opposite a canal. We did spot a Grey Heron that posed obligingly on a fence right by the road.

Just then, my phone pinged with good news from Gérard. He'd made the ferry Saturday afternoon and was now on Ouessant—hooray! Relieved, I texted back *Excellent news and happy birding*, adding clapping hands, a thumbs-up, and a big bird emoji.

In preparation for our gourmet dinner, we made time for a little snooze before our 7:30 p.m. reservation. I wanted to be rested and have all my wits about me to appreciate the repast to the fullest. The night before had been our minimalist salmon meal thanks to the spinach and green bean thief, so tonight we were planning on making up for that meager supper.

We arrived a few minutes early, traffic not being much of an issue on the short stroll through the courtyard. Several tables were already in full dinner mode, making for a lively ambience, though a certain formality prevailed this Saturday evening. Equipped with tongs in one hand and a woven basket in the other, waiters served an assortment of bread slices by carefully lifting the pieces as if they were fragile eggshells.

Soon after we ordered, a pair of amuse-bouches appeared in front of us—always a welcome surprise. My favorite was a shallow bowl of creamy cauliflower froth served with a crispy phyllo stick laid across the dish. The smoked salmon and eel appetizer we shared didn't knock our gastronomic socks off, but *oh là là*, my main course sure did. The *lotte*, or monkfish, was extraordinarily luscious. Although it may be known as the "poor man's lobster," it came with a substantial price tag. But it was a feast for both the eyes and palate. The succulent knotty chunk of fish was lightly grilled and had a bit of bounce. Served on a bed of spinach and mushrooms and surrounded by a vegetable garden of potato, broccoli, and a mild red pepper stuffed with grains, what a pretty plate it was. I told Ralph, who received a generous bite, that the fish dish alone merited a return visit.

"C'est noté," he said, adding that if we ever did return, he would forgo his braised beef, as tender and deliciously rich as it was, for my fish dish.

"Duly noted by me as well," I said. "Then I won't have to share!"

"What's that buzzing?" I whined the next morning, rolling over toward Ralph and the racket.

"Oh, sorry, honey. I set the alarm on my watch," Ralph said.

"For the middle of the night? It's dark!"

"Uh, not really—the curtains are thick. Actually, it's 8:00 a.m., and we'd better get moving."

"Oh, right. Next stop, Carcassonne." It would be over five hours in the car, but the next day we'd be home in three. I forced myself up.

We debated over whether to have a full breakfast in the hotel restaurant or head south after having a cup of coffee in the room. A simple *petit déjeuner* made a lot of sense considering the previous night's gourmet meal, but we were curious what tasty treats might be on offer. Since we had resisted the scrumptious-looking desserts at dinner, we rationalized our way to a morning indulgence.

The buffet was extensive and superb, with something for every palate and even a little machine to soft-boil eggs. All carbed up, we packed up and paid up. The breakfast was included in the room price, which was a gracious parting gift.

Leaving the peaceful enclave that was commerce-free except for one small post office–grocery store combo, we pointed our Golf toward the medieval citadel of Carcassonne. Our long-time buddies Louis and Sophia, whom we've known since our Heidelberg days, had lived there for several years, along with their heart-melting golden retriever Rudolph. We crossed paths with them periodically somewhere between our two towns, and we were looking forward to taking a leisurely stroll with their dog and catching up over dinner.

During my driving shift, flat fields that stretched as far as the eye could see were the main feature of the landscape. Without daunting bridges to scale, the region won my approval. Maybe because the scenery wasn't entertainingly eye-popping, Ralph offered to take over the driving thirty minutes early, which would be around the rest stop after the toll station by Toulouse.

"Cool," I said. "That's so kind of you."

"Well, there's a catch."

"Oh, darn. What is it?"

"We'll listen to covers of classic tunes by ukulele."

"Ukulele, seriously?" I said, unaware that ukulele musicians actually did covers of classics. "Nah, I'll pass. What else you got on your playlist?"

"No problem. We also have bluegrass at the ready."

"Bluegrass? Also not my fave. In that case, fine—ukulele classic covers it is."

"You may not be pleased to know there are more than a hundred."

A favorite sarcastic riposte of Ralph's came to mind: *Your kindness is only exceeded by your good looks and winning ways.* But I kept it to myself in case it might trigger a retaliation in the form of bluegrass. No offense to bluegrass fans, but it's an acquired taste.

As the first ukulele ditty began, Ralph said, "I think I might get one."

"One what? A ukulele?"

"Yeah."

"Fine, I'll get a karaoke mic," I threatened. I can't sing. I mean, seriously, I cannot begin to carry a tune. It's painful to hear. Even in the shower.

"Okay, truce," Ralph conceded.

In all honesty, the ukulele covers were pretty cool. "Perfect," which Ed Sheeran made famous, "La Vie en Rose," "Shallows" of Lady Gaga fame, "I Can't Help Falling in Love with You," "Take Me Home, Country Roads," "The Lion

Sleeps Tonight," "Stand by Me," "Over the Rainbow," "Here Comes the Sun, "Build Me Up Buttercup," and "Don't Worry, Be Happy." *Ukulele Moments* got me to Toulouse, toe-tapping all the way. (I was on cruise control.)

Suddenly, the don't worry, be happy vibes conjured up by the sweet ukulele versions dissipated as we neared the pay station. Our toll ticket had vanished. Slowly approaching the multi-lane complex, I pawed around for the piece of paper, which we normally placed in the open cubby space below the radio. It wasn't there. Ralph looked under his feet and felt all around his seat. No ticket.

Wow, this is pathetic, I thought. *How could we lose the ticket?* "Have we stopped anywhere or let it fly out the window?"

"No to both those actions."

"Then it must be here, right?"

"One would think."

Closing in on the toll station, I pulled way over to the right to a place that seemed safe to stop, far from the incoming streams of vehicles. We flung both doors open and took turns searching around the seats. We were at a total loss as to where it could have gone since we hadn't stopped anywhere or rolled the windows down after picking up the ticket. Again we pushed the seats back, looked under them, and even checked in the backseat. I couldn't believe this was happening. Were we idiots or what? Idiots, I concluded. This takes the honors in the idiot category. Who loses an autoroute ticket?

Finally, we resigned ourselves to paying a hefty fee for the lost scrap of paper and scanned the area for the administration building where we'd go confess to being idiots and pay whatever it was. We had no choice. We just hoped it would not take long. The sooner we put this idiotic move behind us, the better.

We needed to get back on the road to make our rendezvous in Carcassonne.

"Okay," I said, "before we go to confession, let's try again." I was convinced the result would be the same, but we did it anyway.

"One more time with feeling," Ralph said. We both went through the motions of looking around the seats, Ralph on the passenger's side and I on the driver's side, duplicating our previous searches. Then, on the driver's side, tucked into the track that the seat slides on, I saw a piece of paper that I swore hadn't been there before. I lifted it and turned it over.

"Check this out," I said to Ralph, extending my hand.

"The ticket?"

"In plain sight."

And miracle of miracles, our credit card was where it was supposed to be, so at last we were ready to head toward the toll booth.

With the ticket fumble behind us, Ralph took control for the last leg. "Buckle up, Buttercup," he quipped, the ukulele tune still in his head. He explained he had to swing over ten lanes from our impromptu parking spot on the far right side of the toll lanes, about fifty meters from the pay station, to the far left, dodging the incoming cars in the process. This maneuver was essential for accessing the autoroute we needed on the other side, he said.

"No, no," I insisted. "Why go through all that? Just head straight—crossing over to the far left will be easier on the other side, after we pay. All lanes lead to the same place."

Ralph's cocked head indicated nonconcurrence, but he was anxious to go somewhere, even if it was the wrong somewhere.

After he fed our newfound ticket into the machine, paid, replaced the credit card in its protected space, and accelerated under the raised arm, a low cement barrier loomed on the left, making it impossible to charge over to the preferred autoroute.

"Oops. Oh, dang. Sorry, honey," I said. "I didn't see that barrier from where we were."

Ralph didn't utter a syllable but turned his head toward me, eyebrows raised, which said it all. Because of my misguided advice, we ended up cruising the longer west side of Toulouse, a new experience for us. Since we typically swung around the east side of the metropolis, this meant that now we had circled it, albeit in stages.

This novel route prompted the question: Why hadn't we toured Toulouse? "One of these days," I said, "we should visit Toulouse, not just loop it." For one thing, it would be neat to see the rose-colored stone buildings, the reason for its Pink City nickname.

Ralph agreed, adding, "Maybe take a train from Avignon that goes directly into the city center. Probably the safest way— no possibility of navigational errors."

"You well might think that," I said, smiling. "We're awfully creative."

Traffic moved fluidly, so we both went mindless, letting more ukulele music soothe our frenetic thoughts after the pay station ordeal. Twenty minutes shy of Carcassonne, Ralph exclaimed, "I think I'm ukulele'd out."

Miracles do happen, I thought. But just to annoy him, which I felt was my duty periodically to keep him alert, I said with dramatized emotion, "Nooo! I'm hooked now. Don't take my ukulele tunes away!"

"Clearly, you've met and exceeded your quota—on to the next. Jimmy Buffett?"

"If you insist," I said, feigning disappointment. In fact, I was elated to join the search for a lost shaker of salt in Margaritaville.

When we arrived at the hotel, we were pleased to find our room ready, so we checked in early. It was sunny and 20.5°C, perfect for a walk around the ramparts and maybe spotting some birds flying over the plain. A raptor would be most appropriate for the majestic fortress-castle setting.

After a shower and a short snooze, we were ready for dinner at our friends' place, and hopefully, beforehand, a walk with Rudolph, my canine soulmate. Tonight, we'd get a good night's sleep, and by tomorrow afternoon, we'd be sailing past the Saint-Rémy city limits.

At Louis and Sophia's house in the New Town below the citadel, we enjoyed a delish barbecued salmon supper, but no walk with Rudolph. He was tuckered out and happy enough playing with us inside. It's always sweet sorrow in parting from this upbeat, fun couple and their pooch, but it helps when we plan another rendezvous soon. The following spring, some friends of theirs would be visiting from New Zealand, and they planned to rent a place together for a week in Isle-sur-la-Sorgue, not far from Saint-Rémy. "How about if we all get together then?" Sophia suggested.

"Excellent," we replied, each adding two thumbs-up. Rudolph barked in agreement.

Joie de Vivre Highlights

A ukulele lesson in music appreciation
An ivy-covered, riverside auberge
Kids fishing on the river by an ancient stone bridge
An almost-lobster dinner
A reunion with pals and their pup in Carcassonne

13

Bonaparte, Boats, and Bruises

Corsica, Mediterranean Sea

"The best-laid plans of mice and men often go awry," goes the saying by Robert Burns. The Scottish poet's words had special meaning for this island outing. Appreciating the highlights meant managing some lowlights—all mere hiccups, except for one.

The port strike wasn't planned, but it was comprehensive, including all seaports, airports, and every other kind of port on Corsica, the French island where we had just spent an eventful week, our first trip to the Île de Beauté. This disturbing information came to light during breakfast on our sunny apartment terrace in Calvi, a town on the northwestern coast. It was the morning of the day before our scheduled flight from the beguiling mountainous island, famous as the birthplace of Napoleon, not to mention Christopher Columbus. Yes, this is where the global explorer was born—if you quiz a Calvi resident. A plaque installed by the citadel says so.

Although controversy abounds about Columbus's birth-place, there was none regarding the striking factions that had slammed our travel plans. Early the next day, we were to vacate our holiday rental and fly back to Marseille, where our car was parked. Unless we sprouted wings, there would be no liftoff from the island. In other words, we were up the proverbial creek without a paddle, an instrument that now seemed essential for exiting the island.

Scrambling to prioritize all the ramifications related to our captivity on Corsica for who knew how long had not been programmed for the final day of our vacation in gorgeous Calvi. The last-day plan had been to leisurely soak up the glorious 180-degree view from our fourth-floor *terrasse* overlooking the pleasure boat port, citadel, and beach. After that, we were to have a carefree day indulging in strictly holiday activities such as strolling, swimming, lunching, napping, *apéro*-ing, and watching the twinkly lights spring to life at sunset, followed by dinner quayside. A consummately stressless day it was to be. But it was not to be.

Predawn the previous Saturday morning, we'd left Saint-Rémy to reach the airport in Marseille in plenty of time for our 9:10 a.m. departure to Corse, the French name for Corsica. We'd parked the car in the cheapest airport lot, aptly named the Super Eco lot, which was jammed. Consequently, we'd had to drive to the far reaches to find an open slot, so the estimated ten-minute walk became a twenty-minute schlepp to Terminal One. There used to be a shuttle, but we saw no sign of one. Maybe it was on hiatus during the construction of the parking towers and enlarged terminals? We were amazed at all the new structures that had been erected in the last few years as France's second-largest city angled to become a major international airport hub with flights to the US. Thankfully, our rolling carry-on suitcases executed their duties well, and check-in was a snap.

An hour after takeoff, the Isle of Beauty came into view. Stunning! The landing was particularly smooth and our luggage emerged quickly. Jeremy, our taxi driver, had already texted me that he was outside waiting for us. It was a comfort to have a reservation with the reliable taxi-driving friend of our Saint-Rémy neighbors' son-in-law. One less potential hassle to deal with. The ten-minute drive to Calvi passed through lush countryside with impressive mountains in the distance. As we approached the town, the beautiful bay came into view, boding well for the vista from our seafront apartment.

Emilie, the accommodating manager, had agreed to let us leave our luggage in the apartment while the cleaners prepped it, and we happily took her up on the offer. As we entered the spare lobby, decorated with only a few dismal plants, we noted that the plain building needed a refresher and the elevator was antiquated. Just like our apartment in Brittany, up we went to the fourth floor, but unlike the apartment in Brittany, this elevator, as rickety as it was, performed its job well enough. We held our breath for the view. The door was open to the open-plan living area, and Emilie was right there, along with a few other helpers.

Before I could greet her, I saw the fabulous vista we had been waiting for. Wow, just as advertised—shimmery, expansive, and half a dozen shades of blue. Emilie was smiley and welcoming, but I knew we had to scoot so they could get on with their work. She'd text when the place was ready, and the key would be in the lockbox.

The anticipation of how a new place will (or will not) measure up can be anxiety inducing, and I began to unclench only after seeing that the apartment and view were in fine form. We walked to the supermarket a few blocks away to give it a once-over so when we returned to shop, the chore would be efficient. And then it was *pieds-dans-l'eau* time—feet in the water—or at least toes in the sand. We walked a few blocks to the beach and did both. An hour later, Emilie texted that the apartment was ready.

Now that we'd gained possession of the apartment with its terrific view, we took to the terrace to take it all in. High on the hill to our left stood the citadel, watching over the pleasure boat marina, straight ahead was the horseshoe bay ringed with commanding mountains, and to the right was the wide arch of impossibly white sand called Plage de Calvi. Simply enthralling. Friends had gushed over the town and its proximity to the beautiful beach, but I'd taken some of that enthusiasm with a realistic pinch of salt. Now, seeing it with my own eyes, I needed no sodium sprinkles. It was stunning. And to top it off, a Hooded Crow flew by, reminding Ralph of the island's promise of new birds.

Before we became too comfortable, we turned our attention to provisioning. With an empty roller suitcase in hand and both our backpacks strapped on, we headed back to the store. Motivated to make it to a restaurant for lunch, we did a quick shop and were back in a flash. With supplies put away, we took off in search of a casual bistro where we could relax and officially kick off our Corsica week.

Following Emilie's restaurant tips, we found an appealing establishment called Via Marine Le Bistrot on a pedestrian street. From outside we could see straight through the dining room to the terrace overlooking the sea. Inside, a greeter with a warm smile asked whether we wanted a table inside or out. The weather was great, so to the view we went.

It was *moules* for me. I was no doubt gilding the lily by choosing the version infused with a Corsican cheese sauce, but it was so much fun to try a local specialty. The mussels were fresh and plump, and the sauce deeply rich. Ralph chose an enormous *chèvre chaud* salad that was piled dangerously high and stacked with a couple of fist-sized balls of goat cheese slightly melted on dark toast rounds. It could have fed us both. Of course, magnanimous me offered to help him. And in return, some golden *frites* that had accompanied my mussels migrated his way.

Exploring the town was part of what we dubbed our feline familiarization protocol. Like cats circling an area before deciding where to curl up, we like to prowl around new surroundings, getting a feel for the place. So following our leisurely lunch, we wandered the maze of narrow lanes, noting the many attractive boutiques, brasseries, and wine bars, one right after the other. The waterside stretch was also chockablock with inviting restaurants and boat excursion kiosks, most of which went to the Scandola Nature Reserve, which topped our must-do list.

We paused at several of the excursion booths to size up their vessels and departure times. It appeared there were two types of crafts. One looked like a proper boat, and the others more like glorified rubber rafts. I took a photo of the vessel that suited us and also the schedules. A wide choice of times was available, so we felt comfortable putting off booking a trip until later, when we were rested and had figured out our agenda. Satisfied that our week would be filled with fun, we wandered back to the apartment.

We were now exhausted after our early-morning departure, and a snooze held great appeal. But once we returned to the terrace, it was hard to tear ourselves away from the sparkling Mediterranean view. When our eyelids began fluttering, we took the hint, gave in, and laid our heads down, dreaming of the sunset that awaited us.

And it was spellbinding: Barbie pink, deep persimmon, and coral streaks splashed across the horizon, contrasting with the darkening sea that bobbed below. Sipping our *apéros* while watching the sky morph into night made us wonder how we could arrange our lives to have this scene every day forever. What would that be like?

As tender as the dawn may be, we easily surrendered to the reality of being on a Mediterranean island getaway and savored our sleep-in and a slow wake-up. Between steaming cups of espresso I popped over to the Maison de la Presse a block away to check for any English-language newspapers, and I returned with the *Financial Times*, direct from London. The previous afternoon, I'd been told it would arrive a day or two late. Life in the slow lane, I'd thought—clearly that approach was de rigueur on the island. But how nice to receive a bonus that I hadn't counted on it. The day looked promising. We relaxed with our paper over lots of coffee until the beach beckoned.

A sunny sky reigned during our stroll on the fine white sand. Families and couples sunbathed, many stretched out on the loungers belonging to the seasonal pop-up restaurants.

Kids built sandcastles, splashed in the water, and threw Frisbees. I'd come prepared to do some ocean walking, called *longe-côte* in France, so I was wearing my reef walkers and a brightly colored ensemble that screamed *seaside*. My surfer tights and long-sleeved rash guard were printed with bright blue and purple palm fronds, the top trimmed in coral. Ralph, or anybody else for that matter, would not have a hard time spotting me if I were swept out to sea. The outfit also provided protection from sun and floaty stuff, plus some insulation, not that I needed that in the warm water. I didn't feel the slightest shiver, even in late September. While I walked laps in the waist-high surf, Ralph put his binoculars to use. A friendly Red Kite visited several times as if to remind us that wildlife was present and accounted for on this island paradise.

Early Monday morning, while Ralph relaxed in the apartment, I walked over to the covered market to check out the action. It wasn't the bustling produce market I had imagined but just a handful of specialty vendors selling sausages, honey, and such. I found out later that the town up the coast called Île-Rousse was *the* place to find a full-on, busy *marché*. On the way back to the apartment, I more carefully studied the information boards for the Scandola Nature Reserve boat excursions and settled on one that offered the boat we preferred and that left that afternoon after lunch.

Back at the apartment, Ralph and I discussed seizing the moment to take the cruise since the weather was nice and the water seemed calm, always a plus when boating. No iffy conditions for us. I'd made that mistake once years ago when we were on the Isle of Jersey in the English Channel off the Brittany coast. I'd had my heart set on visiting the island of nearby Guernsey to visit the house where Victor Hugo had lived while in exile from France, reachable by ferry in a couple of hours. The day I intended to go, sea conditions were rough and the ferry companies had canceled all crossings— except one. Sensible tourists would probably have considered the canceled trips reason enough to stay put, but irrationally, I only saw my good fortune. Ralph was reluctant to let me go, but I assured him that I didn't get seasick and that I'd be a good sailor.

I didn't know that what I needed were rodeo skills. The ferry bucked fiercely like a bronco with a blazing tail. The crew was frantic trying to keep up with demands for barf bags from seated passengers and assisting those swaying down the aisles in the direction of the restrooms. I was certain my time had come. Back then I had no cell phone, so I accepted my fate was to be swallowed up sans goodbyes. I closed my eyes and waited for the inundation.

Instead of sinking, the ferry docked at the port in Guernsey. I visited Hugo's house, ate lunch, and returned a few hours later by the same ferry across silky-smooth waters to Jersey. And to Ralph, who I hugged like there was no tomorrow. Because I hadn't expected one.

With that traumatic Jersey trip in mind, we headed to the excursion office to buy tickets. The young lady on duty behind a tall counter relinquished her post to direct our attention to the wall displaying an aerial photo of the boat we would sail on. I already knew the type of boat they used from the photos at the kiosk on the dock. And I even had a picture of it on my phone, so there was no need to dwell on it. I barely glanced at the photo on the wall. We paid and agreed to be at the dock ten minutes before departure.

At the appointed time, we joined dozens of other people on the pier waiting to board in front of the boats. A young man appeared and informed everyone that three boats would be going to Scandola at the same time that day. He called out the names of twelve people assigned to the first boat and another twelve to the second. We were still there.

Then another young skipper appeared, hollering our names along with six others and asking us to follow him. Obediently we walked down the pier, through a gate, and along another dock. He stopped us at an excuse for a vessel, hopped aboard, turned to the eight people trailing behind him, and held out his hand to help us board … a raft. At least from my perspective, it seemed like a blown-up rubber toy. Known as a Zodiac, it boasted two engines and seating for twelve, but there were just eight of us and the captain. A pair of twenty-somethings marched to the bow. *Wait*, I thought. *This is precisely the floaty thing we did not want to go on.* It was made of rubber. It could pop at any moment. All it would take was the stab of a fish's spiky snout—and *bam*!

Ralph and I stared at each other with pained expressions. Should we bail, or should we take the plunge and have an experience outside our comfort zone? Perhaps being more flexible wasn't a bad thing? We hadn't planned on this, but maybe being spontaneous on vacation is part of what it means to be *en vacances*? Lots of companies used these types of inflatable boats, I reasoned, and had for decades. We'd seen plenty of them motoring in various harbors and beaches on our travels. The sea looked calm, and the sun was shining. Ralph and I exchanged shrugs and hopped aboard.

Cruising through the harbor was like sliding over ice. We didn't even begin to bounce, and the view of the city and the towering citadel from that vantage point was worth the ticket right there. But once we were on the open sea, the wham-banging began. The bow would soar for a second and then slam hard into the water. *Soar, slam! Soar, slam!* We soared-slammed our way to a quiet cove in the Scandola Nature Reserve, pausing in a calm, crystalline lagoon where swimming was an option. At first, Ralph and I sat glued to our seats, waiting for our brains to register the quiet. There was no need to speak. We were where we were, so we moved on with the program.

The pristine water was inviting, though crowded with schools of little silvery fish. I hesitated to join them, thinking back on what a friend had told me about her upcoming trip to Saint Helena off the coast of West Africa. She and her husband were headed to the tiny island, where Napoleon had spent his second exile, to swim with whale sharks. My adventurous friends didn't intend to "swim" in a cage because they had been assured that consuming humans didn't appeal to these huge animals. While telling me this, she paused, reflected, and added, "So if we don't return, you'll know that we were … well …"

"Misinformed," I offered, trying to negate the gruesome visual she'd painted.

Although my shark-swimming friend had returned unscathed—the adventure had been extraordinary—I asked our captain about the fish. He assured me they were very friendly. In reality, I was likely the one who scared them because they took off as soon as I jumped in and didn't return. They left me alone to paddle around peacefully, perhaps better to admire the deeply carved cliffs that plunged into the sea. A stunningly dramatic scene.

The captain expertly navigated our blow-up boat into a couple of narrow grottos, gently backing out each time. The nature park had strict rules about speed, and our captain took them to heart. We admired unique rock formations, some topped with elaborate Osprey nests, but saw few birds, which was surprising and disappointing for Ralph. With large schools of fish visible just beneath the surface, we wondered where all the fish-eating birds were. The small cove seemed like an extravagant seafood smorgasbord, but maybe the birds knew of other buffets where they could snack without an audience.

Despite the dearth of birds, there was some remarkable wildlife. In front of some small caves tucked into the lofty rocks, mountain goats sporting huge curled horns stood firm as if they knew they were part of a photo shoot. Considering the location of their chosen dwellings, these animals tended toward the introverted end of the personality spectrum and appeared to highly prize their alone time. Like nature paparazzi, we all went berserk snapping photos with our zoom lenses as the four-legged hermits posed in front of their impossibly steep havens.

The return trip to Calvi was not nearly as bouncy as the outbound trip, to the relief of all three couples sitting at the rear of the boat, who now began to chat, smile, and laugh. Maybe the young pair sprawled on the cushioned bow missed the bouncing, but those seated aft were much happier sailors.

As we approached the harbor, we plowed into a big swell that landed squarely on the couple next to Ralph, completely drenching them. Ralph took only a partial hit from that wave, but avoiding a full soak before finding terra firma would prove a challenge.

Once we arrived at the port, two of the couples hopped off the Zodiac and up onto the dock while the captain was occupied elsewhere, probably securing our raft-craft. One of the men who had jumped onto the dock extended his hand toward me, asking whether he could help. Welcoming his assistance, I said, "Oh yes, please," grabbed his hand, and up I went.

Ralph was behind me, and I expected the man who had assisted me to perform the same maneuver. But as I turned around I saw Ralph try to scramble onto the dock, lose his balance, then tip to his right and slam hard onto the concrete, with momentum propelling him into a slow roll toward the edge. I dropped on him, attempting to prevent his sliding off into the water. But to no avail. As if in a slow-motion nightmare where villains are chasing you but you can't run, I couldn't control Ralph's roll and he disappeared over the side of the dock, dropping into the drink. His backpack was loose and I reached down to grab it along with his eyeglasses, which miraculously were on top of his pack.

I heard myself frantically yelling, "Ralph! Are you okay? Are you okay?" I didn't know whether he'd hit his head on either the dock or the boat. He didn't respond, but one of his arms reached for the metal ladder on the craft. By then, the captain had reappeared and helped Ralph up onto the boat and then onto the dock.

Again I asked, "Are you okay?"

"I think so," he finally answered, looking stunned.

"Did you hit your head?"

Shaking his—hopefully—undamaged head, he said, "No, no, I didn't. I don't think so."

I handed him his glasses, and he stretched his arms and bent his legs. I did the same. My left elbow was screaming, but it functioned. I must have landed on it when I landed on Ralph.

We hugged, holding our embrace for a while as everyone looked on, forming a silent semicircle around us. In a daze, I thanked the captain for the tour, following polite protocol like a robot as if nothing untoward had happened. He assured us Ralph would be fine but gave us directions to a pharmacy just in case. Bidding the group adieu, we picked up our backpacks and walked to our apartment, trailing rivulets of seawater behind us.

Ralph stripped and got into a hot shower as fast as possible. A deep purple bruise had appeared on his right side above his hip, and two big red scrapes curved across his back. But no blood. And no protruding bones.

Sitting on the couch, wrapped in warm, clean clothes, we sat side by side in mild shock for a while, processing the surreal ordeal. It had happened in a flash. Ralph had watched two other couples and me pop onto the dock, and he was following suit. A seemingly ordinary maneuver. But not. Had the boat shifted as he pushed off forward, or had the helper released his grip a split second too soon, or both? Or was something else at play? Whatever the cause in this particular case, vulnerability was all I could think about. *What a fragile life we lead,* I thought. Potential disasters were everywhere we were. That we humans avert near misses all day long every day is something of a marvel at the miracle level.

But at least one lesson was to be learned. In an unfamiliar environment, slowing down and assessing the situation is essential. After experiencing a bouncy and wet cruise, once at the dock, all the passengers—including us—were anxious to exit. But we all should have taken a deep breath and waited for the captain to finish tying up the boat and come back around to oversee the disembarkation process.

As it happened, we ran into the captain the next day. I delivered my suggestion by way of an airplane analogy. When a plane lands, I said, the pilot announces that everyone must remain seated until the seat belt sign goes off. Maybe he should issue a similar but boat-appropriate directive. Monsieur le Capitaine was gracious about my idea, saying that an exit warning was in fact the official protocol, carried out by an assistant. But with a staff shortage that day, he remembered the unannounced safety precaution only when securing the craft. He promised to deliver the announcement on all future excursions, without fail. We parted ways, wishing each other a wonderful week.

We took his wish to heart. Instead of dwelling on the near miss, we recognized that we were on a beautiful island we'd been anxious to visit for years, and this was our chance. We would find ways to make the most of our remaining time on the island, keeping Ralph's bruised body foremost in our minds. We'd take it slow and make no sudden moves. Rushing, as we'd discovered, was begging for trouble.

The next few days were filled with walks on the beach, exploring the citadel, easy hikes to small, exquisitely sandy coves around the town, and a discovery lunch at a pizzeria called A Punta. I took my chances with a new ingredient, a spicy local sausage called *figatelli*. It was love at first bite, and before I knew it only one slice remained to offer Ralph. The meal at the quaint enclave was also fun. The skilled Italian pizza maker put on a show, tossing the dough high and artfully assembling the toppings with dramatic flourishes, then pivoting gracefully to slide the pies into the oven. His antics might sound gimmicky, but his playfulness belied a high skill level. After we watched him for just a few minutes, it was clear he truly loved his work, which perhaps was mainly about bringing joy to his patrons. He succeeded with that one.

Then we kicked back and left the driving to a conductor aboard the train to Île-Rousse, the bustling market town farther up the coast. Since Calvi was the origin station, finding seats was no problem, but other passengers weren't so lucky. After a dozen stops along the coastline route, the two-car train was stuffed when it pulled into the station at Île-Rousse.

On the short stroll to the quaint town center, a multigenerational group gathering in a parking lot caught our attention. They were unmissable because everyone wore various red and black outfits, some with feathered headdresses or gigantic angel wings. With all the drums, bells, and tambourines on display, it seemed they were preparing to put on a parade. A Las Vegas showgirl lookalike in a skimpy black satin ensemble festooned with sparkly fringe wound around and through her colleagues, carrying out costume adjustments—in stilettos.

We continued our walk to town, hoping to catch the show during our brief stay. We navigated the maze of narrow pedestrian lanes crammed with boutiques and cafés and wandered through the covered open-air market where vendors sold local specialties like goat and sheep cheeses, cured meats, honey, and garlic. A tree-filled square adjacent to the outdoor market was lined with white canopied stalls—some serving up Corsican goodies and others selling jewelry, home décor, or clothing. And next to that area, gigantic carnival rides were welcoming thrill seekers. It all added up to a Corsican county fair.

Soon, we did indeed come upon the musical festivities. Happily, our visit coincided with an annual festival, the Fiera di Lisula—not its 5th or 25th or even its 105th edition, but its 195th edition, no less. As we were making our way through the crowds, a loudspeaker announced that a musical interlude was about to begin. The group from the parking lot had assembled, and soon drumbeating, bell rattling, and tambourine shaking exploded in a repetitive samba-like beat. They entertained us for a while before beginning a slow slalom through the carnival throngs, making music and grinning broadly, just like the enthusiastic audience.

After the concert, we found seats at a café under tall trees where a gangly lad who hailed from Normandy served us coffees. He was crazy about living in the US one day, but even crazier about his basketball hero, Steph Curry of the Golden State Warriors. He was convinced Curry was the greatest basketball player of all time. He didn't know where he would live in the US, but he *did* know in his heart that Curry was the best ever. Basketball-loving Ralph didn't want to burst this eager young guy's bubble with b-ball stats about most wins, championships, all-star appearances, and Most Valuable Player awards attributed to other stellar basketballers like Kareem Abdul-Jabbar, Michael Jordan, LeBron James, Bill Russell, Wilt Chamberlain, and others. In Ralph's opinion, the best is nearly impossible to define. *Just like a lot of things, including* la belle vie, I thought.

But defining a good lunch spot was surely possible. After exploring the town some more, we followed a tip from a tourist office lady and found our way to the family-run U Spuntinu. I voted for my old standby *salade de chèvre chaud* because a bright, light dish appealed, and it's always interesting to experience different versions of one of my favorite lunch dishes. On this one, the melted goat cheese oozed over slices of dense, toasted multigrain bread on top of crunchy greens. Ralph made a more adventurous choice of an assortment of appetizers, including a spinach tart and eggplant mélange, all subtly flavored. I knew this because I helped.

While paying at the counter, I chatted with the owner. She explained that the restaurant had been started in the 1970s by her grandmother, whose framed photograph was positioned on the wall above the cash register. Still a family affair, the eatery hummed along, overseen by her and her brother. I commented on the other vintage photographs in the dining room, which captured the restaurant's extensive history. Before I could elaborate, madame excused herself, as duty called from the *cuisine*. Appreciating the tradition the restaurant upheld, I called after her, "Here's to another fifty years and beyond!"

Walking off lunch took us along a beachside promenade with direct views of the pretty beach, across a causeway, and up to the lighthouse. Well, nearly there. We were just shy of the summit when strong gusts forced us to slow down and finally turn around. It was for the best, though, as we didn't want to risk missing our ride home. The trains kept a light schedule; the one following ours didn't depart for hours.

We weren't alone preparing for the 3:30 p.m. return trip. Loads of other passengers had gathered on the train station platform too. Thinking that the train doors opened on both sides, we walked briskly over to the far side of the tracks, where the crowd waiting to board was smaller. That would have worked had the train been the same model and the conductor followed the same protocol as the one on the earlier trip. Wrong on both counts. While the passengers poured out the other side of the train, none exited on our side, as the doors refused to open no matter how many times we anxious travelers pushed the button. So we all walked back to the opposite side, where we joined the tail end of a lengthy line waiting to board. Needless to say, we didn't snag prize seats. Ralph stood on some stairs with a wall to lean against, careful not to nudge his wounded back, which was healing but still sore. I balanced myself on the luggage rack railing, which was a bit of a trick. *Mais oui*, we were happy to disembark.

Overnight, our good luck with the weather washed up. It started to rain before dawn, poured throughout the morning, and was still gushing into the afternoon. Our tentative plan to take the two-hour bus ride to Bastia, the main town on the island's northern tip, dissolved. Wheeling around hairpin turns on steep and now slick mountain roads lacked luster, to say the least. Not to mention that the scenery would be a bit blurry.

Finally, around 5:00 p.m., the sun appeared. And *mon Dieu*, was it beautiful. There was no doubt what we wanted to do— feel the sand in our toes. We hightailed it to the beach to wander. On the way back to town, we crossed the train tracks and hiked into the woods. There, we happened to get a clear look at a Great Spotted Woodpecker. It put on a rousing show, hopping around on a tree limb with a large, round shape in its beak. It was hard to tell whether the black-and-white bird with a scarlet cap was trying to crack or store the morsel, but we enjoyed its entertaining antics.

The sun greeted us again on our last full day, and we hoped to make the most of it with a stress-free last-day plan. That is, until the strike news broke. Now, that dreamy agenda looked decidedly improbable. The port strike had begun on Thursday afternoon, unbeknownst to us. But not to the people who were scheduled to depart that evening from Bastia, forcing them to spend the night in a gymnasium. That jolting news forced us to leap to our action stations.

First, we contacted the apartment managers and asked whether the travelers following us in the apartment were already on the island or arriving from elsewhere. If they couldn't get here, then perhaps we could stay in the apartment, I ventured. They didn't know the status of the next vacationers but said they had room at another residence not far away. Okay, fine. Shelter—check.

The next order of business was to get a refill of a vital prescription for Ralph. He hadn't brought a strike stash, and though he could go a day or two without the medication, it was anybody's guess how long the grievous *grève* would last. We'd better be prepared. Due to France's stellar health-care system, Ralph was able to access his prescription online, making a refill a snap. At a local pharmacy, a stunning-looking pharmacist à la Taylor Swift greeted us, causing Ralph to forget the purpose of our visit momentarily. "She wants to see the prescription, honey—your phone," I whispered, nudging his arm.

Composure regained, Ralph said, "Oh, right. Here you are." He extended his hand cradling the *portable*.

"C'est bon," she said, ushering us to another pharmacist who would take our request to the next step. Her colleague was a friendly woman who swiftly punched in the vital information on her computer and informed us it would be just a minute. While we waited for the process to finish, we exchanged back-stories. She learned how we fell for France, traveled all over the country, and ended up settling in Provence. And we discovered

she came from Slovenia, married a Frenchman, started a family, and had lived on Corsica for many years. Maybe because we were all expats living in France by choice, I sensed we shared a silent camaraderie. So when she said she hoped the strike would end soon so we could return *home*, we all understood that the *home* she emphasized was more than a mere building. With the prescription pickup set for the following morning, we wished the intuitive pharmacist all the best for a *bonne journée*. Health—check.

As for the car at the Marseille airport parking lot, well, we'd just have to pay whatever the overtime cost was. And prepare for a potentially overblown bill. Sadly, for the category of parking, there was no chance of a check.

Another unsettling thought was that I had a hospital procedure scheduled for the following week. It had taken months to arrange. It wasn't urgent, but if I had to postpone the checkup it would be very disruptive to many, and most certainly, a new time slot wouldn't be available until next year, impacting our planned trip back to the US. The ripple effect rattled my nerves. *Stay calm, stay cool,* I told myself.

Now all we could do was wait. And try not to think about it. Which was impossible, of course. We were compelled to check for strike updates every few minutes to see how the talks between the warring factions were going. How long would it take them to work out a deal? Based on our experience with other strikes, there was no way to tell. Sometimes they gathered momentum and kept on rolling. I also idly wondered whether the decision-makers went their separate ways for lunch. Or did they keep at it and order in? Perhaps breaking bread together would deliver a breakthrough.

We sure weren't in the mood for a leisurely lunch ourselves, so we skipped discovering another culinary winner and pieced together a picnic at the apartment. After cleaning up and packing, we checked the news for the umpteenth time. There was none, which in this case was *not* good news. To distract ourselves, we hoofed it back to the closest beach.

We couldn't get enough of the gorgeous horseshoe-shaped bay with its white sand and stunningly clear water. It's shallow for a long way, so you can walk out quite far before the azure water reaches waist height. During our walk beyond the lifeguard station and back, one of the local Red Kites came swooping past very low, giving us a good look at its long, fingered wings. While we watched the magnificent eagle-like creature cruise the shoreline so elegantly, port strikes seemed a world away.

Ralph returned to the apartment to read while I stuck my head into a couple of boutiques. One was a cute shop with a clever name, Il Était une Île (Once Upon an Island), a play on words from the common phrase *il était une fois* (once upon a time). A few boutiques later, a customer was jabbering with the *vendeuse* about the strike and how happy they were that it was over.

Before I could stop myself, I interrupted, *"C'est vrai? C'est terminé—la grève?"*

"Oui, oui," they insisted. It was true. The strike had ended.

Two seconds later, Ralph called with the good news. "It's over! For sure, for sure. Yes, it's official," he yelled into the phone.

Although definitely not sweet, the strike had been mercifully short, and grateful were we. Now we could relax and be worry-free for the evening. We honored our original docket, which appropriately indicated dinner at the dock. In a laid-back bistro, a short stroll from our apartment, we savored seafood and sipped chardonnay by the seashore.

On departure day, we reluctantly bid adieu to our glorious view of captivating Calvi. With an hour to spare before our taxi would arrive, we wheeled our suitcases to a café terrace for a goodbye coffee. We sat quietly, contemplating the gentle rhythms of the easygoing seaside city—boats puttering across the harbor, parents herding their kids to school, customers drifting in and out of the stylish boutiques. I pondered leaving Ralph with the suitcases while I squeezed in some last-minute shopping, but thought better of it. And then just as quickly I countered my own decision, but this time my retail motivation wasn't self-centered. The cool polo sweater I bought was for Ralph.

The flight home was uncomplicated, as was picking up the car and driving *chez nous*. What was not so painless was compiling our trip report, as we typically enjoy doing after a getaway. This meant reliving the accident, which gave us pause. Considering the rather dramatic mishap that had befallen Ralph at the beginning of the week when he took an unplanned dip, we could have concluded it was best to file the excursion under Trips Best to Forget, especially when factoring in the strike that capped off the finale.

But it would have been misguided to overlook the middle portion of the trip. After Ralph's misstep, we'd dusted ourselves off, or in this case *dried* Ralph off. We kept to the travel program throughout the rest of the week, chalking up loads of exceptional memories. And with a seafood dinner quayside, we'd orchestrated a perfectly fine farewell. All in all, the major portion in between had been a dream.

Our positive evaluation included a cautionary addendum: Spontaneity and some risk-taking added zest to our lives. By flinging us into the moment, this approach could pave the way to cherished joie de vivre—as long as it didn't pitch us off the pier in the process.

Joie de Vivre Highlights*

The first sight of Corsica from the plane
The view of Calvi Bay from the apartment terrace
Dancers and the roving band in Île-Rousse
A dough-tossing pizza maker and the *figatelli* at A Punta
Walking barefoot on the beach at Calvi

**Despite the initial injurious lowlight*

14

Beguiling Bonnieux

The Luberon Valley, South of France

Both sides of the Luberon mountain range are home to many attractive stone villages such as Gordes, Roussillon, Lacoste, and Lourmarin. These picturesque enclaves are huge tourist draws, especially in the summer months. We visit often, as they are only an hour or so away—just not in peak season. But exceptions happen …

Gastronomic restaurant, here we come. The lunch reservation for my birthday had been locked in for weeks. We'd dine at a Michelin-starred eatery, tucked into Bonnieux, a hilltop town close to Ménerbes, where Peter Mayle wrote *A Year in Provence,* a book that had inspired me for decades. Since the village is only an hour from Saint-Rémy, our plan was to enjoy an exquisite meal, stroll the bijou enclave, take in the views over the verdant valley, and return home. There would be no need to pack, face daunting August crowds, or set up an augmented watering system for the garden. Easy-peasy.

But as the date approached, the idea of staying overnight gained momentum. And soon thereafter, the notion of arriving a day early hitched a ride on the single-night concept. But what were the chances of finding a room at the very last minute for a weekend in the popular Luberon area in August, the highest point of the high season? It was ludicrous to try, but I checked hotel availability online anyway.

Lo and behold, it must have been meant to be because the last available *chambre* at an attractive hotel, Le Clos du Buis, just across the street from the restaurant, was waiting for us. Not wanting to waste a minute fiddling with online booking, I picked up the phone and booked it for a two-night stay. What had begun as a no-fuss *déjeuner* idea to celebrate my special day became a mini-getaway—a surprising development for us during high season in Provence.

Reaching the village by scenic backroads rather than the autoroute, which would no doubt be daunting in summer, made the outing seem even more like a leisurely escape. And by staying two nights we had nearly three full days to fill, so my agenda blossomed. First we drove directly to the Friday market in Bonnieux, which flows throughout the hilltop village. Even though the market in Saint-Rémy is one of the best, I don't typically spend much time shopping for nonfood items there, except with visitors. Real-life demands typically take priority, and when I do visit it, I tend to rush through. But when *en vacances*, I take the time to browse. Even though many of the wares on sale are similar throughout Provence— lavender sachets, woven baskets, olive wood utensils, flowing linen dresses—I like to study the novel presentations at each stall and the diverse settings. From hilltop Bonnieux, the views stretched beyond the church to the Luberon Valley—a scene of quiet, natural beauty.

We were too early to check in to the hotel, so we'd left our luggage in the car parked outside the town center. But we popped in anyway to let the owner know we had arrived and would return later. Surprisingly, she took us to our room, where the cleaners were nearly done. She gave us the key and said the room was ours in half an hour. *Parfait.*

With the small hotel parking lot still full, we couldn't relocate the car to unload, so we decided to address lunch first. For that, we doubled back a few kilometers through sun-kissed vineyards to the Bistrot de la Citadelle, conveniently located at the winery, Domaine de la Citadelle, where we would pick up some bottles—rosé, of course—for summer sipping.

I hadn't reserved, but we were early enough to snag a table in the attractive vaulted dining room that looked directly out onto the vines through a large arched window. I love a vineyard view, especially in the dazzling Luberon, and sometimes played a little game with myself: Given a choice of a vineyard or water vista, which one would I pick? Whenever I'm in one of them, inevitably that's the one I choose.

Since we'd be eating out for dinner and had an elaborate lunch the following day, selecting salads was the thing to do. Not a sacrifice. Both of our oversized bowls of garden greens, topped with melted goat cheese on hearty toast discs, prosciutto, and walnuts, were particularly satisfying. And so was the wine.

Sipping my rosé serenely was a challenge, however. The young family across the aisle from us provided some drama, with a baby declaring lunch was over with piercing shrieks and his older sister throwing fits and food. Not to mention a ceramic bowl that landed on the floor. Following a smashing crash, a server appeared and calmly swept up the debris. *"Pas de soucis"*—no worries, she assured the overwrought couple. As they prepared to leave, the kiddos now spent and silent, I handed the father a soft toy that had skidded across the tiles and landed near my feet and wished them a *bon après-midi*. Dad thanked me, replying in kind. Having assumed a vacation frame of mind, I could almost guarantee our afternoon was going to be even better than *bon*.

After our delicious meal, we bellied up to the tasting room bar to discover a new wine to celebrate my birthday the following day. As we sipped our way through a series of classic blends, we chatted with the friendly young guy in charge. Topics ranged from our love of Provence to birds. He told us he'd helped band flamingos at the nature research center, Tour du Valat. I was stunned by his vivid description of the extraordinary event to protect my favorite bird. I imagined the marvelous honking chaos and immediately wanted to be a part of it. Maybe one day? He also told us his brother had recently opened a bookstore in the unique town, known as the Venice of Provence for its web of canals. We promised to visit Isle-sur-la-Sorgue soon to support his entrepreneurial brother and placed our wine order—we both agreed on wine number three.

The nearby town of Ménerbes was next on the agenda to visit the home of Dora Maar, the acclaimed artist and photographer and Picasso's long-time partner and muse. In 1944, after her nearly decade-long turbulent relationship with Picasso ended, she bought an eighteenth-century townhouse in the pretty hilltop village where she spent summers pursuing her art. After her passing in 1997, Nancy Brown Negley, an

American arts patron, bought the property and converted it into an artist and writer residence and cultural center.

Guided tours of the house's private rooms were available only two days a week, and this wasn't one of them. Simply experiencing the setting and visiting the public section, however, would help satisfy my curiosity about the muse mystique that engulfed Maar. Picasso's portraits of her primarily reveal anguish, but Maar also influenced him politically, resulting in one of his most famous paintings, *Guernica*, about the horrors of the Spanish Civil War.

Maar's life was surely tumultuous, and I wondered whether by coming to Provence she was hiding or seeking. If it was a refuge for her, had she found peace?

Once inside the village, we took a misguided turn that spat us out onto an impossibly narrow lane that was billed as a two-way street. The town was jammed, and no parking was available anywhere. So Ralph pulled into a residents-only space and remained in the car while I hoofed it through the village lanes to Maison Dora Maar.

Even before I went inside the building, I understood the appeal. From the upper floors of the stately structure, the view of the valley would be unobstructed and stunning. This alone must have been heaven for an artist like Maar. And also a safe haven. Perhaps the rural setting provided the serenity she so desperately coveted.

Aware that Ralph was in a precarious parking situation, I wasn't able to do justice to the current exhibition in the public gallery, which featured the intriguing engravings of Argentinian-Italian surrealist artist Leonor Fini, a friend of Maar's from Paris. During the 1930s both women had moved in the heady circles of some of the artistic titans of the time such as Man Ray, Salvador Dali, and Max Ernst. By comparison, rural Provence must have been shocking to Maar in its silence. Considering the clash of ambience between the two regions jolted me back to reality and Ralph.

By the time I reached the car, Ralph had already been reprimanded for his parking choice and was feeling guilty. It wasn't a gruff patrolling policeman who read him the riot act but an even more effective keeper of the peace. A wizened, white-haired local lady in a flowered housedress had gently explained to him that he was in a spot reserved for the town's residents. He responded by gently assuring her that he would be on his way in minutes, as soon as his wife returned. She smiled sweetly and retreated to the threshold of her house across the street. There, she unlocked the door, turned, and glared at Ralph, tapping her wristwatch. Her message was clear: "You're on the clock, buddy." Luckily, I arrived sooner than *tout de suite*, so Madame Neighborhood Watch didn't have time to raise the alarm. I hopped in and we made our escape.

Instead of driving straight back to the hotel, where poolside chaise longues awaited, we made a detour to another winery. This was not any old wine *domaine*. It was none other than Château La Canorgue—the property where the movie *A Good Year* with Russell Crowe and Marion Cotillard was filmed. As we turned off the main road and headed down a lane to the winery, the impressive villa appeared. It was exactly how we remembered it from the film, which we watch every year, maybe twice. For us, it only gets better as we find another aspect to applaud, just like Provence.

From the parking lot by the boutique, we marveled at the beautiful château. As I moved closer, trying for more creative angles with my camera, some serious warning signs came into view. In strict terms, they warn tourists that the filming is over, and it is a private residence now. Do not even *think* about entering. *Point taken*, I thought as I backed off. But it was fun being on the set and imagining the flurry of filming activity in this tranquil corner of Provence.

As a matter of fact, the allure of the area wasn't lost on the film's director, Ridley Scott. In 1992 he purchased his own vineyard nearby, Mas des Infermières. At first the property covered only eleven hectares of vines, and he sent the grapes to a cooperative for wine production. Now it had expanded to thirty hectares, and Scott had built his own winery, making two hundred thousand bottles of wine annually.

On our first visit to the winery earlier in the year, we had been surprised to find that an expansive tasting room doubled as a film museum. On display were the tennis racquet Russell Crowe played with in *A Good Year*, the Peugeot bicycle that Adam Driver rode in *House of Gucci,* and some of the space-suits Matt Damon wore in *The Martian*. And outside in the courtyard, cannons used in *Napoleon* guarded the property. On the lower floor, more museum displays were open to the public but were only accessible by guided tour. Interestingly, the multi-talented, indefatigable dog-loving director and vintner designed his own wine labels. Every version had a pup on it. If Mr. Scott ever had a casting call for dogs, our friends' dog Rudolph from Carcassonne would land the part, paws down.

But there were no canines on patrol here at Château La Canorgue and we roamed around freely, checking out differ-ent views of the villa, making sure we didn't get too close. Before leaving, we popped into the boutique where it was de rigueur to buy a bottle—primarily a sentimental purchase, but one we would thoroughly enjoy as it transported us back to the movie set.

Back at the hotel, we stretched out on the lounge chairs by the pool, read, swam, and snoozed away the afternoon. The lush grounds were much more expansive than the front of the building had led us to expect, with benches scattered all around, some under mature trees and others in the open. And the view of the valley was marvelous, very close to the one Dora Maar would have had from her house in Ménerbes.

Lunch the next day at the gastronomic restaurant Ju-Maison de Cuisine was stellar. After a warm welcome, we chose a table inside under the pale stone vaulted ceilings with a view to the terrace. Simple elegance reigned, from the sleek furniture to the glassware and cutlery. Nothing fussy, just tastefully stylish décor and oh-so-tasty food. Chef Julien Allano and his team delivered stunning cuisine and service from beginning to end. The trio of amuse-bouches included a falafel ball on fluffy goat cheese, spiced with chorizo. The inventive zucchini-citrus starter in a delicate anchovy sauce and the succulent guinea fowl with fresh basil were rave-worthy. We especially enjoyed the ramekin of mixed potatoes in a rich, flavorful sauce—prepared without butter, the server told us.

After the dazzling finale of creamy polenta covered with slices of peach and apricot on a quenelle of almond ice cream with a maple leaf-shaped cookie on top, we were completely sated. But there was more. We passed on coffee, but three saucers appeared, each with a phenomenal bite-sized chocolate treat. And to cap off the celebratory meal, the server presented me with another surprise—a platter emblazoned with *Joyeux*

Anniversaire written in a fancy font with chocolate sauce, next to a single candle. I made a wish to return.

On our way out, we passed along our enthusiastic sentiments to Chef Allano. I told the superb *chef de cuisine* how pleased I was to have discovered the restaurant from a magazine article and that it had inspired our trip. He was exceedingly gracious and even brought in a staff member for a group photo to commemorate the occasion. It was my birthday, after all.

Our hotel was only about fifteen meters away, a blessing since I was teetering on some ridiculous car-to-bar heels. Valuing style over comfort, I'd acquired them for a French garden wedding, but they were not made for actual walking. Back in the room, I changed into some tennis shoes before we took a stroll through the village.

That afternoon, our demanding schedule involved more lollygagging by and in the pool, reading, and watching Pied Wagtails dipping into the *piscine* for a sip while zooming around. All the loungers were occupied, but the extensive grounds allowed everyone their own wide space. The tranquil setting gave us the feeling we had the place to ourselves, the perfect place to let thoughts loose, mostly about why we didn't do more of these limited-range, exploratory excursions more often and how we could change that.

When dinnertime rolled around, only a snack appealed after such an elaborate lunch. Since guests can access the hotel's large kitchen, we'd stashed some cheese and charcuterie there, which we now collected. Declaring it a dinner *pique-nique*, we spread it out on a garden table, where we munched, entertained by the twinkling lights of the Luberon Valley.

The next morning, with our appetites intact, we splurged on a big breakfast in the hotel dining room with the big Luberon vista. We lingered over extra cups of coffee before hiking with our binoculars into the hills above the village. We didn't see many birds, but we guessed that the heat was causing them to hunker down.

Since home was only an hour away and our route took us past the crossroads of a town called Coustellet that stages a sprawling Sunday farmers' market, we decided to take advantage of it and pull over. I bought some snacks to nibble on in the car and a roast chicken for dinner. This way, we wouldn't mess up our kitchen and could continue our free-as-a-bird getaway mentality even after we unloaded the luggage.

It was a better birthday than I could have imagined. At this crowded time of year in the south of France, I'd feared it would be a madhouse, full of ornery tourists clamoring for space. Except for the parking problem in Ménerbes and Ralph receiving the dressing-down from the elderly local, it had been hiccup-free and full of memorable moments. And one especially unexpected conversation—we'd learned about the thrill of banding flamingos in the Camargue from a young wine expert. I never would have thought we could have pulled off such a rewarding, easygoing mini-adventure at the last minute in Provence in August.

Never saying never won the day.

Joie de Vivre Highlights

A flamingo-banding discussion at a winery
The Luberon Valley view from the hotel pool
Visiting the Dora Maar house
Wandering the grounds by the set of *A Good Year*
The gastronomy *and* hospitality at Ju-Maison de Cuisine

15

The Inside Loop

Saint-Rémy-de-Provence

Behind open doors, a world of camaraderie, friendship, and goodwill awaits. And so a sense of belonging builds …

Adventures near and far from Saint-Rémy revved our engines in a multitude of marvelous ways. But that was only part of the joie de vivre story. Routine life right here in our familiar but vibrant patch told the rest from two perspectives. On the one hand, there were our breezy town-and-country walking routes that meandered past shops, cafés, boutiques, galleries, pretty squares, and through the Alpilles woods. During these carefree outdoor forays, we inevitably crossed paths with friends, acquaintances, and wildlife, building and deepening social and nature bonds as we went.

On the other hand, managing the practical demands of daily life—along with supporting the local café culture and restaurant scene—offered the potential for a steady stream of memorable moments. Plus something else: They presented more heartfelt reminders that we'd become part of this little community. My journals made that very clear, countless times.

Once we pushed through a door, any old *porte* in town, delightful moments had a chance to blossom. Our go-to drugstore next to the church was staffed with exceptionally capable and amicable pharmacists who greeted us and treated us with smiles and good cheer throughout the year. One day in the foyer of the *pharmacie*, we bumped into our angelic house call nurse. (Yes, house calls were routine here.) We'd once surprised her with a lightweight sport hat for a fundraising hike in Morocco. It had a wide rim and long flap in the back for sun protection. The cap was her lucky charm, she said, pulling her phone from her bag. She scrolled through photos to find one of her wearing it on the desert circuit, which she shared with us and the interested pharmacists. Just maybe the flapped hat had helped her come in third, she enthused. No, no, we insisted, all the credit went to her. After the hugs, I felt so full of well-being that I nearly forgot to fill my prescription.

While I was waiting in line to pay for my newspaper in the town's small *presse*, which also sold books, toys, and sundry items, the six-year-old son of the owners showed me the raffle tickets he was selling for a school project and asked me whether I would buy some. His mother, overhearing the exchange, gently admonished her sweet boy.

"Ask her if she'd like to buy *one* ticket, dear. That's enough."

I bought two. Mom mouthed *merci*.

"Avec plaisir!" With pleasure, I whispered back.

Another time when the weather was grim, as summer slipped into autumn, Florence, the more reserved owner of the shop, was on duty. We chatted about saying goodbye to the toasty sunshine and welcoming the cooler season, which she hated doing. I knew both owners were sun worshipers, but she seemed inordinately down about it. While picking up a hearty loaf called *pain Nordique* next door at Maison Bergese, I noticed the tempting sacristans stacked on the counter. They're insanely decadent twisted sticks of puff pastry dusted with confectioner's sugar and toasted sliced almonds. I knew the other owner of the *presse*, who wasn't working that morning, favored them because she had mentioned it once in passing. So on this day, along with my healthy bread, I asked for three sacristans, thinking they'd cheer up Florence. She was usually low-key, so I didn't expect more than a quiet *merci*. When I reentered the shop, she looked up from behind the counter with the same dour look as a few minutes before.

Extending my arm with the pastries, I said, "Maybe these will compensate a little for the lack of sunshine." Her face burst into a broad smile, and she stepped down from her elevated position behind the counter and offered me three *bises*, the traditional number of cheek kisses given in these parts. I couldn't wait to tell Ralph how Florence's reaction to that trio of treats made my day, and I hadn't even had my second cup of coffee yet.

Across the street from the newspaper shop was our favorite takeout pizza place, Glanum Pizza, named after the Roman ruins in Saint-Rémy, just like our pie of choice. So at Glanum

Pizza, we'd order the classic Glanum pizza, a veggie version with goat cheese, olives, and eggplant, but with one alteration—extra aubergine. When I placed the order, I started with *"Comme d'hab,"* short for *comme d'habitude*, meaning "as usual." The owner always remembered and got a kick out of it, making me chuckle every time, which wasn't often since we considered pizza a special treat. If we were planning to splurge on pizza for dinner after our regular Friday night get-together for drinks with friends, we ordered it on the way to the café so it would be ready for pickup on the way home, thereby avoiding a wait. Because it was a popular place, it was constantly busy and particularly so on a weekend night.

Recently, however, we forgot about efficiency. So when we stopped by on our way home during the supper rush, the owner's wife, who was minding the till, informed us the wait would be forty-five minutes. We weren't surprised and politely declined, telling them not to worry—it was our fault for not ordering earlier. As we turned to go, the husband and wife exchanged looks and indicated we should wait a minute. They assessed their workload, shuffling through the orders and checking the boxed pizzas ready for pickup.

Then monsieur said, "Will twenty minutes be okay?"

"Oh! That would be great!" I said, completely surprised. I settled up right then and made sure I'd added more than a bit extra so they knew they were appreciated.

This short wait would be put to use. After securing our bikes, we popped into the quaint Bar Provençal next door. This was where, many years before when we'd first arrived in Saint-Rémy, we bought our *timbres fiscaux*. Back then, these "fiscal" stamps that looked like ordinary postage stamps were used to pay for the temporary French visa we had to apply for each year. Oddly, these special stamps couldn't be purchased at a post office or government office but rather at a bona fide pub, where folks pop in for a pint. It was one of the multitudes of "who knew?" learning-curve challenges that we strove to conquer in the early years of our life here.

We'd had our ten-year card for many years, so we didn't need fiscal stamps, and I'd heard the process had changed. The bar, however, hadn't. Aside from some big flat screens showing music videos and sports, the establishment was the same—the prices were still very reasonable, and the authentic zinc countertop still shone. We had always liked to sit on the tall chairs in the front, a great place to people watch. Patrons read newspapers, gathered for a beer, or rushed in and out for cigarettes and lotto tickets. The busy waitstaff was always welcoming, even though we hadn't earned "regular" status. But it seemed on this night that the young guy who brought our Perriers recognized us. He returned with a little tub of peanuts and a warm smile, giving the impression he was genuinely happy we'd stopped by. So were we.

Early for an appointment for a recent routine medical checkup, we had our choice of seats in the general reception area, shared by several doctors, with only a couple of other adults there. I flashed back to a previous visit when it had been more crowded and much livelier. It was like a Bring Your Kids to Work day because Dr. Mom's two young daughters were there, helping the office manager make photocopies.

They were poised and polite and demonstrated exemplary efficiency, suggesting they would complete their training program with honors. The eldest girl stood tall next to the printer, showing excellent posture, with the younger one at her side. As each sheet emerged from the machine, the oldest would extract it, pivot, and hand it to the younger as if she were placing a scalpel into a surgeon's palm. The younger one would then pass it to the manager, who in turn handed it to the patient. In my mind's eye, I saw them both walking confidently across a stage to receive their doctorates, in medicine or maybe astrophysics. The sky was the limit for these two, I felt certain, giving a boost to my faith in the future.

At that moment, our personable GP had appeared and glanced at the girls performing their tasks before motioning us into her office. As if channeling my thoughts about her capable daughters, who might increase the number of doctors in the family one day, she said wryly, "Three for the price of one."

On this day, just as we were leaving, I asked about the girls. Our doctor replied that they were doing well and growing up fast. Her eldest had attended a nine-year-old's birthday party the other day and for entertainment, everyone had gotten a facial. "Wow," I said, adding, "that's very grown-up." She nodded with resignation and a warm smile, bidding us adieu.

Our excellent doctor's comment had allowed a poignant insight into her humanity, which made me feel cared for even more. It also was a reminder that time was flying for me too. Since it was unlikely I could wrangle an invitation to a preteen party with a self-care theme, perhaps I needed to stop procrastinating about some pampering and book my own facial? Maybe a massage too for good measure.

On the foodie front, we were thrilled to hear some splendid news. After the closing of the restaurant most dear to our hearts, located in a hamlet near Saint-Rémy, the considerate Belgian owners opened another, conveniently located within walking distance of our house. The setting was much more casual, but the cuisine was equally stellar. One example was a first-course dish, typical of the autumn lineup that I yearned for throughout the year—a plump cannelloni made with feather light pasta stuffed with duck confit.

At a pre-opening chat we'd had with Michèle, a co-owner, she explained that they would have limited hours because they wanted to slow down and take their downtime seriously. So much so, she joked that "if my husband makes me work on the weekends, I'm making a divorce." Her point was made. The new schedule for Le Capoun was set for dinner two nights a week and lunch every day during the week except for holidays. This would work perfectly for us since we preferred to schedule special-occasion meals at lunchtime. And we couldn't wait to share the experience with our gourmand friends from the Luberon Valley, who met us for a meal every few months. Former fixtures in the London theater scene, this worldly couple had exacting and refined tastes. It had been a long time since they'd eaten at the restaurant's original location, but they surely would remember its top-notch cuisine and its very desirable *bon rapport qualité-prix*, meaning good value, not to mention the warm welcome from irrepressible Michèle. The next time they were free to trek over to our neck of the woods, I'd know just where to make reservations. Of course, in the meantime, we would be regulars.

All our day-to-day encounters with the usual suspects enhanced our understanding and appreciation of our local lifestyle, but it was an out-of-left-field interaction that added another valuable dimension. The early-spring morning was crisp, clear, and calm. Our backyard was birdless—no Great Tit, no Sardinian Warbler, not even sparrows were taking turns entertaining us at the birdbath or pecking at the seed balls hanging from the still leafless grapevine.

But Ralph was hopeful he'd find some winged creatures where he was headed—the eastern part of the Camargue called Salin de Giraud. Bird reports revealed some good sightings. He wasn't doing a dedicated birding year as we'd done in 2019 when we traversed France to find as many birds as possible in twelve months; this year, he was making a more casual but still concerted effort, counting as he went. I was pretty sure he hoped to beat his 2019 record, but minus the countrywide travel and internal pressure to keep up a high-pitched pace. On this day he hoped to see a Woodchat Shrike, a Marmora Warbler, and a Jack Snipe. The last two would be lifers, new species for him, and all of them would be new for the year.

But I would be missing out because I was due to pay a visit to my yoga class. I wasn't flitting about all day, burning calories and toning muscles like my feathered friends, and my core needed work. Also, my spirited, indefatigable friend Lana would be there. There was no need to flip a switch when Lana entered the room—her beaming smile provided all the light you needed. No matter what state my spirits might be in, Lana would boost them, so it was always a treat to see her. In addition, she always relayed the latest information about Saint-Rémy happenings before they became printed news. (Her husband was a city planner.) Lana knew everyone and always kindly included me in conversations, so I was able to interact with the other ladies as a semi-insider. And I could relax and chat in French worry-free. If I backed myself into a linguistic corner, Lana would come to the rescue—she was fluently bilingual.

But on this particular morning, Lana wasn't there, which surprised me, as she'd texted me asking whether I intended to go. This was the last class before our teacher Suzanne was going to her hometown in Brittany for a month to give some dance courses. I planned to impress Suzanne with my Breton knowledge of how to say hello—*demat*—which she'd taught me the week prior, and miraculously I still remembered.

In the absence of Lana, to fill the gap before Suzanne called us to order, I turned to a woman next to me who I recognized as part of Lana's entourage. I seized the moment and engaged her with an Easter question, which I thought was a safe bet since it's an elaborate event around here.

"Did you have a nice Easter fête?" I asked.

"Oh, yes, but *oh là là*, I ate so much. So much food." She patted her tummy. "I bought a lot of chocolate for all my grandkids—five of them—but the ones who live in La Ciotat didn't come. The weather was so horrible."

Driving an hour and a half in heavy rain from the Mediterranean town would have been difficult, I knew. "Oh, too bad," I said in sympathy. Suddenly I was curious about her chocolate preference. I suspected she, like most of her French compatriots, harbored strong opinions about everything culinary. Often folks here were devoutly loyal to particular producers of particular products, and no substitute would do. One friend wouldn't ever eat oysters from the Mediterranean—only oysters from Brittany were acceptable. A truffle-loving neighbor advised us to never go to the young seller at the market—only the older one. In this country where folks are often fanatical about food, I wondered what my new friend's take on chocolate was. So I asked what kind she preferred.

"You mean the brand or the type?" she replied.

"Well, both. For example, do you like Joël Durand?" This renowned chocolatier was a local favorite. His shop in Saint-Rémy might be tiny, but it boasted an impressive chocolate-sauce fountain and a variety of chocolate infused with intense and inventive flavors. During a purchase, a petite square of the chocolate du jour was usually offered gratis.

"Durand is wonderful," she said thoughtfully, nodding her approval. "And Lindt," she added, "for their Easter bunnies."

"And what type do you like—milk or dark?"

"Oh, dark is my favorite."

"With nuts?"

Her eyes lit up. "*Oui!* I love chocolate with nuts."

Being a nut fan myself, I wanted to ask her more about them, starting with hazelnuts, a popular nut here. At that moment, however, I drew a blank on *noisette*, so I filled in with an upbeat statement in French that I thought would be easily understood: "So many delicious temptations this time of year." But communication failed, according to her pursed lips and cocked head, a look I've grown to know well considering my near-constant flow of undecipherable phrases.

I explained further. "I mean something that is truly good and is hard to resist, but sometimes comes with consequences." But that didn't clear things up at all. An even more confused expression settled on her face.

In that instant, it occurred to me that perhaps in French, the idea of temptation has a distinctively sexual connotation.

Oops! This would be fodder for my group French session on Friday, conducted over Zoom. My feisty nonagenarian professor, Sylvie, loves to comment on slight variations in pronunciation or word usage that make the difference between a completely benign comment and an off-color one, like the classic newbie faux pas involving heat. When the ambient temperature is high and so is your body's, you might say, *J'ai chaud,* I *have* heat. But if you say, *Je suis chaud(e),* I *am* hot, you indicate you are hot to trot. *Attention!* Careful! Sylvie will warn, convulsing with laughter.

Now my yoga classmate was leaning in, preparing to crack the code on the attempted translation. Before I could muddy the waters further, Lana appeared. Wanting to solve the linguistic mystery before moving on to other news of the day, I barely said bonjour before asking her how to say *temptation* in French.

"Ah, c'est une tentation," she said.

So very close—I just needed to adjust some consonants. I turned to my patient conversation partner. "What I meant to say was, *chocolat est une délicieuse* tentation."

Judging by my new friend's grin, I'd managed a comprehension breakthrough. "Yes, it certainly is!" she said, nodding.

"But you know," I added, trying once again to be supportive, "they say dark chocolate is much better for you. It has less sugar, so it's healthier."

"Yes, but for the kids, I bought all sorts of chocolate, and since some didn't come, a lot of it was still in my house—all left for me."

"Milk, dark, nuts, and no nuts?"

"Yes, *all* kinds, and I ate *all* of it!" she blurted.

My new French friend, still nameless, had been seduced by mounds of milk and dark chocolate with and without nuts, binging her way through a grim and drizzly Easter in Provence. Her indulgence confession was delivered in a matter-of-fact manner, seemingly without fear of retribution from me. Suggestive of a sense of mutual trust, her story provided a bonding moment. She could have kept her weakness for dark chocolate a dark secret, but instead she had shared it, and that was much appreciated in a deeper way than she could have known.

My impulse was to follow up by sharing a secret back, thereby boosting our budding friendship. A clever quip about succumbing to a *tentation* of my own, perhaps? After all, our conversation was just between us girls, so why shouldn't I seize the opportunity to fess up in the name of *amitié*, friendship? But class was about to start, and I didn't want to risk my comment getting mangled in translation, thereby requiring Lana's interpretive assistance to unravel some non-PC phrasing I might come up with.

Truth be told, my story of seduction is not a closely held secret. I share it often, and often with near-strangers like my yoga mate. But it would keep for another day. When that time came, I'd tell her about falling for France decades ago. I'd find a way to explain how, since that moment, the country—and Provence, in particular—has continued to seduce me, season in, season out.

However, seduction minus substance didn't equal staying power over the long haul. Ralph and I might have met with arrows from Cupid's French arsenal, but the forces that held us in thrall for so long weren't the stuff of fleeting fancies. Our attraction to this life amounted to more than a string of holiday romances motivated exclusively by lust.

What had begun as a flirty fantasy flourished and ended up nourishing our souls, not to mention putting a bounce in our bebop, a saying Ralph insisted was the best way to capture the sentiment. His unique take on the power of joie de vivre defied an easy English translation—we only knew when we had it. While it might be difficult to explain a bouncing bebop to a French person, my journals confirmed we were experiencing it all the time, all over the place.

Joie de Vivre Highlights

An angelic nurse happy with her hat
From glum to glee at the newspaper shop
Doctor Mom's healing powers
Lunch at Le Capoun
A chocolatey yoga friendship

16

Quartier Characters

Saint-Rémy-de-Provence

Three hundred days a year, sunshine sets Provence aglow, tourist sites boasted. Except for the mistral days when the mighty wind endeavored to send rooftop tiles soaring, there were plenty of calm, sunny days, and then everyone wanted to feel the heat. Especially after a cold snap, when the sun appeared so did the neighbors, and relationships blossomed.

As long as it was not scorching or blustery, when sunbeams spread over Clos Mozart, where we lived, chances were good we'd cross paths with other residents. Some would be trimming bushes, others washing cars or performing other routine maintenance chores. Or they were cruising the streets either by bike or on foot to run errands or just plain run. My journals were filled with interactions with our personable neighbors, who lent our little *quartier* a buzz all its own.

Part of the energy came from Philippe, a tall, shaggy-haired, eternally upbeat guy, whose family owned several houses in the neighborhood. Our conversations were typically lively as we bantered about the weather, tennis, or trekking in the Alpilles. One day, though, our discussion turned serious. When he told us his honey-hued stone house was going on the market, we didn't hesitate to ask him for a big favor. Without pausing, he made us a promise to find a genuinely lovely new neighbor to join our friendly enclave. We thanked him in advance, confident he would comply. He lived next door.

A couple of other neighbors emanated a similar vibe. On our return from the Loop one bright mid-March morning, we saw them chatting and laughing at our *quartier*'s entrance. The fellow was Antoine, one of the most helpful and funny people in the neighborhood, who lived around the corner from us. His companion on this day was pretty, petite Marianne, always carefully dressed, coifed, and made up. She was married to Patrice, who kept me updated with the latest French music videos and significant news stories, which he regularly sent by text. He also shared philosophical insights like "when you love, you don't count," referring to his wife's latest birthday. The couple spent part of the year near Lille by the Belgian border, skipping the sizzling summers in Saint-Rémy. It was warm enough there to enjoy their pool with their grandkids, so the dual-home balance worked nicely for them. For my part, I much preferred seeing their grey-blue shutters open so I knew they were around, but happily, they were never gone long.

Today Marianne was wheeling a stuffed rolling cart, a tip-off that she'd already been to town to shop and was on her way home. Antoine, with a folded shopping bag under his arm, was just beginning his errands. Because the town was so close, walking was a practical way to go—it negated the need to park.

The other advantage was social. With folks strolling around outside, we had more chances to chat.

As we approached our good-natured neighbors, I waved and called out, "Is this a meeting of the Clos Mozart Community Association?"

"Yes, and you're late!" Antoine joked, jabbing at his watch.

"Sorry about that," I said, playing along. "Lost track of time."

"Well, we'll let it go just this once." We all laughed, parted ways, and wished each other a *bonne journée*. To Marianne I added, "Please tell Patrice hi."

Another time we crossed paths with Antoine as he was riding his bicycle. Flashing an impish grin, he pointed his bike straight in our direction and accelerated, veering off at the last second, teasing us, much like another prankster neighbor, Didier, used to do.

Didier was Antoine's close friend and our across-the-street neighbor. He took every opportunity to try to run us over with his tiny yellow Citroën. Whenever Didier would see us walking down the road, he'd swerve in an exaggerated loop as if he were aiming directly for us. He got such a big kick out of watching us scurry to the sidewalk, and we always played along, feeling privileged to scurry for Didier. Every time he toyed with us, we felt cared for and that we belonged here just a little bit more. Then he'd stop the car, roll down the window, grinning just like Antoine had today, and we'd find out about his latest adventures at his primary home in Paris and his family vacation spot in Corsica.

When we stopped laughing, I said to Antoine, "That's exactly what Didier did whenever he saw us—with his car!"

But he doesn't do that anymore. Covid-19 took him in the first wave. I wanted to say, "I miss him, Antoine," but I didn't, due to a perceived unspoken bond. Sadly, it's partly based on a shared loss, something I certainly never counted on from a French neighbor. Confronting that painful sentiment is not how I envisioned feeling at home here. He looked down at his bike and back at me, his smile having vanished. He said nothing for a second, but during that instant, I saw the "I miss him too" understanding in his eyes.

Typical funeral events like a church or memorial service didn't take place in early 2020. Didier was in Paris then, but no formal ceremony happened here either. Soon afterward, his wife Jeanne sold the house and moved to a small apartment elsewhere in Saint-Rémy. But we rarely saw her. Eventually, she gave up her second home and returned to Paris. Our communication was now reduced to infrequent emails.

Had we had closure about Didier? Did we need it? How would we get it? I thought about discussing my feelings with Patrice, also a close friend of Didier. I should have done that sooner. It was he who had called to tell me about Didier. He'd listened to me sob for a while, so I knew he'd understand about the closure issue. Maybe we could get together to celebrate Didier's upbeat life, full of joie de vivre—we'd toast and tell Didier jokes. I could tell the one he'd made when he first met us. He had bounded across the street and stuck out his hand, telling us his name and that he was French. We told him our names and that we were American. He quipped, "Well, no one's perfect." That was the first time I'd heard that line, and it stuck with me. Ever since then, whenever I hear it my thoughts go to our wonderful friend and how much we miss him.

And so began our lighthearted friendship, filled with easy teasing. Over the years, it developed into a heartfelt, affectionate one, with Didier assuming the role of culture teacher. He would remind us of important local events, give us tickets to a popular concert, or surprise us with a bouquet of *muguet*, lilies of the valley, a first-of-May tradition celebrating friendship. One of the most touching gestures from Didier and Jeanne was a coffee-table book on Provence, commemorating our first ten-year residency cards. They dedicated it to us, the new Franco-Americans of Provence.

But right now, not wanting to dwell on sadness, I switched to small talk with Antoine. "So you're off to town to run errands?"

"Yes—just a few things."

"Try not to run over anybody!" I said, wagging my finger at him.

"I'll do my best!" He offered his big expressive grin and waved goodbye.

A block from home, we passed the multigenerational abode of a young family with Corsican roots, with two kids *and* a grandfather. When their son Lucas was a child, he had walked a platter of hors d'oeuvres around to all the guests during a party at Antoine's house. Now that little boy was over six feet tall and had just returned from a high school trip to Louisiana. We gave him a few dollars to eat some local specialties like jambalaya. But when he returned, his cuisine comments hadn't included raves about that famous rice casserole. It hadn't been on the menu at the budget-friendly fast-food outlets where he'd found himself. However, in one of them, he discovered his pièce de résistance: spicy chicken wings. He couldn't get enough of them—high praise from a Frenchman.

Across the street was the home of a Belgian couple, Samuel and Violette, who had us over for dinner years ago for a big reveal—an elaborate absinthe contraption, a source of pride for Samuel. The towering dispenser involved manipulating multiple spigots positioned over tall glasses filled with ice and topped with a sugar cube. It was hilarious watching Samuel manage the device, but he was intent on seeing the procedure through, with Violette egging him on. On another occasion, she revealed her irrepressible enthusiasm at our house during the celebration of Ralph's major birding year. She guessed the precise number of birds Ralph had spotted and snagged the game's grand prize—a big bag of birdseed. Cradling the bundle like a newborn, she laughed at her winnings as tears streamed down her cheeks. Violette is gone now, and Samuel lives in a residence in Brussels near their daughter Sarah and her family. Luckily, Sarah and her husband use the Saint-Rémy house on holidays. On their last visit, I recalled the silliness of the absinthe evening to Sarah. Like her good-humored mother, she began grinning, and for a few seconds Violette was with us.

A woman named Francine lived around the corner from us. Alone for several years since her affable husband Gilles passed away, Francine could often be seen sweeping her drive-way or tending to her plants, especially in summer. Our little chats were often about nothing special, but Francine's smile was special with a capital S. As much as it lit up the world, brimming with optimism, I knew it belied a broken heart. One Christmas, she told me with her eyes welling, "Losing Gilles was like ...," and then emotion took over. Her sorrow left me speechless too, so hugging her was all I could think of doing. Since then, when I buzzed by her house on my bike or our cars passed each other and we exchanged waves, I'd feel as if those fleeting gestures doubled as airborne embraces.

Where Didier and Jeanne used to live, we now had terrific new neighbors, Frank and Jacqueline. Low-key and kind, they always put us at ease whenever we had a French interchange. English, however, was the lingua franca with their translator daughter Elle, who lived in coastal Spain with her twinkle-in-his-eye Texan husband John. Like Ralph, who also hailed from a southern state, John had a soft spot for black-eyed peas. The legume wasn't readily accessible where they lived in Spain, so when we stumbled upon a source near Saint-Rémy, we bought an extra bag to share. We gave it to them as a quirky Christmas *cadeau*, thinking it would elicit a laugh. As expected, they cracked up, but Elle's father got the biggest kick out of it. As a professional musician and songwriter, Frank was familiar with the rock group the Black Eyed Peas. Still, he had never known the band name's origin—until then. To some degree, we felt like ambassadors of American culture, albeit unwittingly. And all by means of a humble bean.

The legume gift was undisputably down-to-earth, but the travel possibilities for this energetic Franco-American couple were sky-high. They were constantly zipping off to exotic destinations such as Svalbard and the Faroe Islands, where they were married. They showed us dreamy, surreal photos of the bride in a flowing gown that she had hand-carried on the wind-up toy plane that had brought them there. We were captivated by their intrepid spirits and their take-it-to-the-bank travel tips. When we met up with them in their beach town in Spain, they offered insider info such as where to watch the sunset, eat the best tapas, and find feathered friends. And recently they'd bought a house and were remodeling it, all without a car. They were confident about the life they wanted and took their time to carefully mold that life. I applauded their wise worldview and marveled at how they had acquired it as thirty-somethings. Whenever they offered us advice, we listened.

And last came our fabulous next-door neighbors. Since our driveways ran parallel and our cars were parked side by side, we often crossed paths. Until she retired early, Agathe was a *notaire*, which is a lawyer in France. Fabrice was a business consultant and took consulting to heart. He advised us about the best oyster vendor, pool-cleaning gizmo, convertible sofa, and bean-grinding coffee maker. He also told us how to buy fresh liver for foie gras. I'm not a huge foie gras fan, but I made an exception for Fabrice's version, decadently rich and silky. If I ever did find the magic in mushed liver, I would be sure to follow our neighbor's advice and go early on market day to the nearby village of Fontvieille, to have my pick of the liver.

Eventually, the time came for them to semi-retire—great for them, but not for us. After nearly eight years as our neighbors, they moved to Corsica to be near their daughter, her husband, and grandkids. In the days before their departure, Agathe brought us some homemade panna cotta with raspberry coulis and *mousse au chocolat*—the best we'd ever had. In addition to all the support they'd given us as neighbors and friends, I now added luscious dessert recipes to the list of gifts they'd bestowed on us over the years.

But it was more than tips, advice, or Agathe's superlative dessert-making skills that endeared them to us. It was the little things, like their comforting neighborly soundtrack—listening to Fabrice buzz off on his Vespa or being greeted with his signature "Hellooooo." We also loved chatting about their renovation progress on their Alpine retreat near the Italian border, exchanging reviews of restaurants we enjoyed, sharing *apéros*, and looking out for each other. If we left the garage door open as dusk arrived, a text would come: "Did you know your garage door is open?"

After we said au revoir for good, I missed them greatly, but my sorrow was eased by knowing how happy they were. The video they sent of their stroll on the beach on Christmas Eve underscored that message. They were having a blast, and we were thrilled for them. I hoped they wouldn't forget us; I knew we wouldn't forget them and how they had enriched our lives. They might have sailed across the Med to an island paradise, but our memories of them would remain secure in our hearts.

Maybe our new neighbors would prove to be as wonderful. Unbeknownst to them, they had some enormous neighborly shoes to fill. This challenge was laid out for four pairs of feet instead of two. In place of Fabrice and Agathe, the new residents were a local couple with two little girls who attended the elementary school around the corner. Now there were new cars in the driveway, new daily rhythms, new interactions, new topics of conversation, and from over the wall, new voices, some young and tender. It was a new beginning, and not just for the incoming family but also for us. Shifting gears after saying goodbye to our beloved neighbors wasn't easy, but the new community dynamic meant a chance for new friendships. Already, we had sparked some smiles from the girls and their parents for our welcome-to-the-neighborhood offering—my specialty, homemade chocolate chip cookies. If the girls had show-and-tell at school, I would volunteer. They could present me as the strange creature from America who lived next door and spoke funny but made yummy treats (the secret was the chips I brought back from the US).

In our compact *quartier*, there were many other families we hadn't formally met but recognized and acknowledged with hellos, waves, or both when they cruised by in their cars or on bicycles. Regular passersby were the young movie-star-handsome film director who would sail through on his road bike, a weathered olive oil producer, and a farming family who had supplied us with fresh veggies and fruits during the pandemic. After school, their kids played in the cul-de-sac down the block, their whoops and hollers reminding us of childhood enthusiasm and making me wonder where we'd stashed our hula hoops. Attic, maybe?

When I sized up our backyard community, where we felt accepted and connected, I saw independent moving parts, each with stories to tell and secrets to save. It was young and old, traditional and contemporary. It was an intriguing place, this zone we called home, where we'd shaped a life. Like all sections of the Loop, the small corner where it began and ended was never dull, never the same. Happy surprises were tucked in everywhere—when we not only looked but saw, and not only heard but listened.

Joie de Vivre Highlights

Antoine's silly bicycle antics
Patrice's caring oversight and philosophical insights
Elle and John's zest for life
Frank's discovery of what a bean means
Sharing hopes and dreams with Agathe and Fabrice

17

Cracking the Joie de Vivre Case

Saint-Rémy-de-Provence

After I closed the last of my journals, they all found homes in special boxes for safekeeping. Like our belle vie, *they were precious and deserved protection. Reading through them had proved Ralph right. Two dozen days after the Big Puff, much wiser now about joie de vivre, I knew what I needed to do.*

How did Parisian showgirls performing a rousing cancan join my joie de vivre journey? No clue. The backstory wasn't detailed in the revelatory dream I had the night after I'd finished mulling over my last journal. But the spectacle's costumes and choreography were breathtaking. What *did* appear as transparent as the champagne the rapt audience sipped was the answer to my *je ne sais quoi* quest. The precision dancers of my dream delivered the sought-after message, cracking the joie de vivre case wide open.

The revelation I'd been seeking arrived unannounced. But surprise is the calling card of eureka moments, *n'est-ce pas?* It was predawn when I awoke from the convoluted dream about my quest. The *rêve* read like the playbook from a theatrical production called *Frenchification: Making the Most of La Belle Vie*, and I was the star. The gist of the dramedy was that reveling in the pleasures of French culture was one thing—and it was a marvelous thing—but connecting to the heart of those pleasures was another. And a much more powerful *another* at that.

By deciphering the code of this connection, the code cracker was in for more rewarding benefits. And these benefits would make for a *belle vie* that was fuller, deeper, and sparked more joie de vivre—wherever one happened to be. Furthermore, the script implied that there would be countless other beneficiaries. In fact, everyone who made contact with the code cracker would benefit. Joy had a ripple effect. Whoever those joyful ripples reached—with all their diverse interests from *tarte flambée* to flamingos—would naturally strive to protect the source of whatever they valued. So the planet would be a winner too.

This was the aspirational storyline anyway, and as the lead in this play, my job was to wrestle with the conundrum until a solution made its grand entrance. Throughout two acts, thoughts boomeranged around my head as I considered various angles, searching for clarity, but only hazy hypotheses surfaced. In the third act, I suddenly heard an impromptu cue, three words whispered from an invisible source in the wings. The answer had arrived. Standing still, staring directly at the audience, I processed the information with eyes wide, as if witnessing a surprise cameo from an A-list celebrity.

The breakthrough to the solution was showcased in theatrical fashion in the form of Moulin Rouge chorus line dancers called the Pleasure Principles. They filed past me, taking center stage, lining up straight and tall, the three in the center each with a one-word pleasure principle emblazoned on their towering feathered headdresses. With arms linked, the Pleasure Principles perfectly executed their signature high kicks, marking the celebratory finale. Applause erupted, the curtain closed, and the house lights eased to full illumination. Dream done.

Without my head leaving the pillow, my eyes popped open. In my foggy state, I considered the performance from my dream. Despite the lack of encores, the show deserved a Tony Award for the rousing climax alone, delivering the solution I sought. But did the pleasure principles of my dream make real-life sense? At 3:00 a.m., reality was far from clear, but these pleasure principles seemed to have squarely hit the mark like tumblers sliding into position on a vault's safe. Just maybe, I thought, this was *the* information about joie de vivre I'd been searching for—a compact set of three components.

To ensure my dreamland epiphany would endure the night, I jotted down the keywords in the notebook I kept on my nightstand. Feeling as if a burden had been lifted, I closed my eyes, hoping my dark-of-night insight would hold up in the sunshine. If the pleasure principles were still intact in the morning, sharing them with Ralph would make for its own joie de vivre moment. I knew he didn't need to know as much as I needed to know, but I also knew he understood my need to know. Soon, we'd both know that we both knew and we'd both then be on the same page of knowing, even without any musical accompaniment.

Throughout the next day, my insight gained traction. The more I scrutinized it, the more it felt right. It seemed to align perfectly with the quest I had set out for myself. But before saying anything to Ralph, I wanted to make sure, so I reflected on the chain of events that had brought me to this point. Ralph's brush with the law, which could have disrupted or even derailed our cherished *belle vie*, had jolted me into acknowledging I had been taking it for granted. I'd been prompted to search for a better understanding of what we'd put on the line, the meaning of our *belle vie*. Only then could I hope to protect it. I had no road map, but one thing was certain—joie de vivre moments were at the heart.

Although I'd accepted that these pleasurable experiences primarily resulted from mysterious serendipity, I theorized that identifying some special dimension of joie de vivre *was* possible. How to begin? What to search for? Where to look? All I'd had was a messy quest until master analyst Ralph suggested a way to break down the task into manageable parts. This approach led to my journals, a compilation of daily musings full of joie de vivre scenes, which would hopefully yield valuable clues. I'd aimed to illuminate a critical common denominator by shining a light on these happy times, perhaps reconnecting with their vitalizing power. Ready or not, joie de vivre moments faced a close-up.

Combing through our local experiences and far-flung adventures spanning hundreds of Provençal sunsets provided many trips down memory lane, most of them upbeat. But reviving the we'll-laugh-about-this-later experiences gave me pause because some still didn't elicit chuckles. It occurred to me that had I known the elusive answer earlier—and paid particular attention to the operating instructions—maybe the distress of those challenging episodes could have been either avoided altogether or at least deflated somewhat. Be that as it may, I chose to consider them valuable as character-building reminders that we'd successfully met some challenges.

Although difficult scenarios played out occasionally, the key to my quest rested with the remarkable moments. They ranged radically from the rustic to the refined, the ordinary to the extraordinary. Ralph and I had learned historical viticulture lessons near Les Baux, rode the rails to a marvelous meal in the Nîmes covered market, and twitched for avian nobility by the Med. We'd admired a special collection of Van Gogh's masterpieces at the Musée d'Orsay in Paris, met a watchmaking artisan skilled in restoring more than timepieces, and deciphered delicate flavors from a Michelin-starred kitchen on the Brittany coast. We'd tracked wildlife and roamed with sheep around wild Ouessant, the island at the end of the earth, and sipped bubbly in a bubble bath with an Alpine view. We'd strolled by a famous film set in the Luberon Valley where Marion Cotillard and Russell Crowe had once cavorted, bounced in a boat along the rugged Corsican coast, walked the Loop in Saint-Rémy, forged friendships with locals, and bonded with neighbors.

During my deliberate recall of the joie de vivre moments and delving into their meaning over the last few weeks, a promising pattern had emerged, suggesting that the answer to my quest was at hand. I had felt tantalizingly close to solving my joie de vivre riddle that would enhance our *belle vie*. It seemed the French universe forces had agreed and guided me to the solution, and I had listened. The dispatch was unmistakable, delivered by a dream. Fait accompli.

Playing it safe, I decided to let the dream-answer percolate another day. By the following afternoon, it still seemed to make sense—to me, anyway. I wondered whether it would to Ralph.

As the light was beginning to fade, turning the Alpilles peaks pastel pink, Ralph was at the piano playing one of my favorite romantic tunes, "All I Ask of You" from *The Phantom of the Opera*. It was time. I drifted downstairs and perched on the banquette by the baby grand, preparing to ask something of *him*. After he'd landed the last chord and lowered the keyboard lid, I gave him a standing ovation, clapping enthusiastically.

"I love that song," I said.

"I know—and it's my pleasure to play it for you."

Bending down to deliver an appreciative peck, I said, "I've got news."

"About?"

"My *je ne sais quoi* quest. I had an aha moment—an epiphany, really."

"Seriously?" Ralph's eyes were wide, filled with expectation.

"Seriously. The answer to my quest became clear to me in a dream, just like that, out of the blue. Or technically out of the black … It was definitely dark at 3:00 a.m."

Before the big reveal, I reminded Ralph that I wasn't trying to unlock the secret of *how* or *why* joie de vivre happened when and where it did—the answer to that question would forever remain in the mystical department, having sprung from some mysterious realm of alchemy that required credentials I hadn't earned. Even if I owned basic wizard gear like a tall pointy cap and a cape, I still couldn't pretend to know. However, without any bewitching accoutrements, I'd followed a hunch that there was a *notable* and *knowable* way to connect more deeply with joie de vivre—finding that way was my goal.

Ralph said, "So, back to the dream … What happened?"

"While falling asleep the other night—maybe because we'd been talking about London and theater reservations—I started thinking about setting the stage for joie de vivre. Anyway, it led to a dream about a stage play. Or it might have been a musical …"

"But the genre is beside the point, right?" Ralph said, trying to harness the storyline.

"Yes, sorry. So I was in this dream sequence with Moulin Rouge dancers and bingo, the answer popped up … in the form of the Pleasure Principles," I said, emphasizing the last two words.

"The principles of pleasure? I'm liking the sound of this."

"Can you guess them?"

"Sure. Why didn't you ask sooner? Got 'em right here," Ralph teased, patting his pockets. He made himself comfortable on the couch before lifting his feet to the ottoman. "Oh, come on, come on—do tell!" Considering it had taken me a few weeks to unravel the *je ne sais quoi*, he understandably thought he was in for a long haul. I was about to surprise him.

"In the end, there's only a trio of principles, plus a postscript."

"Start with the PS first. That's usually where the important message is."

"This one won't divulge much. It's to repeat the principles—repeatedly."

"They must be tricky."

"Nothing worth having comes easy, goes the saying."

"Touché. Bring it on, baby. The first principle is …?"

"Oh, wait. Before I tell you, I should explain why I think it's a good fit." I recapped how reading through my journals had helped me realize that the most meaningful joie de vivre moments happened when we set off on adventures or treated each day like one, curious about what we might find, open to new experiences. "So," I went on, "if you let your curious mind-set take charge, where does it take you?"

"I think I know where you're headed."

Though I sensed he was on the verge of the answer, I couldn't resist giving him a little nudge: "This is the ritual we follow whenever we land somewhere for the first time, like cats carrying out recon in a new location."

"Got it—no question," he said. "*Explore* is Pleasure Principle Number One."

"Yay!" I said, giving him two thumbs-up. As I added details about how I'd arrived at my first finding, Ralph nodded in agreement. I was relieved because while I knew he would have questions, at least so far he wasn't objecting. We talked about how exploring meant embracing the promise of possibilities and the advantages of making routines more like explorations, even basic chores like the weekly shopping. If we were *exploring*, not just mindlessly throwing items in the cart, chances were that something intriguing might surprise us, perhaps something as commonplace as a spice or veggie. A joie de vivre moment might be in the next aisle waiting to be found.

"And speaking of finding," I said, "what do you think Pleasure Principle Number Two is?"

"Has to be *discover*, correct?"

"Yes, sir. *Discover* is Pleasure Principle Number Two." More discussion followed about how having the *intent* to discover nurtures discoveries. And these prized discoveries could appear in all sorts of forms, in all sorts of places, under all sorts of circumstances.

Ralph put the first two pleasure principles to the ultimate test: birding. In his early birdwatching days, he recalled outings when he had been so focused on spotting a specific bird that he'd ignored other species. Over the years, he'd been most successful with overall sightings when he kept the target birds in mind while also considering whatever else might be flying around.

"As for your last principle," Ralph said, "it seems to me that exploring and discovering create the conditions for joie de vivre moments, so the last principle probably fires them up somehow."

"That's exactly what it does." I told Ralph that the last pleasure principle was the most critical because it allowed the first two to do their best work. "Wait," I said, "I'll give you a hint. Think of a word that rhymes with *favor*. While you're thinking about it, how about doing me one by pouring some of that red you picked up at the winery the other day?"

We moved to the kitchen, where Ralph uncorked the *bouteille* and poured a healthy splash into two wine glasses, his internal light bulb beginning to blink. I could tell by the smile creeping across his face as he handed me a stem, weighty with *vin rouge* from a favorite local vintner, Domaine du Val de l'Oule.

"Here you go," he said. "This is for you to … *savor*."

"*Très bien, chéri. Santé!*" I said as we clinked our glasses the French way, looking directly into each other's eyes. This toasting custom allows clinkers to acknowledge a shared convivial experience, infused with the pleasure of being together. This one certainly qualified as a top joie de vivre moment. For weeks, I had struggled to understand how to connect to these special moments that added spark to our *belle vie*, to better appreciate and protect the French life we loved. Now, after sharing the core of my new understanding with Ralph and seeing it had passed muster with him, I was elated. I felt as if I'd hit a homer—or three.

For a few seconds, we silently sipped our *bon vin*, which coincidentally was called Séduction—a fitting name, I mused, considering the sensuous dimension of the pleasure principles I was introducing to Ralph. As seductive as the wine was, I hoped he would find the details of my savor principle even more irresistible.

Settling back into the sofa, Ralph said, "You said savoring was the most critical principle. There's more to it, isn't there?"

"There is," I said, preparing myself to deliver my senses-centered summary. My explanation centered on realizing that my senses were more than automatic sensory mechanisms, extraordinary as they might be. I'd made a game-changing discovery—there was a way to finesse the *je ne sais quoi*, namely, a technique to jump-start the set of pleasure principles. Since the three were interconnected, each affected the other like a feedback loop. By fine-tuning one—in this case, savoring—the entire system tapped into more vitality.

Ralph gave me a puzzled look.

"Drumroll," I said, slapping my thighs. "Okay, this is it. Senses are equipped with a secret setting—specially designed for savoring."

"There's a secret savor setting?"

"My sight, smell, taste, touch, and hearing each have one. These savor sensors let me make more of joie de vivre moments—when they're activated."

With those last two words, Ralph's eyes narrowed. Frowning, he asked, "And this activation process of the savor sensors is rather complicated, is it—is that the kicker?"

"Au contraire, *chéri*. As a matter of fact, I simply have to *thoughtfully* switch a sensor to savor mode and voilà, it springs to life." Granted, my experiments were based on a sample size of one, I explained to Ralph, but the results were indisputable. Over the course of only a couple of days, each of the hundreds of times I woke up my savor sensors, they detected finer details about whatever I saw, heard, smelled, touched, or tasted. What might have been ho-hum or ignored before was now attention-grabbing.

"I'm waiting for the catch," Ralph said with a hint of apprehension.

"It's a tiny one," I admitted. "The transition isn't exactly instantaneous. *Springing* to life may be an overstatement. The savor sensors need a moment to move from cruise control to fully operational savor mode."

"Waiting a moment isn't that hard," Ralph said, nodding.

One would think that to tarry for the span of a deep breath wouldn't be such a challenge. But we had to take *moi* into account. I knew Ralph would soon see that as titillating as savoring itself might be, the practical side of the process provided an excellent lesson for me. Savoring requires pausing the pace. No one knew better than Ralph that I had a long way to go to grasp downshifting, a key element for mastering the art of savoring. This was a formidable challenge for someone who was often compelled to complete just one more action from the day's impossibly unrealistic to-do (or *want*-to-do) lists before tomorrow's dawn. Now, I had issued myself what amounted to a mandate to slow down, to decelerate, in a stress-free, natural way.

Reading the mood of the room, I sensed Ralph was coming to the same conclusion—that the pausing part of the savoring process could work wonders for me and for us. I could tell it wasn't lost on him that embracing my intuitive approach to savoring would reduce my penchant for overprogramming, which sometimes snatched the wind from our sails. The rewards for merging into the slow lane were mounting.

After taking all this in, Ralph asked, "So as long as senses are functioning fine, ...this method will work for everybody?"

"Should, if they want it to."

"So, to have more captivating joie de vivre moments—"

"—putting more bounce in your bebop, as you like to say—"

"—we need to learn to Explore—Discover—Savor," he said. "And make sure to give the sensors time to rev up." Staring at me, Ralph added, "Pausing might be a big stretch for *some people*, but it's actionable, something you can actually *do*."

"That's the beauty of it," I said. "Theoretically, everyone, *including me*, can control waking up their savor sensors."

"So it seems plausible that activating the sensors will lead to more joie de vivre."

"Possibly. That would be a significant upside."

"With no downside, as far as I can tell," Ralph said. "So far, so good."

"Good gets better. Savor sensor activation can happen wherever you go. *La belle vie* can flourish more fully wherever you are, as long as you pack your joie de vivre mind-set. Since it's weightless, no worries about baggage fees. Simple as that."

"I especially like the simplicity part, though it's not the slam dunk you might think at first glance," Ralph said. "Decelerating in a hyper-accelerated world can present challenges."

I agreed that making savoring second nature took more than a quick click. "It would be more like athletes creating muscle memory," I said.

Now that I had the pleasure principles lined up, taking the time to Explore-Discover-Savor was imperative. The more I perfected the principles, the more deeply I'd connect with joie de vivre moments, enriching my *belle vie*, which, in turn, would positively affect everyone and everything I encountered. It was a win across the board. Certainly, enacting the principles would take considerable effort sometimes. Other times, not so much—like the scenario Ralph was about to suggest.

Following up with the sports comparison, Ralph asked, "So we need to train then?"

"Yes, regularly."

"Well then, shall we take our savor sensors out for a spin?"

"At your earliest convenience, monsieur." I took a slow sip of Séduction.

"Since the sunset promises to be spectacular tonight"—Ralph held his glass in one hand and extended his other arm toward me, palm up—"would madame care to join me on the deck for our inaugural practice session of the pleasure principles?"

Resting my hand on his, I answered, *"Avec plaisir."*

Acknowledgments

A wise writer friend advised me that ushering a book project over the finish line wasn't a sprint but a marathon. Fortunately, during every step of the seemingly never-ending trek, I could count on support from many, and I am deeply indebted to each and every one:

My courageous editor, Arlene Prunkl, who welcomed my third book with enthusiasm, and hawkeyed proofreader Caroline Kaiser; Carol Kline for her insights, and the Spun Yarn readers for their candid feedback; and publishing guru Geoff Affleck, project manager Maria Connor, and the dedicated team at AuthorPreneur Publishing for the cover design, interior layout, technical production, and marketing.

Mollie and David Regan, who braved the initial draft with wit and generosity, Beth Woodford for her astute and upbeat French culture guidance, and Rena Pederson for her writing acumen and priceless life lessons.

Simone Sanchette and the Groupies for boosting my spirits and French proficiency; my writer and blogger pals, expat and French buddies in *la Belle France*, as well as family and friends scattered across the globe, for listening and providing encouragement.

The *formidable famille* Mistral, the Clos Mozart community, the village of Saint-Rémy-de-Provence, the Anglo-American Group of Provence, the American Club of the Riviera, and all the engaging people who inspired me and this story—including my birder *amis*, whose efforts have helped expand my knowledge of birdlife and biodiversity. And importantly, to France and her celebration of *la belle vie*.

And lastly, to *mon amour*, Ralph, my intrepid adventure partner, who keeps surprising me, paving the way for more joie de vivre moments.

About the Author

Gayle Smith Padgett is the author of *Passion for Provence: 22 Keys to La Belle Vie* and *The Birdwatcher's Wife: A Quest across France for Birds and La Belle Vie*. She is a UCLA graduate with two master's degrees, neither in French. (The first is in Latin American studies and the second in English linguistics.) After studying in Mexico and South America, she worked as a language specialist in California and Virginia and later as a management analyst and US government liaison in Heidelberg, Germany. Since 2011, she and her husband have lived in Provence, where they continue to shape their *belle vie*.

For more information, go to:
gaylesmithpadgett.com